getting loaded

D0311499

PETER G. BIELAGUS

getting loaded

MAKE A MILLION . . .
WHILE YOU'RE STILL
YOUNG ENOUGH TO
ENJOY IT

New American Library

New American Library
Published by New American Library, a division of
Penguin Putnam Inc., 375 Hudson Street,
New York, New York 10014, U.S.A.
Penguin Books Ltd, 80 Strand,
London WC2R 0RL, England
Penguin Books Australia Ltd, 250 Camberwell Road,
Camberwell, Victoria 3124, Australia
Penguin Books Canada Ltd, 10 Alcorn Avenue,
Toronto, Ontario, Canada M4V 3B2
Penguin Books (N.Z.) Ltd, 182–190 Wairau Road,
Auckland 10, New Zealand

Penguin Books Ltd, Registered Offices:
Harmondsworth, Middlesex, England

First published by New American Library, a division of Penguin Putnam Inc.

First Printing, January 2003
10 9 8 7 6 5 4 3 2 1

Copyright © Peter G. Bielagus, 2003
Illustrations by Rick Shagoury
All rights reserved

REGISTERED TRADEMARK—MARCA REGISTRADA

LIBRARY OF CONGRESS CATALOGING-IN-PUBLICATION DATA:

Bielagus, Peter.
Getting loaded : Make a million:
while you're still young enough to enjoy it / by Peter Bielagus.
p.   cm.
Includes index.
ISBN 0-451-20592-8 (alk. paper)
1. Finance, Personal. I. Title: Make a million:
while you're still young enough to enjoy it. II. Title.
HG179 .B476 2003

332.024'01—dc21   2002070983

Set in Adobe Garamond
Designed by Patrice Sheridan

Printed in the United States of America

Without limiting the rights under copyright reserved above, no part of this publication may
be reproduced, stored in or introduced into a retrieval system, or transmitted, in any form, or
by any means (electronic, mechanical, photocopying, recording, or otherwise), without the
prior written permission of both the copyright owner and the above publisher of this book.

PUBLISHER'S NOTE
This publication is designed to provide accurate and authoritative information in regard
to the subject matter covered. It is sold with the understanding that the publisher is not
engaged in rendering legal, accounting, or other professional services. If you require legal
advice or other expert assistance, you should seek the services of a competent professional.
While the author has made every effort to provide accurate telephone numbers and Internet
addresses at the time of publication, neither the publisher nor the author assumes any
responsibility for errors, or for changes that occur after publication.

BOOKS ARE AVAILABLE AT QUANTITY DISCOUNTS WHEN USED
TO PROMOTE PRODUCTS OR SERVICES. FOR INFORMATION
PLEASE WRITE TO PREMIUM MARKETING DIVISION,
PENGUIN PUTNAM INC., 375 HUDSON STREET,
NEW YORK, NEW YORK 10014.

This book is dedicated to my teachers, especially the first three, Mom, Dad and Ryan.

contents

preface

Of All the Places a
Life-changing Event Could Occur

When I was younger, someone once told me that "the little things make all the difference." That's one of those sayings that you don't pay any attention to until one of those "little things" actually happens to you. A few years back, two such "little things" happened to me that changed my life. They happened within twenty-four hours of each other, and the first one occurred simply because I was sitting in the one place where you'd least expect a life-changing event to occur:

A bar.

I was enjoying a beer with a rather unique friend of mine—unique because he's one of the few people who does exactly what he wants. He is a stubborn SOB, but I give him a lot of credit for the way he lives his life. On weekends, I would go to work, and he would go wild. At a moment's notice, he would drop everything to go live in Europe for six months. If it's last-minute, this guy is in. He'll visit a friend for a weekend and stay the whole week. He'll start a business, have the whole thing blow up in his face, and not break a sweat. And while this guy's lifestyle isn't for everyone, I can't help but recognize the fact that he is truly happy.

As we were propped up on our bar stools, I asked him, "How do you do it? How do you live like you do? Why is society pushing and pulling everyone else in every direction but not you?"

As his empty beer glass hit the counter, he looked at me and said, "You got to live life on your own terms." With that, he left the bar and left me to reflect on what he had said. He really didn't give me much to go on. For a moment, I stared into my bottle of Budweiser as if it were a crystal ball, or a glass telescope that let me peer into a universe of answers.

Then that little thing happened.

Now, I had known this friend a long time. But for the first time in my life, it hit me why this guy was able to live the way he did.

He's loaded.

The smell of crushed cigarette butts and the thumping techno music faded away. I couldn't stop thinking about my friend and his sense of freedom. And all because he was loaded. The thin line that separated this guy, who can pretty much do whatever he wants, from the rest of the us, who spend their lives being told what to do, was money.

It was money that was on my mind as I swished down the last of my beer and left the bar. In fact, money was on my mind all night and all the next morning, until I happened upon another one of those "little things."

I had been thinking about my friend, his money, and his freedom, when I suddenly asked, "What about me? Am I loaded?" I decided to really look at my own finances. I owned some stocks I'd bought myself, some stocks that had been given to me, a few bonds, and even some gold coins. Not bad for a young guy. But what about the future? I asked a friend, whose Microsoft Excel skills put mine to shame, to create a spreadsheet to track how my investments would look ten, twenty, thirty, even forty years from today. We took their value today and projected what they would be worth if they just did nothing but earn interest—compounded.

"Wow."

I was stunned because the little things *do* make all the difference and I had just *stumbled* upon the mathematical formula to prove it. I had heard about the magic of something called compound interest before, but it wasn't until I saw it working there, line by line on that spreadsheet, *my spreadsheet,* that I fully appreciated this phenomenon. The concept that "the little things make all the difference" was no longer some cheesy line to me.

Looking at that spreadsheet, I realized that because of compound interest my investments would one day grow to a fortune. This wouldn't happen because I'm particularly smart; it would simply happen because I'm young, so I could afford to give compound interest enough time to work its magic.

Instantly, and not because of my hangover, I began to see the world in a different light. I began to see life in the same way as my bankrolled buddy. For the first time, I wasn't worried about money. As long as I continued to save and invest, I could live life on my own terms. I was *getting loaded*.

That's what this book is all about: the *other* way to get loaded. Think about the term "getting loaded." I think we all get loaded in our own way. Some people get loaded on alcohol. Some cigarettes. Many *many* others get loaded every morning on coffee. If and when you go to buy a car, the salesperson will tell you the price of the car is $15,000, but it's $18,000 if you get it loaded with all the doohickeys like power windows and air conditioning.

But what are all these things adding up to? Nothing really. We're all getting loaded on the wrong things and that's why so many of us are in financial trouble. Take a moment to think about how much you worry about money. And if you're still bankrolled by your parents, think about how much they worry about money. People spend so much time working for money. What else do you spend forty hours a week doing? Okay, maybe sleeping. The quest for cash sucks up most of our time, second only to sleep. And many people sleep less so they can use that extra time to work more. The only break from such a stressful lifestyle is to get loaded on something short term, like beer, coffee, or power windows.

My compound-interest epiphany changed the way I thought. I started to think about what I spent my money on in terms of what it would be worth in thirty years. Suppose I had saved the $3.50 I spent on that beer? What would it be worth in thirty years? The answer? $231.74.* Sure that's not a fortune, but that's $231.74 for *every* beer. Now I'm not saying you should give up everything you enjoy just to save for the future. What fun is that? My point is that

---

* Keep reading, and I'll show you how this works.

there are two ways to get loaded, and hopefully this book will get you thinking about the other way. Somewhere, between the two, there's a balance. For me, I found that the more I learned about finance, the easier my life got.

And as things got easier, I wanted to learn more about my finances. What did I have? What should I have? I gathered every scrap of financial information I could find about myself: bank statements, stock accounts, everything. I found that I had more than I thought and also discovered areas where I was losing money unnecessarily. Soon my interest became an obsession. I wanted to use my youth to become wealthy. I began surfing the web for info. I began going to seminars. I read over three hundred books—some enjoyable, some horrifically dull—in the area of personal finance and investing. I interviewed accountants, stockbrokers, real estate agents, bankers, lawyers, cheapskates, insurance agents, car salespeople, and recruiters. When I left college, I started working as a real estate consultant, but my primary goal was to find out how someone could use their youth to become wealthy.

I'm going to show you the fifty most important things you need to know about the financial world and how you can use your youth to take full advantage of them. I call them "secrets" because this information is rarely imparted to people under thirty-five.

After five years of research, seminars, hundreds of books and websites, and over a thousand magazine articles, I felt I had enough information about the financial world to craft a life I could live on my own terms. Now it was time to share it. But I knew most people wouldn't take the time to do all the research I had done and I wouldn't wish it upon anyone anyway.

I wrote *Getting Loaded* because I want you to live life on your own terms too. Whether your dream is to backpack through Brazil, spend more time with your family, or play more with your Sega, the way you live should be the way you want to live. We're young. Life shouldn't be about the money.

Money won't bring you happiness. But it *will* bring you the freedom to live your life the way you want to live it, both today and in the future, and that does bring happiness.

Getting Loaded is about using your youth, and all the benefits that come with it, to take control of your financial future. Once you control your financial future, you can control your *entire* future. I'm going to show you the fifty most important things you need to know about the financial world and how you can use your youth to take full advantage of them. I call them "secrets" because this information is rarely imparted to people under thirty-five. They're the secrets that will allow you to live life on your own terms—the secrets to *getting loaded*.

I'd like to thank my parents, Justin and Barbara Bielagus, and my brother Ryan Bielagus for their complete and total support of this project. Also a special thanks to Ken Atchity and the AEI team for their belief in both me and this book. I'd like to thank the editorial staff of Penguin Putnam for seeing the importance of the subject, most notably Marie Timell and Jennifer Jahner for their constructive and creative comments.

Many thanks to my friends, readers, reviewers, and interviewees, especially (these are in no particular order) Ernesto Anguilla, Tim Golden, Dan Zevin, Holly Reynolds, Laura Mackey, Dr. Antonio Paradis, Ernest Famiglietti, Paul Hendrickson, Jen Melvin, Lori Kramer, Joseph Reilly, Ann Sage, Todd Norwood, Andrew Roberts, Meredith Brown, Lindsay Curran and Joel Gould, Carolyn Scott, Chris Norwood, Donald Barley, Damon Degner, and Kathy Parker. Also thanks to Rick Shagoury for his excellent icons.

If I have accidentally left anyone out, I apologize.

And thank you dear reader for buying this book. By buying it, you've made me a bit richer. By writing it, I hope I did the same for you.

introduction

How This Book Will Work

Taking control of your financial life today is not only the responsible thing to do, it's also the cool thing to do. Whether you're sixteen or sixty-five, the moment you decide to live your life the way you want to live it you should begin to spend some time on financial management. If you don't, your boss is telling you what to do. He's telling you when to wake up, when to have lunch, and when to go home. Or perhaps your parents are telling you what to do. They're telling you that your car is too expensive or that you should not study art history because you can't get a job with an art history degree. Everyone but you is calling the shots. Financial planning is more than just being responsible. It's about being who you want to be.

I've juiced up the book to be more than just sentences and charts.

I realize that for some people the world of finance is not as exciting as the Jerry Springer special titled "I used to be a man, now I'm a woman in love with the man I used to be." But what can top that? Yes, trust me, finance can be dry. That's why you have me, and that's why I've juiced up the book to be more than just sentences and charts.

Let's take a *Where's Waldo* approach. I've sprinkled key sentences throughout the book for you to find. Be on the lookout for:

- *The most arrogant sentence in the book.*
- *The most important thing you can know about economics.*
- *The sentence you least want to read in the book.*
- *The only free lunch in the credit card industry.*
- *The most important sentence in the book.*
- *The scariest thought in this book.*

The information in this book is really quite simple because the world of money is, like Dr. Seuss's *Whoville*, a simple world. But every Whoville has its Grinch, and the world of money is no exception. There are financial "advisors" who invade and complicate things. These invaders try to make us believe that we can't manage our own money, and they eventually part us from it. Don't believe them. In truth, learning money management is almost as easy as falling off a ladder and certainly a lot less painful. The tough part isn't learning money management, the tough part is managing your money the way you learned how to. All too often people try to take the fast road to riches and all too often they are disappointed. But I'll preach that sermon later. For now, let's talk book structure.

The world of money is, like Dr. Seuss's Whoville, a simple world. But every Whoville has its Grinch.

Remember the book is divided into fifty secrets. I've made it easy to skip around and feel free to do so. Each secret has three sections:

- **Why It Works**—This section simply explains why that particular secret makes sense. It includes stuff like how much money it will make you, or how much money it will save you.
- **How It Works**—You may be surprised to learn that it took me years to come up with these section headings, but this section explains the secret in detail, either how to actually implement the secret itself or its specific components.

- **Secret at Work**—This will show either an example of what happens when you implement the secret or provide an exercise to help you complete the secret.

I've also thrown a few of my own icons:

Free Lunch—When you see this icon, you're about to read about one of life's free lunches. And yes, there are plenty of free lunches in the world. Anyone who disagrees with this statement simply fails to recognize the fact that one can have the Victoria's Secret catalog mailed to one's home, free of charge for the rest of one's life, without one ever ordering a single item. There, my male and female friends, is one of life's free lunches. Look for this icon to find others.

Recycle Bin—There's a lot of garbage out there, and I don't want you throwing your money away on any of it. If I come across a common misconception or something that's outright crap, I'll highlight it for you in the Recycle Bin.

In a Nutshell—Our society's peanut fetish has reached an alarming level because we want to hear everything "in a nutshell." But I'm fine with that. So I crammed the most important stuff into a sentence or two and highlighted it with the In-a-Nutshell icon.

Surf's Up—Scanning the web can save you thousands of dollars because of the bargains offered online. The Surf's-Up icon will point you to some of these great money-saving sites.

Rule of Thumb—Personal finance is ... well, personal. I can't possibly address your exact needs to the penny, but I will give you a general idea under the Rule-of-Thumb icon.

Fountain of Youth—This icon will show you how to use your youth to a financial advantage.

Hey Pete—This icon indicates a question is being asked that relates to the subject at hand. By the way, this guy to the left here is Buck, the hero of *Getting Loaded.*

End of the Rainbow—Legend tells us there's gold at the end of the rainbow, and I believe that. Only I use the term "rainbow" a little loosely. (There will be no chasing of leprechauns in this book.) Had I invested the $3.50 I spent on that beer it would have been worth $231.74 in the future. This icon will point out the future value of some other everyday expenses. Hopefully it will prove to you that the little things do make all the difference.

The Big Picture—Whatever you do, don't ignore these. The realm of personal finance is filled with countless concepts. That's the bad news. The good news is that you really only need a few of these concepts to do well financially. When you see this icon, pay attention.

Don't think, however, that it's okay for you to be that guy who stands in the aisles of Barnes & Noble thumbing through this book looking for all the Big-Picture icons. Most likely they won't make sense all on their own, and even if they did, you'll miss a smaller, but crucial step.

My Quick and Corny Speech

Compound interest is going to be your best financial friend. But I'll get to that in a minute. After I learned about compound interest, I scrounged around for other ways that young people have a financial edge over the rest of the world. Here's what I came up with:

We Have the Ability to Take More Risks. One key to investing is that the more risk you assume the more money you stand to make. Could it work any other way? Some readers of this book will be trying to buy a condo, others a car, others a computer game. I don't know you personally but whatever your situation is, you at least have plenty of time to make up for any financial mistakes you may make in your life. You invest in a stock, and it tanks. No problem, just ride it out. You lose some money in your own business. Don't worry, you've got time to get it back. Such is not the case for the sixty-nine-year-old.

We Haven't Lost It Yet. I don't mean your sanity, I mean your money. Most people, people much older than you and me, pick up a personal finance book not because they've made a bunch of dough but because they're tired of losing it. They pay their stockbroker too much, they've lost tens of thousands of dollars because they bought the wrong life insurance, they paid too much for their house, or their credit card bills are choking the life out of them, so, out of desperation, they mosey on down to the bookstore thinking this journey will solve their problems. By then it's often too late. If you learn about personal finance now, you'll be prepared when the salesperson tries to sell you overpriced insurance. You won't lose your shirt in the stock market, because your stock analysis will consist of more than just looking for the words "dot com." You'll not only begin earning more money right away, you'll also never lose it.

Computer Savvy. There are countless bargains on the internet. You can save on everything from banks to bongos to books. But you have to know how to use a computer. Those who don't know how to use one sink. Those who finally learned how to use one swim. Those of us who grew up with computers surf.

Abundance of Creativity. While I can't prove this, I believe that the younger you are the more creative you are. Each day of our lives we get more and more of society's rules thrown at us. Every time you're told a rule, you limit your possibilities. The keep-off-the-grass sign eliminates one possible way to get across campus. As Cat Stevens points out, "From the moment I could talk, I was ordered to listen." Some of these rules are justified, but many of them greatly hinder your creative mind. And in this day and age, creativity is your most valuable asset.

This idea hit me like a *Midnight Train to Georgia* while I was watching the Mel Gibson film *The Patriot* (not as good as *Braveheart* but worth the rental.) In the film, which is set during the Revolutionary War, an ambitiously evil British colonel asks his commanding officer what he will receive for his efforts in the war. His commanding officer offers him a generous land grant and begins with an explanation of how in America "the new aristocracy will be landowners." As I munched down my fifteen-dollar popcorn, I wondered, who is the new aristocracy today? Before the movie was over, I had the answer.

> *Today, the new aristocracy is creative people.*

Today, the new aristocracy is creative people. In the past, you had to have huge tracts of land or inherit a manufacturing plant to be rich, but now you can write a computer program in your garage that could be worth millions. (This is the story of Apple Computers.) If computers aren't your shtick, you and your friends can always prank call people, record the calls, and sell 'em. (This is the story of The Jerky Boys.) And if computers and prank calls still don't do it, you can always find yourself a lovely lady who is bringing up three very lovely girls. (This is the story of a man named Brady.)

Creativity alone isn't enough. The recent dot com bombs—which I'll discuss in detail later—prove that some rules are necessary. But even though the playing field still isn't perfectly even, because of our creativity it favors young people now more than ever. Anyway, I hate the word "aristocracy" (I picture funny wigs and croquet games.) When I use it, I simply mean a class of people who have the financial freedom to live life on their own terms, whatever those terms may be. Maybe that's sailing around the world, or giving all your money to charity. I don't know. I'm not here to tell you how to spend your money, just how to get control of it before it gets control of you.

I want people to realize that the strongest attributes of our generation also happen to be the most desired attributes for achieving financial freedom. You have more than you think.

Compound Interest. Finally we get to what Ben Franklin called the "eighth wonder of the world": compound interest. Here's how it's going to make you a millionaire.

Interest is a rental fee for money. People pay a fee to rent cars or videos, and likewise, when money is borrowed, the borrower pays interest to the lender to compensate for the use of the money. If I loan you $100 at 10% annual interest, you owe me $110 at the end of the year. Chili Palmer (a.k.a. John Travolta in the movie *Get Shorty*) made his money by making high-interest loans. You too can make money this way; only it's commonly known as loan sharking and it's illegal.

But you don't need to break the law to make money when you've got compound interest. Compound interest is simply interest paid on your initial investment (a.k.a. *principal*) and on the interest already earned. Imagine you invest $100 at 10% annual interest compounded (stick with me, I'm going somewhere with this). After the first year, your investment is worth $110 because you were paid 10% (or $10) in interest on $100. After the second year, your investment swells to $121 because now you're being paid 10% (or $11) interest on $110. The third year, you're paid $12 in interest (10% of $121), so your investment is worth $133.

 After forty-five years, compound interest turned your $100 investment into almost $7,000. Now, on top of your initial investment, if you invested an additional $100 a year, you'd end up with eighty grand after forty-five years. Invest one dollar a day at a 15% interest rate and after forty-five years, you'll have over a million dollars. Do you blame me for becoming obsessed with this stuff?

Hey Pete, you really expect me to wait forty-five years? I know it's a long time, but it's the easiest money you will ever make. Who else is going to pay you a million dollars to sit on your butt?

Want proof? Check out the chart below. It shows how compound interest turns a dollar a day ($365 a year) into a million.*

Year	Starting Cash	Interest Earned	Deposit	Ending Cash	
1	—	—	365	360	
2	360	50	365	770	I know this
3	770	110	365	1,240	looks boring
4	1,240	180	365	1,780	but
5	1,780	260	365	2,400	you wanted
6	2,400	360	365	3,120	proof.
7	3,120	460	365	3,940	
8	3,940	590	365	4,890	
9	4,890	730	365	5,980	
10	5,980	890	365	7,230	It takes twelve
11	7,230	1,080	365	8,670	years to get
12	8,670	1,300	365	10,330	to ten grand.
13	10,330	1,540	365	12,230	
14	12,230	1,830	365	14,420	
15	14,420	2,160	365	16,940	
16	16,940	2,540	365	19,840	Five more
17	19,840	2,970	365	23,170	years and
18	23,170	3,470	365	27,000	that money
19	27,000	4,050	365	31,410	doubles to over
20	31,410	4,710	365	36,480	twenty grand.
21	36,480	5,470	365	42,310	
22	42,310	6,340	365	49,010	

* This chart assumes an annual return of 15%, and all numbers have been rounded down. Since 1929, the stock market has returned about 11.8% but for the last ten years, the market's return has been much higher. We can play with interest rates all day long, but the fact remains that the earlier you start investing the larger your fortune will be.

23	49,010	7,350	365	56,720	
24	56,720	8,500	365	65,580	
25	65,580	9,830	365	75,770	
26	75,770	11,360	365	87,490	
27	87,490	13,120	365	100,970	Now the
28	100,970	15,140	365	116,470	numbers
29	116,470	17,470	365	134,300	start to look
30	134,300	20,140	365	154,800	really
31	154,800	23,220	365	178,380	attractive.
32	178,380	26,750	365	205,490	
33	205,490	30,820	365	236,670	
34	236,670	35,500	365	272,530	
35	272,530	40,870	365	313,760	
36	313,760	47,060	365	361,180	
37	361,180	54,170	365	415,710	
38	415,710	62,350	365	478,420	
39	478,420	71,760	365	550,540	Crossed
40	**550,540**	**82,580**	**365**	**633,480**	the half
41	633,480	95,020	365	728,860	million
42	728,860	109,320	365	838,540	mark.
43	838,540	125,780	365	964,680	
44	964,680	144,700	365	1,109,740	
45	1,109,740	166,460	365	1,276,560	One million!

You made it! Now let's take a closer look. Notice that your money doubles in value about every five years. Find year 40 on the chart (in bold). After forty years of investing a dollar a day, you've built a fortune worth $550,540. But at year 45, you have over a million dollars because every five years your fortune doubles. You've made half your fortune in the last five years. This is the big picture. **You have to start *today*.** In this example, waiting just five years would have cost you a half-million bucks. Painful procrastination.

Whatever your age, just start! At a young age, it isn't about money, it's about time. Don't have forty-five years left? So what? So you have to invest $2 a day. Big deal. Skip on that extra beer. Skip the Diet Coke. What's that compared to being a millionaire? There is no better or cheaper way to get your hands on a fortune than by investing small amounts of green over a long period of time. And compound interest does all the work.

If you were looking for a way to earn a million dollars in three weeks, you got the wrong book. The books that promises millions within months can be found just after the infomercial for spray-on hair and right before the infomercial for breast enlargement creams. All three will give you the same results. By the way, the average millionaire is fifty-four years old. It takes time, but anyone can do it.

There is no better or cheaper way to get your hands on a fortune than by investing small amounts of green over a long period of time. And compound interest does all the work.

Hey Pete, wait a minute, the subtitle of this book says, "Make a million . . . while you're still young enough to enjoy it." I won't be so young in 45 years. True. But believe it or not, you will start enjoying this money even before you get your hands on it. Personally, I'm still a ways away from a million, but I'm enjoying that million right now, not because I have it, but because I know I *will* have it. I think in life we all have a Plan A and a Plan B. Ya know, Plan A was to study singing and then hit Broadway, and if that didn't work out Plan B was to get a second major in education and then teach music. But I see a lot of people go straight to their Plan B and I think they do this because of the money. What if Broadway doesn't work out they ask themselves.

Getting started on a complete financial plan can be your catchall Plan B. Sure you won't see all the fruits of your financial plan for many many years, but knowing they're at least growing can instantly change your life. You're enjoying tomorrow's millions today.

I just told you why I think you should start investing today. Now it's your turn. You tell me why you should start investing today. Go to Part I to see what I mean.

PART ONE

call the shots

The first part of this book deals with organizing your finances. I know many of you want to jump straight ahead to Part V, which discusses investing, but the *Getting Loaded* plan doesn't work that way. Remember that financial planning is about your plans first and then your finances.

You want to save, maybe buy some stock, but why do you want to buy it? What are your goals? And whatever happened to that stock your grandfather gave you? What's in that safe deposit box you have at the bank? How much is all this stuff from the Franklin Mint worth anyway?

There's no point in buying a stock unless you have a reason for buying it. There's no point in saving money unless saving money is part of your plans. So we'll start with the planning and the organization.

go for the goals

Give me a stock clerk with a goal and I will give you a man who will make history. Give me a man without a goal and I will give you a stock clerk.

JAMES CASH PENNEY
(FOUNDER OF JCPENNEY)

Let me tell you the secret that has led me to my goal. My strength lies solely in my tenacity.

LOUIS PASTEUR

Why It Works

If this book is about living life on your own terms, it's time you thought about what those terms are. "What do you want?" is the question for this secret.

Yeah, yeah, I know you know what you want. But if you really want it to happen, you'll put it in writing. Think about it. These days, if it's important, people make you write it down. When you apply for student loans, does your college hand you a fistful of twenties and say, "Get crackin' Einstein"? Of course not. You sign off

on a written agreement to pay back those loans. That's what this secret is about. Making a written commitment to achieve your goals.
When a goal is in writing, you know clearly what you are trying to
achieve and when you are going to achieve it. When a goal is not in
writing, it's a wish.

How It Works

There are good goals and bad goals. Neither has anything to do with
ethics. To enter the *Guinness Book of World Records* as the World's
Most Committed Chain-smoker is not a bad goal (though a rather
stupid one). A bad goal is one that is unspecific and
one that cannot be measured. The following goals are
examples:

When a goal is

not in writing,

it's a wish.

- *"I want to be rich."* When? And how rich is rich?
- *"I want a date."* Don't we all? Who do you want a
  date with? Steve Urkel? Janet Reno?
- *"By the end of next year, I want to have more money."* A dollar
  more? A thousand dollars more?
- *"I want a new car before winter."* A Pinto? A Ferrari?
- *"I have only one burning desire, let me stand next to your fire."*
  Ummm . . .

A good goal is one that is in writing and is as specific as possible. It
should describe exactly what you want and when you want it. Specific
dollar amounts, product brands and features, and locations should all
be named in your goals. This makes your goals *measurable*, which
means you are clearly able to tell when you have achieved them. Finally, each goal should have one or two sentences attached that explain
what you need to do to achieve that goal. Good goals look like this:

- *"By age fifty-five, I want to retire with $1.5 million. That means I
  have to invest two dollars a day."*
- *"I want a date with Brad Pitt, so I must call the* National Enquirer
  and start some nasty rumors about Jennifer Aniston."

- *"By the end of June, I want my monthly income to increase by $100. That means I have to either cut back on my spending, approach my boss for a raise, or make better investments to provide additional income."*
- *"Before I graduate from high school, I want a cherry red El Camino dropped down real low, twice pipes, base cannon, and lift kit. This will cost $24,000 (plus $10 for the fuzzy dice). I can probably get $2,000 for my jalopy on a trade-in, so I need to save $150 a month in order to pay cash."*
- *"Ideally I'd like to be standing six to eight feet from your fire, sometime between now and St. Patrick's Day."*

Specific, measurable, with a brief explanation of what needs to be done. Perfect.

Secret #1 at Work

Grab a sheet of paper and start writing down your goals. Be specific. You can follow the format I provided below or create your own.

I want _____

_____

_____

I want it by _____

_____

_____

Here is what I have to do to get it _____

_____

_____

_____

Follow this format for each one of your goals. Go ahead and write anything down, no matter how big or outrageous it seems. The next secret, which talks about organizing and prioritizing your goals, is where we start crossing off things like the life-size ceramic Godzilla lawn ornament.

 When people write down their goals, a big-picture idea often pops up. Look at your goal sheets. Do your goals say anything about buying a gourmet coffee every morning? How about anything about eating lunch out every day? Typically people don't write down such trivial goals as buying gourmet coffee or a Pizza Hut all-you-can-eat buffet. People's written goals are about big things like trips to Paris, or having $10,000 saved up within three years. But think for a second: in the last month, how much money have you allocated to the gourmet coffee fund, and how much toward the trip-to-Paris fund? Hey, if you want the coffee, buy the coffee. But I hope you're not reading this book so you can upgrade from the tall to the grande. Personal finance is about financing your plans, your *big* plans. This is something to think about next time you are standing in line at Starbucks.

To help you remember your big-picture goals, turn your big goals into a picture. Get a picture of each one of your goals and put it where you'll see it every day. Some great places to put pictures of your goals are:

- The refrigerator. The only art gallery in the world that turns no one away.
- Your key chain. Get a small picture of your goal and have it lami-

nated. Most people carry around a bottle opener, but hey, whatever reminds you about *Getting Loaded*.

- Your screen saver. Why look at psychedelic cubes (unless your goal is to be on acid) or an underwater world (unless your goal is to be a fish)? Download a picture of your goal and slap it on the screen saver. In fact, you can get two for one off your computer. One goal is your screen saver and one is the background of your desktop.

 ### Secret #1 in a Nutshell
Goals should be specific, measurable, and tied to a timeline.

---

wake up and prioritize your dreams

The man who can master his time can master nearly anything.

WINSTON CHURCHILL

Why It Works

A twelve-room penthouse. A vacation to Trinidad. The Grand Funk Railroad boxed set. Unless your last name is Trump, you can't have it all—yet. If you're going to succeed in achieving your goals, you first have to choose the goals most important to you and then focus on obtaining them. Try to get everything and you will end up with nothing. I admit that dreams are like songs. It's tough to pick your favorite. ("Wild Horses" by The Rolling Stones if you're curious). Remember the wise words of John Rogers and Peter McWilliams, authors of *Wealth 101*, "You can have anything you want, but you can't have *everything* you want." It's time we picked your pleasures. Secret #2 will make this task easy on you by sorting your goals by cost.

How It Works

The idea is to determine how much each goal will cost you and how important that particular goal is to you. Some goals have hidden costs. For example, if your goal is to spend more time with your friends, you may need to find out what it will cost you to cut back on your work hours, or how much it will cost you to purchase a computer so you can do more work at home. You must figure out how the decision will impact your finances.

Some goals have hidden costs.

First, look at your list of goals from Secret #1 and see if there is anything you can eliminate. You may have thought at the time that you couldn't live without that six-foot velvet Elvis but compared to all your other goals, the King becomes insignificant. Cross out as many as you can.

Now make four separate lists in which your goals are organized by how much they will cost you. Create an under $1,000 category, a $1,000 to $5,000 category, a $5,000 to $25,000 category, and a category for purchases over $25,000. Now that your list of goals is organized by cost, it's easier to prioritize them. And don't forget, as boring as it may sound, paying off debt—unless it's a mortgage payment or college loans—is a major goal, because high interest from credit cards and car loans will impede all your other goals. If you have debts and if your bookie carries a gun, your debts must have top priority. (See more on this in Secret #10.)

Paying off debt—unless it's a mortgage payment or college loans— is a major goal, because high interest from credit cards and car loans will impede all your other goals.

Keep this list handy and make copies so it won't get lost. Read your goals over from time to time. The more you look at your goals, the more likely you are to achieve them. Have those Beanie Babies you wanted gone down in price? Did the dealer finally agree to shave $100 off that Harley? And don't keep Secret #2 a secret. Tell your goals to other people; they might be able to help you.

Secret #2 at Work

Use the following blank goal sheets to complete Secret #2.

- **Goals under $1,000**

  1. _____
  2. _____
  3. _____
  4. _____
  5. _____

- **Goals from $1,000 to $5,000**

  1. _____
  2. _____
  3. _____
  4. _____
  5. _____

- **Goals from $5,000 to $25,000**

  1. _____
  2. _____
  3. _____
  4. _____
  5. _____

- **Goals over $25,000**

  1. _____
  2. _____

3. _____

4. _____

5. _____

Quickie Over 35% of Americans have written wills, but less than 5% have written goals.

Secret #2 in a Nutshell
Divide your goals up by how much they will cost you to achieve them. Once they are placed in categories, you can prioritize them, which puts you that much closer to achieving them.

---

find your net worth

The greatest good you can do for another is not just to share your riches, but to reveal to him his own.

BENJAMIN DISRAELI

Why It Works

Now you know what you want, how badly you want it, and what it's gonna cost you to get it. You see the light at the end of your tunnel, but how long is the tunnel? If your goal is to have $1 million and you've got $975,000, well, this should be easy. But for the rest of us, we need to know exactly how much money we have and where that money is located, so we can rearrange it to get what we want. Take U.S. Savings Bonds. If you've got anything to show for yourself, this is probably it. A favorite gift of relatives, U.S. Savings Bonds can be bought in small amounts, making them a staple of the birthday or the bar mitzvah. These bonds pay peanuts in interest but because they're cheap, safe, and patriotic (and since no one knows your shirt size anyway), they were gifted to you. By finding your net worth, you may discover that you have way too much green in these low-interest Savings Bonds and a readjustment is necessary.

How It Works

Net worth is the number you wind up with when you subtract your *liabilities* from your *assets*. My *what* from my *who*? An asset is anything you own. Assets can be gold, cash, real estate, even a pair of socks. A liability is anything you owe, what you are liable for. Liabilities include debt, mortgages, phone bills, or car loans. To find your net worth, you have to compare what you own with what you owe.

Secret #3 at Work

Grab the following:

1. A pad of paper
2. A pen
3. A calculator
4. A cup of coffee or cold drink (Depending on when you do this. No alcohol! This is important!)

Next, gather all the financial information you have about yourself: credit card bills, bank statements, stock certificates, gold coins, student loan statements, or outstanding criminal fines (they warned you not to copy those VHS cassettes). Now, make two piles—you guessed it—one for assets and one for liabilities. As you glance over each bit of financial information, decide whether it is an asset or a liability and chuck it into the appropriate pile.

Once you've made two piles, start listing your assets and liabilities on the sheets provided. Notice that the assets sheet doesn't include everything you could possibly own. Your car is probably worth several thousand dollars, but don't bother listing that as an asset. When you calculate your net worth, you should list only your *appreciable assets* or assets that are most likely to increase in value. Your car, your Levi's jeans, and your Pink Floyd CDs are going to decrease in value. They are *depreciable assets*. They're great for building a wardrobe and a music collection but they're a horrible way to build a financial foundation.

After you have filled in the sheets, just total the assets and liabilities. Then subtract your liabilities from your assets. Congratulations! You now know your net worth.

Don't Panic! At this point, it doesn't matter what your net worth is. Be it high or low, positive or negative, the other forty-seven secrets in this book will help you achieve the net worth you desire.*

Feel free to add your own categories to these worksheets. If a category doesn't apply to you, just write zero.

Net Worth Worksheet

Assets

Current value of home _____

Other real estate _____

Checking account _____

Savings account _____

Eyewitness account (just seeing if you were paying attention)

Gold _____

Stocks _____

Mutual funds _____

Bonds _____

Value of business _____

---

* In fact, since I didn't let you count all your depreciable assets, I bet most people will be in the negative numbers. Only the more reason to start getting loaded—the other way—today.

Cash value of insurance policies _____

Other investments _____

Total value of assets _____

Hey Pete, my asset list sucks! I have like two things on it. I don't have any insurance policies or mutual funds or any of that stuff.

Don't worry about it. At least now you know.

Liabilities

Mortgage _____

Home equity loan, remaining balance _____

Car loan, remaining balance _____

Student loan, remaining balance _____

Credit card, outstanding balance _____

Other loan payment, remaining balance _____

Other _____

Total liabilities _____

TOTAL ASSETS − TOTAL LIABILITIES =

NET WORTH _____

Secret #3 in a Nutshell

Gather every scrap of financial information you have about yourself. Divide this information into two piles, what you own (assets) and what you owe (liabilities). Add up the items in each pile. Then subtract the liabilities pile from your assets pile. That's your net worth.

organize your portfolio

I'm just preparing my impromptu remarks.

WINSTON CHURCHILL

Why It Works

It works because this isn't the dating game. This is the investment game. In the dating game, it's all about vibes. Ya know, vibes, some feeling that the other person likes you. You lock eyes. You catch her staring at you, you catch him looking in your direction. Vibes, however unreliable, are the basis for all decisions made in the dating world.

Not so in the investment world. In the investment world, all decisions should be made based on solid information. The problem is that too many people base investment decisions on vibes. Their investment information is about as organized as a mosh pit. If you're single, just blame the vibes. If you're broke, blame yourself.

If you're sick of being broke, you gotta organize your investments. If you're sick of being single, the answer is clear—no more karaoke.

How It Works

Your investments are grouped together in your *portfolio*. Your portfolio is simply the collection of the investments you own. It can be made up of stocks, bonds, real estate, cash, gold, whatever. We'll get to what should be in your portfolio later. For now, we're just concerned with how to organize it.

Come up with whatever system you want, but I'll offer a simple one. The first step is to get a file cabinet or file box, some hanging file folders, and some of those manila file folders. Each file folder represents the location where you have the investment. For instance, if you trade stocks through the brokerage firm E*Trade, then E*Trade is one folder. Your bank is another. You may have another folder labeled "Valuable stuff in my safe deposit box."

Each of these larger folders should contain manila folders for each specific investment. Say you have an account with E*Trade in which you own Coke, Microsoft, McDonald's, and Enron (Nobody's perfect). Each of these companies should have its own manila folder within the E*Trade folder. You may also have a folder for your bank. At that bank, you may have both a savings and a checking account, so each account has its own folder. Like this:

Bank Folder	E*Trade Account Folder	Safe Deposit Box
Checking Account Folder	Coke Folder	Savings Bond Folder
Savings Account Folder	Microsoft Folder	Gold Coin Folder
	McDonald's Folder	
	Enron Folder	

In these folders, you can put information you come across on each investment—maybe an article on the price of gold or a stock report on the company you own. When you buy and sell investments, you always get a receipt so be sure to stuff the receipt in the appropriate folder.

You can take this financial filing system as far as you want. Some people, folks much more organized than me, have different folders for every different financial document, one for credit cards, another folder for the warranty on their computer and still more for their apartment lease, their car loans, student loans and so on. You do what you want, but if you tend to fall a bit on the lazy side, be sure to at least have one catchall folder where you stuff every financial document. It may not be organized, but at least you have it if you need it. To make it easy on yourself, you could have a folder for every year. At the end of every year you could go through the folder and determine what you can throw out (like supermarket receipts) and what you must keep (like tax information.) If you get scared, just keep everything. Even without knowing your particular financial situation I'm willing to bet ten years of financial information (ten folders) could easily fit into one drawer of a file cabinet.

The only other thing that I like to do is make a few brief notes every time I buy and sell an investment. Writing your thoughts prevents you from acting on your vibes, which will hopefully prevent you from losing thousands of dollars over your lifetime.

You can use a computer to track your investments, or if you use an internet stockbroker, your investments are probably tracked for you over the computer. But you will still receive paper copies of everything, and rather than slam-dunking them in the trash (excuse, recycle bin), you should stuff them in your investment filing system. Your system doesn't have to be perfect (mine certainly isn't), just good enough so you don't do anything stupid.

 Hey Pete, do I really need to do all this? Yes, here's why. Imagine you bought Microsoft at $50, then $75, then $100. Now the Soft is trading at $125 a share. You think that's high and you want to sell some, but not all, of your investment. But which shares? If you were trying to duck the tax man, you should sell the $100 shares. Why? Because then the government only taxes a $25 profit. You bought the stock for $100 and sold it for $125. But if you don't specify which shares, the government will assume you sold the $50 shares and tax the much larger profit of $75 per share. To sell the correct shares, you'll have to know what you purchased, on what date, and for how much. The answer can be found in your investment filing system.

A final folder you should have is for taxes. Just label that folder "Taxes 2002" (or if you really want to be clever try "2002: A Tax Odyssey"), and stuff it with all your tax info for the year. (More on taxes in Secret #16.)

And don't worry if you don't own any investments—you will. The important thing is to be able to get your hands on any financial information quickly and easily.

> *And don't worry if you don't own any investments—you will. The important thing is to be able to get your hands on any financial information quickly and easily.*

Secret #4 at Work

Here is a sheet you can use to jot down a few notes before you buy or sell an investment. Feel free to make up your own.

Date _____

Name of investment_____

Cost of investment_____

Commissions and transaction costs _____

Number of shares_____

I bought/sold this investment because _____

_____

Secret #4 in a Nutshell

Create a file-folder system or use a computer to keep track of your investments. This is especially important when you sell an investment because you'll know what you paid for the investment and what you can expect to give the tax man.

get some green off those goals

> The public may boo me, but when I go home and think of money, I clap.
>
> HORACE

Why It Works

Webster's Dictionary provides the following definitions:

Purchase: To obtain by paying money or its equivalent.

Investment: The outlay of money for income or profit.

What's this mean to you and me? Basically, when you make a purchase, the item you bought will go down in value. When you make an investment, the item you bought will go up in value. Less purchases and more investments equals more money in your pocket.

 Now I know you're thinking, *"Gee Pete, thanks for the obvious advice. If I don't spend any money, of course there will be more money in my pocket."* But I'm not asking you to spend less money, I'm simply asking you to spend less money on things that don't go up in value (like a camera) and spend more money on things that do (like your own photography business).

How It Works

Take a quick look at your goals from Secret #1. Can you turn any of your purchases into investments? You don't have to spend less money, just funnel more money into appreciable assets and less to those that depreciate. As Harvey Mackay, author of *Swim with the Sharks Without Being Eaten Alive*, says, "Buy cheap cars and expensive houses." Cars go down in value, houses go up in value. So if you're gonna splurge, splurge on the house and opt for the Pinto.*
    What else goes up in value?

- Home improvements make your home go up in value. Will it be a jet ski in the garage or a Jacuzzi in the bathroom? A jet ski will start losing money the moment you take it out of the show room. A Jacuzzi won't make you a millionaire, but it could add to the value of your home.
- Investment in education leads to salary increases, job security, and employment flexibility. Education doesn't have to be you in a classroom taking notes. It could mean a trip to France. While you're there, don't just stuff yourself with Bordeaux and beef Bourgogne. Try to learn something that will make you more marketable in the workforce—the local language perhaps. Here's a great Spanish money saver: *"Tiene usted un menu de precio fijo?"* Translation: "Do you have a fixed-price menu?"
- Investment in your own business leads to additional income. Still want that jet ski, huh? Well, can you make a few extra bucks renting it out?

---

* *Hey Pete, why do you keep ragging on the Pinto?* The Pinto's value dropped significantly when it was discovered that the car was likely to EXPLODE when it was hit from behind. I don't ask for much in a car, but spontaneous combustion is where I put my foot down.

Whoa, whoa, whoa Pete, I don't know where you buy your lottery tickets, but I make $26,000 a year and I live in a 300-square-foot studio apartment. I'm scraping by here, and you're talking about buying jet skis and adding a Jacuzzi to my bathroom? Look, I hear ya. But the point of personal finance is to learn about what to do in a jet ski/Jacuzzi dilemma *before* a jet ski/Jacuzzi dilemma comes up. I'm just trying to point out that spending money isn't necessarily a bad thing in itself; it matters where you spend it. Before you throw down your money, think about how you can obtain that same item without paying the full price. True, you're scraping by on $26,000 a year, but why do you keep laying down $3 every day for a caramel mochaccino? Invest (yes invest) in a Mr. Coffee and start earning $3 a day on your investment.

> **Don't ask your wallet for permission to do something.**

Remember the point of *Getting Loaded* is about living your life on your own terms. Stop living on money's terms. What I mean is don't ask your wallet for permission to do something. I don't take orders from my bank account, and neither should you. Stop asking, "Can I afford this," and start asking, "*How* can I afford this?"* Can I convert this purchase into an investment? Can I find something or someone to help shoulder some of the cost? Look, we took two secrets to find out exactly what you want. Now let's be sure you get it. If you want it, make it happen!

Secret #5 at Work

I interviewed several people who changed their purchases into investments. Here's what they did:

- My friend's parents wanted to buy a sailboat, which is a great way to lose money. While they could afford the price of the boat, they didn't want to sink all their money into such an expensive—like $365,000—depreciable asset. So they turned the boat into a

---

* Without using a credit card!

business. They found a company that would rent it out for them and take a cut of the profits. In doing this, they managed to cut about 20% or $73,000 from the purchase price.

- A friend wanted to buy a beer-making kit, which ran about $500. Guess what he got everyone for gifts last Christmas? Guess what everyone will get this Christmas? Guess whose beer-making enterprise has saved him hundreds of dollars in Christmas presents over the years?

- Another friend of mine always wanted to go to Italy but could never scrape together the cash. But then I told her that education is an appreciable asset, so she spent two months there studying abroad and she paid the same price as a regular semester of college. Plus, she is now semifluent in another language, a very marketable trait.

- I got this last one from a college history professor. He wrote to the major cruise-ship lines and told them he'd be happy to lecture on the history of each port the ship visited if they would offer him a free trip. They went for it, and he's traveled all over the world—fo' free. If you have a talent that may be of some use to a cruise line, call them up! See the website directory (p. 361) for help.

Think about it. The possibilities are endless. If you love to travel, can you write for travel magazines? If you love to ski, can you be on the ski patrol? If you love the theater, can you become a critic? If you love pornography, can you . . . well, you get the idea.

Secret #5 in a Nutshell

Take a second and go over that goal sheet. It will be much easier to reach your goals if you can get them to make money for you, or if you can get someone or something to share the cost of your goals. Can you devise a way to turn some of those purchases into investments? Remember, your creativity is an asset. Now's the time to use it.

---

get a college education for $25

If you don't profit from your mistakes, someone else will.

YALE HIRSCH

Why It Works

It works for three reasons:

1. Because you're young.
2. Because they care.
3. Because everyone loves a free lunch.

You know there is such a thing as a free lunch. Everybody loves a free lunch. This secret is about getting the power of a free lunch to work for you.

How It Works

Find someone who is doing what you want to be doing. Tell them you're interested in learning more about what it is they do and offer to buy them lunch. That's how you get a college education for $25.

There are only two types of knowledge: knowledge gained from formal education, and knowledge gained from experience. Schools and colleges offer knowledge in the form of formal education, but they offer little experience. Experience can be found either by doing something yourself or by interviewing someone who has done or is doing what you want to be doing.

Experience can be found either by doing something yourself or by interviewing someone who has done or is doing what you want to be doing.

This is the other half of your college education. It's the part you can't get in school, the part no one does, and the part that's cheap.

Imagine you are a painter. You went to art school and learned all about the masters, and the colors. You learned the brush strokes and heard the art jokes.* But where was the class on how to survive in Manhattan while working two jobs and trying to paint on your day off, which comes every leap year? Few, if any art schools teach such a class.

So you have to go to another school, the Free Lunch University, if you'll allow such a corny name to slide. You need to find a painter who somehow survives in Manhattan on low-wage temp jobs and still finds time to paint. When you find that person, you need to offer them a free lunch.

 I'm certainly not the first author to point out the importance of mentors, but I may just be the first to point out how important it is to do this now. Here's where your age helps you. The older you get, the tougher this is. Picture a successful real estate agent who is approached by a twenty-year-old interested

* How many art students does it take to—ahhh nevermind.

in a career in real estate and wanting to find out how this successful agent sells so many houses. The real estate agent is happy to have lunch with this "kid" because a twenty-year-old poses no threat to his business.

If, on the other hand, a forty-eight-year-old man were to approach the same agent, I think the agent would be cautious. The agent may worry that she is giving up industry secrets to a competitor.

Secret #6 at Work

Grab the goals again. See if you can set up a lunch date with an expert that may be able to help you achieve one of those goals. Perhaps you want to buy a house, but you don't make a lot of money. Find someone who has the same income as you and owns a house. How did that person do it?

 We're going to get into using investments to help you reach your goals. But hell, let's start with the easy stuff. A simple, $25 one-hour lunch with an expert can be an unbelievable investment. What's great about it, and don't ask me why it's this way, is that experts *want* to share their knowledge with young people. Even better, when I have done this, the experts sometimes end up buying *me* lunch!

 Secret #6 in a Nutshell
Find someone who achieved the same goals you have. Ask if you can buy them lunch. Then, over tuna melts and taco salads, ask them how they did it.

---

get a little help

He that won't be counseled can't be helped.

BENJAMIN FRANKLIN,
POOR RICHARD'S ALMANAC

Why It Works

No finance book can cover every topic. If you do try to read a finance book that takes you to every corner of the financial world, you'll probably fall asleep by page 871. You may need a little help from a financial advisor, and this secret is about finding a financial advisor. But the key word in this secret's title is "little" because after you read this book, that's all the help you're going to need. Just a little.

How It Works

There are only three things I hate:

1. One-way streets.
2. That Beach Boys song "Kokomo."
3. The fact that it is extremely difficult to find a financial advisor.

When it comes to one-way streets, I'll just walk. When it comes to "Kokomo," I'll just change the station. But when it comes to financial advisors, it's not so easy.

First let me point out some of the difficulties with selecting a financial advisor:

- **Enormous conflicts of interest.** Some financial planners remind me of authors who deliberately use big words whether they fit or not. I promise I won't do that. (The *last* thing I want is this book to become another insalubrious enchiridion.) Those big-word authors write for themselves, not for you. At times, financial advisors invest *your* money for *themselves*, not for you. Here's what I mean. A large number of financial planners make money by selling people certain investments, not by assisting them with their financial plans. If your financial planner will make $1,000 when you buy investment A—an investment you clearly don't need—or will make $200 when you buy investment B—an investment that's much more in line with your goals— you tell me, which one is she going to push for?

- **It's tough to tell when you get a bad deal.** Financial advising is unlike any other profession. It's true a plastic surgeon has enormous conflicts of interest. The more breast implants and tummy tucks he does, the more money he is going to make, right? That's true, except it would be rather easy to catch a plastic surgeon performing unnecessary surgery—"In my professional opinion ma'am, a healthy size for you would be a EEE." But catching a lousy financial advisor is tough. Imagine you gave your financial advisor $5,000 to invest on your behalf. Ten years later, that $5,000 is worth $8,000. Did you get a bad deal? All you did was write a check and ten years later, you've got an extra $3,000. That was easy, wasn't it? Well, making money is hardly a bad thing but the truth is that over a ten-year period, you probably could have done much better. In fact, whatever investment it was that your financial advisor bought to turn your $5,000 into $8,000 probably could have been bought without paying a fee to your financial advisor. Simply by not paying a fee, you would have ended up with more money.

- **Regulation schmegulation.** The trouble with much of the financial industry is that it is often regulated *by the financial industry.* It's supposed to keep an eye on itself. The government doesn't really keep a watchful eye over the day-to-day practices of financial planners. Many financial organizations are charged with policing themselves. Is it possible to slap one's own wrist?

- **Another overlooked problem with financial advisors is YOU.** Often the good ones will tell you the stuff you *don't* want to hear. Let me tell you about the last time I got hammered (I don't mean hammered like that, I mean hammered in an argument). I was at a party and it came up that I was writing a personal finance book. People began asking me for advice, but one guy in particular really needed some help (in more ways than one!). He asked me what I recently invested in. I told them that I was trying to cut back on my spending so I recently switched all the lightbulbs in my apartment to energy-saving bulbs. He laughed of course and asked for some "better" advice. When I mentioned I found a much better credit card, the laughter got louder. "Come on," he said, "give me something *really* good." Okay, I thought, time to bring out the big guns. I told him about a stock that I had just bought. The stock wasn't Coke, but the company was just as large and well-known and as delightfully boring as Coke and this seemed to piss him off. He wanted a company with the word "tech" in its name. He wouldn't even let me explain my reasons for buying it, he just argued I didn't know anything about finance. I was giving him solid financial advice but because it wasn't sexy, he didn't want to hear it.

Many financial organizations are charged with policing themselves. Is it possible to slap one's own wrist?

The truth about finance is that often the simplest steps will make you the most money. The sad truth is that because the last statement is true, many financial advisors make money by steering you away from the simple yet profitable investments and into the investments that make them—not you—the most money. But the *really* sad truth is that when you finally find a good financial advisor, *you're* often the one who forces that financial advisor to buy a lousy investment you don't need.

These are some of the problems with finding a financial advisor. So how do you sort through all the bull and find a good one?

First, find out your financial advisor's angle. True, it may seem like the financial advisor who has a law degree, a master's degree in business, and who sat on the President's Council of Economics is a qualified woman. But if she tries to sell you overpriced investments you don't need, how much are those qualifications worth? So a great question to ask all financial advisors is, "How do you make your money?"

That's the question; now let me tell you the answer. Ideally the answer you're looking for is "I charge an hourly fee for my advice." A financial advisor who charges by the hour won't try to steer you into investments you don't need, because she doesn't make any more money if you buy these investments. I'm not saying all financial advisors who work on commission are biased, but the temptation is there. You're safest sticking with hourly fee advisors but in the end, it's really a question of the individual person. Partner with the person who makes you feel comfortable.

 Hey Pete, I have an easy way around all this. I'll just look for a financial advisor who's made a lot of money. Obviously they'll know a thing or two about increasing my net worth. Ummm . . . not necessarily. Imagine I sell one million copies of this book within twelve months, thereby putting well over $1 million in my pocket in a year. But does that mean I know a lot about financial advice? Certainly not, it just means I know a lot about selling books.

The reality is that the more honest and reputable financial planners often make less money than their not-so-honest and not-so-reputable comrades. An honest, fee-only financial planner may charge you $300 for a three-hour session. But what about the not-so-honest financial planner who uses that three-hour session to sell you an overpriced investment that makes him a commission of not $300 but $3,000 dollars? The latter financial planner will get richer much quicker than the former, but will do so at the expense of the person they were supposed to help—you.

Another warning sign that your financial planner is thinking solely about themselves is whether or not they ask you about your goals. Remember that financial planning *is first about your plans*. Your finances come second. If a financial advisor opens the meeting with a line like, "it's a great time to buy stocks," grab your coat and a fistful of mints from the candy dish and get out of there. A good financial advisor will always ask you about your goals first and then figure out, based on your goals, the best place for your money.

Beware too, of the ones who skip the simple stuff. For most people, the best things they can do with the first few thousand dollars they save is to pay off credit card debt, buy the proper insurance, and start an emergency reserve fund. If a financial advisor is pushing for you to invest in the stock market and mentions nothing about credit cards, insurance, or emergencies, they probably make money off selling stocks and make nothing off those other things.

Secret #7 at Work

Hey Pete, now I'm really confused. Is there anyone out there who can help me?

There is. First of all there's you. Unless you have a multiple personality disorder, you're never going to cheat yourself. You know what's best for you better than anyone else. After reading this book, you may not need a financial advisor for quite some time. (And if you do have a multiple personality disorder, then you've got it easier than everyone else. One personality reads the first twenty-five secrets, and your other personality reads the last twenty-five secrets. You've cut your reading time in half!)

There is one thing a financial advisor can do that no book or magazine can and that's give you a kick in the ass. I never understood why people paid for personal trainers until my mom got one and her bench press came dangerously close to exceeding mine. I worked out when I could find time, but my mom (or rather my mom's trainer) made sure she worked out consistently. Financial advisors can be that missing link between saying you're going to invest and actually doing it.

There are two financial advisors I'd seriously consider partnering up with. One is a tax advisor, and the other is a lawyer. I say this because while the basics of investing never change, the tax code and the legal code are always changing (There were over 440 new tax laws written in the year 2001).

A *tax advisor* will charge you about $75 to $200 an hour to prepare your taxes depending on their degree of skill, the number of designations they have earned and the complexity of your taxes. If you always prepare your own taxes, I'd go and have a tax professional prepare them at least once. Ask a lot of questions. Work with the tax professional to develop a tax strategy—figure out some ways to reduce your taxes year after year. Your tax advisor will be doing it on the computer (if he isn't, then go somewhere else) so play around. Ask how much more you'll pay in taxes if you get that $3,000 raise. Ask how much you'll save if you go back to school. The money you spend on the tax advisor might pay for itself in tax savings. Unless your tax life is really complex—you own your own business, like an overseas chicken farm—you can get by with a retail tax preparation firm, which will charge around $100. These are firms like H&R Block. If you do have complex taxes, you might want to seek out the help of an enrolled agent or EA, which is someone who has passed a government exam. Many retail firms have at least one enrolled agent on staff. For those with supercomplex taxes—you inherited your uncle's overseas chicken farm, even though he's not really your uncle and technically, they're not really chickens—you may need the help of a certified public accountant or CPA, which is someone who has earned the highest tax designation available (and naturally charges the highest fees possible).

You won't see too many financial books telling young people to seek out a tax advisor and develop a tax strategy, but it is important for many reasons. The first is that many of the simplest tax breaks fit snugly into the lives of students and young professionals. These juicy tax breaks revolve around education expenses, moving expenses, children, working overseas, and earning a low income. Do any of those sound like you? And let's face it—taxes are a painless way to save money. Would you rather save $700 by giving up cable for a year or by getting a tax break?

Finally, the truth is that you're better off spending fifteen minutes going over your taxes to make sure they're done right, and that you've taken every tax break you're entitled to, than you are spending *fifty* minutes researching a stock. A tax break is not subject to the emotional whims of a market, as stocks are. Most retail tax firms will look over your tax return (or past year returns) for free. I ended up saving many of my tax clients hundreds of dollars. If there's a company in your neighborhood who prepares taxes, ask them if they'll look it over free of charge. Pay only if it will save you money. You have nothing to lose.

Lawyers can help you on a variety of things, from structuring your own business to estate planning. Their hourly fees range from "a fortune" all the way up to "Oh my God, you gotta be kidding me." Still we can't seem to do too much these days without the help of a lawyer. It may make sense for you (or rather your parents if they haven't already done so) to contact a qualified estate planning attorney to minimize taxes. Or if you ever start your own business (and I hope you do), talk with a tax advisor or attorney about the most tax-friendly way to structure your business. More about starting your own business in Secret #46.

Hey Pete, I'm eighteen years old and I just got to college. You really expect me to meet with a tax advisor or an attorney?

This question brings up a big-picture idea, and that is that no one is a financial island. The reality is that the way you arrange your finances affects your parent's financial life and vice versa. Perhaps your parents are helping you pay for college. Great idea, but if they're saving money in your name, it will greatly hinder your chances of getting financial aid. What your parents and grandparents do with their money can affect your financial life. It may seem like there's no reason for you to meet with a tax advisor but if you didn't get all the financial aid you were expecting, it may be because your parents, not you, have made a financial mistake. Perhaps your folks need to meet with a tax advisor and since their money affects yours and vice versa, you need to go along. Throughout this book you'll see many, many examples about the importance of talking with your parents about money. For now, just realize that you're not the only person in your personal finance plan.

If you do decide to use a general financial planner, they'll charge anywhere from $75 to $150 an hour. Your first meeting will be about three hours, probably less if you followed all the secrets in this book. If you're married, bring your spouse. If the plan is "free" that means the planner makes money by selling investments.

So you have three hours. What should you do? Well this person is a financial *planner*, as opposed to a financial bowler or a financial belly dancer, so you should spend those hours *planning*. Tell her your goals and devise a plan on how you can reach them. Maybe even read this book first.

Some good questions to ask a financial planner are:

- "How much life/car/disability/health/other insurance do I need?"
- "Based on my goals, how much money do I need to be saving every month?"
- "Now that I am married, how should I organize my finances?"
- "I use X credit card. Is there currently a card out there that is a better option?"
- "How can my parents and I work together to build a healthy financial future?"
- "How can I pay for college for myself, my spouse, or my children?"
- "Do you foresee any problems in my financial life?"
- "Can you recommend any places in my life where I can cut back on expenses?"
- "What changes/additions would you make to my financial life?"
- And most important, "Can you validate my parking?"

After reading *Getting Loaded*, you may never need to meet with a planner. But at least you know how to contact and evaluate a qualified professional if a major financial change takes place in your life.

One final thought: you are always your own best financial advisor. You know yourself better than anyone else knows you, and you'll never knowingly cheat yourself out of money. Your financial planner is a human being, so it is important to double-check what she tells you.

Secret #7 in a Nutshell

A good financial planner can be hard to find. Consider using highly specialized planners like tax advisors or attorneys for very specific areas of your financial life. Your finances affect your parents' and vice versa.

PART TWO

put it on my tab

You're through the first part. Believe it or not, simply by doing these first seven secrets, you are more financially prepared than the majority of Americans. Not bad for just the first part of the book.

This next section is about how to get more bang for your buck. Most personal finance books work in the opposite manner. They ask you to cut back on your proverbial bangs—dinners out, movies, concerts, and so on—so you can keep more of your bucks. They'll tell you that if you want to save $50, don't go out for a $50 dinner. Well duh.

I'm not going to tell you to forget about buying a $300 stereo. But I am going to make sure you don't charge that stereo on a credit card, which you pay off with interest over several years, making it a $600 stereo. I'm not going to tell you not to buy a car, but I will show you how to get the lowest possible price for that car and be treated like royalty by the dealership while you're at it.

It is important to save. But it is *inevitable* to spend. Fine. In this section, I'm going to meet you halfway. I'm going to show you how to save as you spend.

spend a week on spending

Lack of money is the root of all evil.

GEORGE BERNARD SHAW

Why It Works

We've all had weak moments in the video store. A lazy Sunday afternoon or perhaps a lonely Friday drives us to rent something we know we'll regret. Whether it's *Mortal Combat 2*, *Half Baked* or something starring Carrot Top, we've all been there. My newest addition to the video rental hall of shame was the cleverly titled treat, *Dude, Where's My Car?*

While I can't salvage my pride from such a purchase, the film does carry a financial lesson that is useful here, especially because it fits in well with this whole getting loaded versus getting loaded theme.

If you missed the film—wait, who am I kidding? *Since* you missed the film, it begins with these two guys recovering from an absolutely wild night of getting loaded. Trouble is, they had such a good time that one character has misplaced his car. Without a single memory to go on, our two hungover heroes try to retrace their steps to find the vehicle.

While many of us don't let our drinking endeavors get this out of control, our financial endeavors are another story.

I'm not a budget guy. Budgets work if people actually stick to them, but nobody actually sticks to them. But you should price your habits. Track your expenses for a brief period so you can find out what you're spending on what. If you don't spend some time tracking your expenses, your life will be a constant state of "Dude, where's my car?" It will be like, "Dude, didn't I have twenty bucks yesterday?" Or, "Dude, I thought I had $200 in my bank account." Or, "Dude, how did my credit card bill get to be $3,000?" When you have no idea where your money goes, you might as well have just lost it.

> **You should price your habits. Track your expenses for a brief period so you can find out what you're spending on what.**

People think that tracking expenses restricts freedom. *Au contraire.* Being broke all the time restricts freedom. Pricing your habits gives you more freedom because you'll know where you're spending money. When you know that, then you have the option of re-arranging your life. You may want to spend more here and less there. You can save up for what you want and not waste money on stuff you don't want.

I'm not going to ask you to stick to a budget week after week. I don't do that, and I don't know anyone who successfully does. But I want you to at least find out how much you spend on what by pricing your habits for a week. Remember, your new question is "How can I afford this?" One week of habit pricing will show you how.

How It Works

The question for this section is, "Dude, where's my notebook so I can keep track of my expenses for next week?"

That's right. I want you to keep track of all your expenses for one week. Write down every expense—every time you swipe that credit card, write a check, or pay cash. (By the way, this week must be an average week in your life. Don't conduct this exercise during spring break or right before a big holiday, when your shopping muscles get a workout. Pick an average week in the life of you.)

Come on Pete, I'm going to look stupid walking around with an expense notebook! You sure will. But it's only for one week and if you're truly embarrassed, excuse yourself and go write it down in the bathroom. Of course, then you're taking notes in a bathroom, which might bring on even bigger problems.

The important thing is that you write down *everything*. Even a 25-cent pack of gum. If you bought Juicy Fruit every day for the next forty years, that's ultimately $3,650 worth of gum. I'm only asking for a week, so go nuts with this.

Whew! The week is over. No more looking like a dork with your little notebook. Using the sheets provided in this section, fill in the blanks. What did you spend on entertainment? Food? Clothes? Juicy Fruit? Add up everything and get a weekly average of your expenses. Multiply this number by four to get your *flexible monthly expenses*, keenly named because these are the expenses you have control over.

Next, grab all your *fixed monthly expenses*. I mean things like your phone bill, cell phone bill, rental payments, car payments, insurance payments, mortgage payments, electric bill—the stuff you don't control over. Total these numbers up by adding your fixed monthly expenses to your flexible monthly expenses to get your *total monthly expenses*.

Multiply the total monthly expenses by twelve and you'll know roughly what you spend each year. Roughly. To be more exact, add in those once-a-year expenses, like vacations, holiday shopping, and the window you broke playing indoor baseball.

Pricing your habits just once will show you all the silly places you spend money. If you ever feel broke, take a week to do this exercise. You'll know where it all went because each expense is itemized, so you know where you can cut back if you need to. You'll notice your questions get more specific, from "Dude, where's my car?" to "Dude, why am I paying so much in car insurance?"

Secret #8 at Work

Below is the worksheet to help you track your expenses. Now I know it looks like a budget, it smells like a budget, but it is *not* a budget. A budget is something one sticks to. *I just want you to do this one time.* That's all I ask.

Expense Tracking Worksheet

Flexible Monthly Expenses:

Food

Grocery Bill _____

Restaurant/Bar/Takeout Bill _____

Entertainment

Movies/Rental Videos _____

Sporting Events _____

Amusement Parks/Concerts _____

Pet Expenses _____

Clubs _____

Bowling/Pool/Arcade _____

Emergency Copy of *Getting Loaded* _____

Transportation

Gasoline _____

Car Products (wax, oil, washer fluid, etc.) _____

Other Transportation (bus, subway) _____

Repairs _____

Personal Expenses

Skin Care _____

Eye Care _____

Hair Care _____

Dental Care _____

Medical Care _____

Remedy Care (cough syrup, etc.) _____

Miscellaneous _____

_____

_____

_____

_____

_____

Total Flexible Monthly Expenses _____

Fixed Monthly Expenses

Housing

Rent _____

Mortgage _____

Bills

Car Payment _____

Electric Bill _____

Water Bill_____

Heating Bill_____

Phone Bill _____

Cell Phone Bill _____

Trash Removal Bill _____

Cable Bill_____

Health Club Bill _____

Credit Card Payment Minimum_____

Student Loan Payment _____

Other Loan Payment_____

Insurance

Renter's Insurance _____

Homeowner's Insurance _____

Health Insurance_____

Disability Insurance _____

Life Insurance _____

Car Insurance _____

Miscellaneous

_____

_____

_____

_____

_____

Fixed Monthly Expenses _____

Fixed Yearly Expenses

Taxes

Property Tax _____

Income Tax _____

Social Security Tax_____

State Tax_____

Local Tax _____

Once-a-Year Expenses

Birthday Expenses_____

Holiday Gift Expenses_____

Vacation Expenses _____

Charity Donations _____

Educational Expenses _____

Professional Advice Expenses (Financial Planning, Johnny Cochran) _____

Miscellaneous _____

_____

Fixed Yearly Expenses _____

(Time for some math.)

Fixed Monthly Expenses _____

+

Flexible Monthly Expenses _____

=

Total Monthly Expenses _____

Total Monthly Expenses × *Twelve Months* = _____

+

Fixed Yearly Expenses _____

=

Total Yearly Expenses _____

Sorry about all the math, but at least you know where all your green is going. Perhaps you were surprised to find that the reason you're so broke is because you spend $600 a year on taxi cabs. Even more, if you want to save up for something, like a trip or a new outfit, you got a whole list of spending categories to cut back on.

Secret #8 in a Nutshell

"Got to find the reason, reason things went wrong, got to find the reason why my money's all gone" goes the Sublime song. Record your expenses for a week so you don't suffer the same fate.

care less

A man will fight harder for his interests than his rights.

NAPOLEON BONAPARTE

Why It Works

I asked you to write down your goals. Writing down what you want only makes it easier for you to get it. But the opposite is also true. Writing down what you *don't* want only makes it easier for you to avoid unnecessary purchases. This secret will leave you more time and money to focus on what you DO care about.

How It Works

Perhaps this is the simplest secret in the book, but it is quite powerful. Grab four pieces of paper each to be titled one of the following:

- Food I don't care about.
- Clothing I don't care about.
- Entertainment items I don't care about.
- Everything else I don't care about.

These lists will be filled with things you don't care about. For instance, you may not care about which brand of trash bags you use. Or maybe you have no preference when it comes to the sheets you sleep on. Must you have a $3 Frappuccino or can you deal with Folger's Crystals? Does it have to be Clinique or will Revlon do? Is the Mach 3 or the Venus that much better a shave?*

Simply by writing down what you don't care about, you plant it in your brain for the next time you're cruising down Retail Lane.

Keep your I-don't-care lists right next to your goals. If you're ever wondering where you can cut back on your spending, these lists should be the first place you look. You may add to them as time goes on. Perhaps you cough up a lot of money for an expensive car thinking it's the final accessory in "the new you." A year goes by, no new friends, no new job, the only thing you've got to be proud of is your collection of car wash receipts and the fact that you put your mechanic's kids through college. You soon realize an expensive car doesn't change anything for you.

Even better, simply by writing down what you don't care about, you plant it in your brain for the next time you're cruising down Retail Lane. You kill the buy impulse. Let me give you some examples of how this secret worked for me.

Secret #9 at Work

After writing my I-don't-care lists I found out:

- I can't tell the difference between brand-name soda and the generic stuff. I had always picked up the brand name, even though it made no real difference to me.
- And while I can tell the difference between beers, I'm a Bud man all the way. Sure, microbrews are nice if someone else is picking

---

* Here I'm actually going to have to say yes, it is. I don't get any endorsement money for this, but I find the Mach 3 to be a sensational shave, so I'm happy to pay the price. The point of these lists isn't to not care about anything, it's just to separate what matters from what doesn't.

up the tab but after writing my list, it's not worth the extra dough. Combined, my suds and soda savings plan yields me just over $300 a year. This is enough to fund a yearly ski retreat, one of my personal goals, for under $1,000.

- It surprised me when I found out I don't really care what kind of car I drive. In fact, it appears I have a Ralph-Naderish affection for public transportation. So I'm not going to kill myself trying to get the Ferrari. The ladies will just have to take me in my Ford.

- I also discovered I don't like spending my money on a vast CD collection. This has saved me at least a thousand bucks over the years. Each time I would pick up a CD and fluster over it, my list would pop into my head and I'd pass. (And I never got caught owning any bands after they went out of style. "What? This isn't my *Polka Party* CD! I'm just holding it for a friend.")

- I also don't give a crap about my brand of toothpaste, floppy disks, toothbrushes, trash bags, dental floss, spaghetti, office supplies, paper towels, ketchup, mayonnaise, bacon, suntan lotion, orange juice, or toilet paper. When it comes to these items, plus countless others, I can just go straight for the generic brand without blinking an eye. I shave an average of 20% off my grocery bills, which float around $200 a month. Sure, it's only $40 in savings, but if I don't care either way, why not?

 Is it really worth saving a buck here and there? Typically, we don't think of a dollar as a lot of money, but stuff adds up. A great rule-of-thumb trick to realize how much your habits really cost you is to think about how much it would cost to pay for that habit in advance, for one year. For instance, a Coke might cost you a dollar a day. No big deal right? It's only a dollar. But if I asked you to prepay me $365 so you could drink one Coke a day for the whole year, would you take it? Probably not, because $365 is a lot of money. So if you think your habits aren't all that expensive, consider how much it would be to prepay for that habit for one whole year.

Secret #9 in a Nutshell

Don't save where it hurts. Save where it doesn't.

cool off the card

> Let us have the courage to stop borrowing
> to meet the continuing deficits. Stop the
> deficits.
>
> —FRANKLIN D. ROOSEVELT

Why It Works

I conducted an interesting experiment one summer. Over the course of two weeks, I counted the number of times I spoke on the phone with my girlfriend. During that same time, I also counted the number of times I was cold-called by a credit card company. I'll give you two guesses who won. Why am I stuck listening to speeches from the nation's credit cartels? Why are these peddlers of plastic so interested in me? It's because they think I'm one of the millions of consumers who spend more than they have.

So what if I spend more than I have? Why do they call so much? The reason our mailboxes are bombarded with brochures, and our phone lines filled with offers, is because financial service companies make big money in credit cards. Here's how they do it.

Financial service companies make big money in credit cards.

How It Works

Currently, the four most popular credit card companies are Visa, MasterCard, American Express, and Discover. These credit card companies are known as the *networks*.

But why so many cards? The Capital One Visa card, the American Airlines Visa card, the General Motors Visa card? This wide variety of cards is the fault of the other half of the system, the *issuers*. Issuers are banks that issue the cards (duh) and control the lines of credit. Discover and American Express are at the same time both networks and issuers.

Visa and MasterCard depend on banks to issue their cards, and they charge these banks an association fee. In addition, all the networks charge merchants a fee when they accept your card. So if you buy a $100 jacket at a store with your credit card, the store doesn't get to keep all $100. Some of it goes to the networks and issuers. You may have noticed that merchants love it when you pay in cash. Now you know why.

Credit cards, with all their components, vary not because of the credit card companies but because of the banks that issue them. The banks get to determine what fees each particular credit card has and how much those fees will be. So you and your friend could both have the same credit card company, say MasterCard, but the fees each of you pay can vary greatly. The big Kahuna of all these fees is the annual percentage rate (APR).

The APR is simply the interest rate the issuer has decided to charge you for the use of its money. If you bought *Getting Loaded* with a credit card, you didn't pay for it with your money. The credit card issuer paid for it with theirs. You don't owe the bookstore anything, but you now have a *balance* (simply the money you owe a lender) with the credit card issuer. If you don't pay them for one year, you've rented their money for one year. This rental fee, better known as the *finance charge*, is determined by your APR.

So you borrowed their money and now you owe them interest plus all their money back, right? Not exactly. Though they'll never admit this, credit card companies don't want you to pay them back all at once. Here's why. Let's say your APR is 15%. Divide that number by twelve (as in twelve months) to determine the monthly finance charge and you get 1.25%. Now, imagine you buy something for $1,000 using the plastic. You get the bill, and it says your minimum payment due is $18 (about 2% of your balance). So, you're like, "I'll just pay the minimum." And you do. Next month (assuming you don't buy anything new), you see the minimum is again around $17. This is so easy!

More like sleazy. If you're just paying the minimum amount, the credit card companies are loving you. Here's why. To calculate your minimum payment, the credit card multiplies your monthly percentage rate (which is 1.25%) by your balance (which is $1,000 for the first month) and they get $12.50. That is what you're paying in interest. Only $5.50 of the $18 minimum payment goes to pay off the balance. When you carry a large balance, the credit card companies are able to keep charging you interest. Next month, the company sees you have a balance of $994.50 because you only paid off $5.50. So to get your minimum payment, they multiply the monthly rate of 1.25% by $994.50 and get a finance charge of $12.43 (only $0.07 less than last month). They slap on another $5 or so to pay down the balance, and it just keeps going. If you paid $18 a month on a $1,000 balance on a card carrying a 15% interest rate, it would take you *over seven and a half years* to pay off that debt and you would have paid over $650 in interest.

Credit card companies don't want you to pay them back all at once.

Even if you pay *nearly* the entire balance, you're still in trouble. Imagine you have a $1,000 balance and pay $999 of it. You're feeling good. You paid nearly your entire balance. Next month, you'll owe just a dollar and what, like five cents in interest? You're so delighted with yourself that you charge a $1 Choco-Wham shake at the local Whammy Burger. But when your bill arrives, you see that you owe over $10!

But before you head down to Whammy Burger with fists

clenched, realize they're not to blame. They didn't overcharge you. *You* overcharged you. See, when you don't pay off the entire balance of a credit card, the credit card company charges you interest based on your *average daily balance* over a thirty-day period. In this example, part of the month you had a $1,000 balance and part of the month (after you sent in your $999 payment) you had a $1 balance. So leave the folks at Whammy Burger alone. It's not their fault. The reason your bill was over $10 (or ten times the going rate of a Choco-Wham shake) was because of the interest from your average daily balance.

If this sounds confusing, that's because it is and, in truth, I even oversimplified it. I wanted to show you how expensive it is to not pay your credit cards off right away. And I wanted to alert you to the fact that credit card companies love people who spend more than they earn and who are forced to make only the minimum payments.

Here's the good news: most credit cards come with a *grace period*. A grace period is a short span of time in which you can pay back the credit card company without being hit with a finance charge. It's a free loan. If you want to win the credit card game, all you have to do is pay your monthly credit card balance off in full and on time.

If the APR is the big Kahuna of all credit card fees, you should do your best to get a card with the lowest APR as possible. Secret #11 will help you do that.

Besides the APR, credit card companies make money off of you in scores of ways, all of which must be legally spelled out in the fine print. This leads me to *the sentence you least wanted to read in the book*:

Always read the fine print.

Sucks, I know, but there's a reason why the fine print is fine: Your mother wears combat boots. See what I mean? Whether you're reading employment contracts, credit card applications, or insurance policies, you gotta read the fine print. If they're hiding something, that's where they hide it.

Hidden within the fine print of your credit card terms will be the additional fees the card issuer charges. How can I charge thee? Let me count the ways:

- If your payment is late, the credit card companies charge you a late payment fee. It's around $29. This late fee I should add does not help pay off your balance. It's pure cash in the credit card company's pocket. And mind you that late payment fees are the same no matter what the balance. If you bought a 69-cent taco with a credit card and paid late, the price of that taco just went up to $30. Even more with interest. There is not enough free hot sauce in the world to justify this price. And if you keep paying your bills late, say half the time out of the year, each year you're generously forking over nearly $175 to the credit card company for nothing. Call it a tip.

- A card will have either a *fixed APR* or a *variable APR*. Fixed APRs don't change, variable APRs change depending on factors in the economy. With a variable APR, you may be paying more or less each month, so be aware. Even with a fixed APR, your rate can still change if you make your payments late. (They couldn't keep it simple, could they?)

- Most cards will have an *introductory APR*. This is simply a gimmick APR designed to get you to apply for the card. It can be as low as 0% and it usually lasts six months. The fine print will tell you how long the intro APR lasts and what the real APR will be when the intro rate is over.

- Convenience checks are another way they make money. You can use these checks just like regular checks, allowing you to pay for things that you might not be able to pay for with a credit card, like an electric bill. The APR on these checks may be different than the APR on your card. It's better to write checks from a bank or money market account. (What's a money market account? Check out Secret #23.)

- Cash advances will suck you dry. That's because the APR on cash advances is usually higher than your normal APR, *and there is no grace period*. In other words, the moment you get the cash, the interest clock starts ticking. What's worse, there's usually a fee for cash advances. Don't use your credit card for cash advances—

you'll get your financial ass kicked. If you absolutely insist on losing money, then just send me an envelope full of fifties. My address is at the back of this book.

- Other stuff. Sometimes you'll get your credit card statement and there will be a free offer for something, like three months of free insurance if you simply fill out this card and send it in with your payment. The fine print will tell you that the first three months are free and then, if you don't cancel, you'll automatically be charged each month for that insurance.

If you

absolutely

insist on losing

money, then

just send me

an envelope full

of fifties.

- Annual fees. This is just an administrative fee (anywhere from $25 to $50 a year) they charge you no matter what. The good news is that annual fees, like roller rinks, are a dying breed. Today there is no reason to have a card with an annual fee unless it has a rewards program (like frequent flyer miles) and you charge like a madman to rack up those miles, yet are somehow able to pay off your balance every month. If your card has an annual fee, call the company and get it waived. If they won't drop the fee, switch cards.
- Whew! I hope I didn't miss anything. Just be sure to read the fine print, because who knows what other fees these companies will come up with.

Secret #10 at Work

Below are two stories from the credit card trenches:

The moment I learned that in this day and age it is silly to pay an annual fee I called up my credit card company and told them to waive the fee.

"I'd be happy to waive the fee this year," the customer service woman told me.

"Great—wait, what do you mean waive the fee *this* year?"

"I'll waive it for this year."

"Then I have to pay the fee next year?"

"Yes."

"Well, I don't want to pay the fee."

"Then call next year and waive it again."

"Then you'll waive it?"

"Yep."

"Can't you just waive it forever?"

"Nope."

"But I can keep calling you year after year to have it waived?"

"Yep."

"Can I do this forever?"

"Yep."

"But you won't waive it forever?"

"Nope."

We sparred a few rounds with this Abbott and Costello–like exchange. The company's hope was that I would forget next year and they could sock me with the fee. I canceled the card altogether.

Another time I charged a $3,000 laptop computer on my card. I had the cash in hand and the moment I got my statement, I paid the full amount. Two weeks went by, and I got a letter from the credit card company asking me if everything was all right! They wondered why I paid up so quickly, as if paying bills in full and on time is a sign of sickness!

 Wait a minute Pete, didn't you tell me my new question is "How can I afford this?" Indeed I did, but to answer that question with "With my credit card" is cheating. I want you to be able to buy what you want, but overextending yourself with high-interest debt is stupid. If you keep doing that, you won't be able to afford anything. If you want to buy something that's expensive, you have to be more creative than leaning on your friends Visa and MasterCard. (And if you are already in trouble, check out Secret #12.)

Secret #10 in a Nutshell

Credit cards are produced from the efforts of both the networks—the big brand names—and the issuers—the banks that offer them. Making just the minimum payment will stretch a $1,000 loan out over many years with hundreds, perhaps thousands in added interest. Read all the fine print because there are scores of ways for the credit card company to charge you. If, however, you charge wisely and pay in full and on time, credit cards are an attractive method of payment.

get the right card

Annual income twenty pounds, annual expenditure nineteen nineteen six, result happiness. Annual income twenty pounds, annual expenditure twenty pounds ought and six, result misery.

CHARLES DICKENS, *DAVID COPPERFIELD*

Why It Works

Whether it's to book a hotel room, or put down the rental deposit on a pair of Rollerblades, most of us will at some point need to call upon a credit card for help. Interest rates and charges vary drastically from card to card, so it is important to know what the ideal card should contain. If you're still using the card you received when you first set foot on your college campus, it's probably a lousy card. Often, people are overpaying simply because they lack the motivation to switch cards. And if you have never set foot on a college campus, if and when you do, the card you get will probably be a lousy card.

How It Works

First, find out what the APR is. Get it as low as possible. Introductory APRs have now hit rock bottom. No, literally they have. You can find an intro APR for 0%. If your credit is good, you should be able to get a fixed APR of less than 10%.

How much difference does the APR really make? Let's suppose you had a $1,000 balance and you paid $20 every month.

- If your card had a 10% APR, it would take sixty-four months (just over five years) to pay off your debt. You would have paid $279 in interest.
- If your card had a 15% APR, it would take seventy-seven months (about six and a half years) to pay off your debt. You would have paid $532 in interest.
- If your credit card had an 18% APR, it would take eighty-nine months (about seven and a half years) to pay off your debt. You would have paid $777 in interest.
- If your credit card had a painful 20% APR, it would take over a hundred months (eight and a half years) to pay off your debt. You would have paid $1,028 in interest.

Simply by switching from an 18% APR card to a 10% APR card, you would have saved $498 in interest.

 Now we come to *the only free lunch in the credit card industry*. Many cards come with some sort of rewards program. For every dollar you charge, you get points toward frequent-flier miles, gasoline, long-distance minutes, whatever. If you have a rewards credit card and pay off your credit card in full each month, you won't be charged any interest and you'll get something for free. This is a fantastic deal if you can handle the temptation of carrying a balance. But if you can't handle the pressure of paying in full every month, the rewards program ain't worth it. Also, be careful if you use a rewards card that has an annual fee. Unless you're spending like Attila the Shopping Hun, the rewards probably won't cover the fee.

Choose a rewards program that is going to suit you. In general, most frequent-flier miles will give you one mile for every dollar you spend. General Motors and Ford will give 5% of what you charge toward a new car.* Discover has a cool cash-back program that gives you a percentage of your purchases back in cash. What card is best for you purely depends on your situation. If you just bought a new car, you may not need Ford's or GM's card, and if you have a war chest of frequent-flier miles from your traveling-encyclopedia sales job, maybe you don't need any more. Whatever card you go with, read the fine print, because sometimes the rewards points expire after a few years. Be aware that some of these rewards programs (and this really ticks me off) reward you only when you carry a balance. It's their way of saying thank you for being irresponsible.

Credit card companies are viciously competing for your business; offers are always changing so be on the lookout for the newest deals. Here are some rule-of-thumb numbers to guide you:

- You want the interest to be charged using the *average daily balance* method. The other method, the *two-cycle average daily balance* will be more costly to you.
- You want a twenty- to thirty-day interest-free grace period.
- You want a late payment fee (if you don't pay on time) of no more than $29.
- You want an over-the-credit-limit fee (if you spend too much) of no more than $29.
- You want transaction fees for cash advances to be 2% of the amount of the advance, usually no less than $3 and no more than $25. But who cares about this fee anyway, because you shouldn't use your credit card for cash advances.
- You don't want to be charged a fee for balance transfers (when you move a balance from one card to another).

* The problem is the car must be new, which is often a waste of your money. I cover cars in Secret #18.

Always remember that credit cards are like martinis—if you have more than two, you could get into serious trouble.

Secret #11 at Work

Despite all my bickering about credit cards, I love 'em. I charge absolutely everything I can on my credit card. It's a great way for me to keep track of my spending—no carrying around that stupid notebook. At the end of the month, my statement tells me exactly what I spent. I don't have to carry a lot of cash, which can be dangerous. Plus if I ever bought a defective product from a dishonest merchant, Visa, MasterCard, or whoever will often argue for me if there is a problem. My card also offers a 1% rewards program, so I can get $1 back for every $100 I spend. Not a fortune, but it does add up.

> *Always remember that credit cards are like martinis—if you have more than two, you could get into serious trouble.*

I say all this because credit cards, at base, are a terrific deal for those who can keep their spending and bill paying under control. What changed things for me was reading about how harmful it was to carry a balance and how great it was to pay on time and get all the perks. My hope is that after reading this secret, you'll stop working for your credit cards and start making them work for you.

 A terrific website to find the perfect credit card is www.cardweb.com. It has a database of credit cards, where you can customize a search. You can search for a rewards card with no annual fee and the website will show you what's currently available. Check it out.

Secret #11 in a Nutshell

If you have good credit, you can get an APR of less than 10%. If you're disciplined, you can actually make a profit off your cards through a rewards program. These rewards programs don't make sense if you don't pay on time. If you develop the discipline to pay in full and on time, credit cards are a great financial tool.

give yourself credit

> No nation ought to be without debt. A national debt is a national blessing.
>
> —THOMAS PAINE

Why It Works

Since day one, our lives are reduced to 8½ × 11 sheets of paper. Your report card, your resume, your driving record are all supposed to define you as a person on a few pages, all because employers, colleges, graduate schools and insurance companies want to get a quick read on who you are. In the financial world, companies can get a quick read on your financial state by reading your credit report. It's the financial form of a report card, and if yours looks ugly, life can suck. As silly as it sounds, the fact that you were six months late paying $15 on your credit card two years ago can affect your ability to borrow $250,000 to buy a house. You're thinking, "Oh, come on. It was only $15," but the credit industry is thinking, "If you weren't able to pay $15 on time, how can we trust you with $250,000?"

Having good credit is like being a nun—people automatically trust you. Good credit means you get the lowest-interest credit cards. When you take out a loan, lenders will charge you less interest because they know you're a sure thing. Your down payments will be smaller. It will be easier to rent an apartment, buy a car, start a business, even get a job with good credit.

But having bad credit is a bit like having bad breath. If your breath is bad, expect a lot of rejections. If your credit is bad, expect a lot of rejections as well. If you have bad breath, I recommend mouthwash. If you have bad credit, I recommend reading on.

On to establishing good credit.

How It Works

Establishing good credit couldn't be easier. All you need to do is pay your bills in full and on time. Simple. For most of us, we begin establishing credit when we get a credit card. Remember, the moment you begin using your credit card, they're watching.

Wait! Who's watching? Big Brother? No, the credit bureaus. These bureaus are like The Police, as in Sting, as in "every move you make, every breath you take, I'll be watching you." These companies keep track of how well you do paying back money that is loaned to you. They watch as you pay your credit card, car loans, student loans—nearly every loan that's through a reputable institution. When you screw up, like if you make a late payment, they make note of it on your credit report. (Although not every late payment will wind up on your report.) These companies then sell your credit report to companies who need your credit information. For instance, if you were going to rent an apartment, your landlord might get your credit report to check you out.

Having good credit is like being a nun—people automatically trust you.

Sucks, doesn't it? Yeah, but that's the way it works. So when you get that first credit card, it's important to pay those bills on time. Note that you may receive your credit card bill on an odd day of the month (a little incentive to help you to forget to pay on time—remember those late fees?). Whatever day your bill usually comes, mark it on your calendar.

What's your credit report look like? I don't know, but you can get a copy by writing the major credit bureaus. The report will cost about $8, but it's worth the money.

Citizens of Colorado, Maryland, Massachusetts, New Jersey, Georgia, and Vermont are entitled to a free lunch, or free credit report once a year. If you ever get turned down for a loan or an apartment because you had bad credit, you are entitled to a free copy of your report to see why you were turned down. (If only you could get such a report when you're turned down for a date.)

To get a credit report, call one (or preferably all) of the major credit bureaus:

- Experian: (888) 397-3742 www.experian.com
- Equifax: (800) 685-1111 www.equifax.com
- TransUnion: (800) 888-4213 www.transunion.com

Be sure to read over the credit report. You are allowed to attach a hundred-word statement that will be seen by everyone who requests your report. For instance, you may have paid several bills late because a family member was ill, and you are entitled to provide an explanation. Also look for mistakes. Lenders are people too and they screw up sometimes. Once, a charge of $1,603.13 accidentally showed up on my credit card bill. Indeed it was from a restaurant in Manhattan but it wasn't *that* expensive. I mean, they still had free refills. (Even though I took some verbal abuse for asking. "Waiter," I asked, "are there free refills?" "Monsieur wants a free refill?" laughed the waiter. "Does Monsieur want a free dinner too?") Be sure everything is accurate.

Secret #12 at Work

*But uhhh ahem . . . uhhh Pete? What do you do if you are already in debt? Like uhhh . . . **deep** in debt? Ya know . . . I'm just asking . . . ya know . . . for my friend.*

High-interest debt is a killer. You'll never live your life on your own terms if you owe the credit card company thousands. You'll be living your life on the credit card company's terms.

You should pay as much as you can right away as opposed to spreading out the payments. If you can scrounge up $800, pay all $800 at once to knock down the overall balance.

Your problems may be solved easily if you can get some free cash from the following sources:

- Interest-free loans from family and friends. *"Hey mom! It's nice to finally talk to you! Listen mom, you were always there for me and uhhh . . . why stop a good thing now?"*
- Selling personal items. Yes, I'm afraid it's time to part with that adorable Olson Twins lunchbox.
- Cutting your expenses by reviewing your . . . wait, dude, where's my notebook?

If you're in debt, now's the time to cut back on spending or clean out the attic and have that garage sale. Use this cash to pay down debt.

Still stuck? Here's a step-by-step process for freeing yourself from the Alcatraz of interest rates:

- First make debt payoff a priority in your life.
- Tell everyone what's going on. If you are deep in debt, you're probably going to have to pass on a few nights out with friends. If you keep ditching them, they're going to start asking questions. Make it easy on yourself *and* them by telling everyone up front that you're in a bit of a financial bind and you need to take a brief hiatus from the social scene. Mind you, being in debt is nothing to be ashamed of. You haven't broken any laws, or for that matter done anything wrong. You just spent more than you had. So tell your friends about it. And you can bet your credit card balance you're not the only one in your group of friends that has credit card debt. If you come out of the credit card closet first, others will follow. It will be much easier to save when many of you are working together—the rent a movie votes will outnumber the dance club votes.

- Shred all your credit cards.
- Make a list of all the money you owe, at what interest rate and to whom.
- Using the cash from garage sales and loans from friends, pay off the highest-interest loans first.
- If your debt is credit card debt, you can transfer all your balances to one card carrying an introductory rate. If, for instance, you have a $1,000 balance on a card with an 18% interest rate, try to transfer that $1,000 to a card with a 0% intro rate. This will free you from a half a year's worth of interest—around $90. Transferring balances to lower rate cards is known as *credit card surfing*. It is possible to roll over the balance many times to take advantage of the low intro rates. While surfing looks a little fishy on your credit report, having mounds of credit card debt looks even worse. But be careful with the transfer. At times, there is a fee for this transfer. Other times only the money you transfer will be charged the introductory rate while new purchases are charged the standard rate. (Of course, if you're in debt, you should not be making any new purchases anyway!)

> **Transferring balances to lower rate cards is known as credit card surfing.**

- Commit to increasing your monthly payments, even if it is only by $10. Adding just $10 could cut your payoff time in half. Where do you get this $10? That's why you tracked your expenses for a week for Secret #8. Where can you cut back?
- Still not there? Here are a few places where you can borrow money that will most likely have a lower interest rate than your credit cards:

  - Borrowing against your employer-sponsored retirement plan.
  - Taking a home equity loan.
  - Borrowing against a cash-value life insurance policy.
  - Selling bonds, precious metals, or stocks. As a rule of thumb, any bonds, precious metals, or stocks that you own aren't making as much money as your credit

card debt is taking away. So long as these investments are outside of a retirement account, it probably makes sense to sell them to pay off debt.

- If you still need to go farther, think again about where you can get some cash. Anyone you forgot to hit up? Look at your net worth worksheets you did for Secret #2. Anything you can get rid of?

Okay. You've had your garage sale. You've sold off investments. You sneak your wash in with someone else's at the Laundromat. You've switched to lower APR credit cards. And you still can't make ends meet. What do you do?

First, don't keep quiet. Many people hide from their creditors, afraid of what their creditors may do. Bad idea. Even if you owe them money, even if it's a lot of money, creditors need to know you didn't hightail it to Tijuana. They are willing to negotiate. Perhaps you don't have the money right now, but you've got a Christmas bonus coming up in a few months. (Even if you don't celebrate Christmas, this can be a great way to stick it to the credit card companies. *"Sure I can send you my Christmas bonus,"* you tell them, *"just let me call the orphanage and tell them the bad news."*) The credit card company may be willing to work something out. You'll never know unless you ask. Creditors know that if you declare bankruptcy, they might get nothing.

 Bankruptcy Pete? Is it going to get that bad? I've seen it happen. (Hell, over one million people a year declare personal bankruptcy.) One friend of mine in college declared personal bankruptcy. Another friend, and this is real bad, couldn't afford personal bankruptcy. She just stopped paying her bills. Neither of these people were over twenty-five.

Filing bankruptcy is a messy process. And the worst part is that it costs even more money! You'll have to pay an attorney to guide you through it. The process is too involved to cover in this book, so if your credit situation reaches the bankruptcy border, talk to a qualified professional. Be sure to get several opinions as to whether or not bankruptcy is right for *you*. Don't file just so the attorney can make money. It's a big step, so take it slowly. And for God's sake, don't do it for the "I Went Bankrupt" key chain.

 Hey Pete, is it true that when I go to get a job, my employer might run a credit check on me? What the hell's up with that?

It does seem weird that an employer would check your credit. After all, you're not borrowing any money from them; they're supposed to be paying you! So why do companies run a credit check?

There are many reasons. It could be argued that poor credit is a sign of irresponsibility. It could be argued that poor credit is a measure of your attitude about money. If you're not thrifty with your own money, how careful will you be with the company's money? One other possibility is that if you're up to your eyeballs in debt, employers may worry you'll do something drastic, like sell the photocopier to a pawn shop.

The fact is that some employers will check your credit, so there is yet another reason why you must pay off your debt and pay your bills on time.

But most likely your credit report is being pulled by a potential employer because it is slowly becoming the only place an employer can go for unbiased information about you. As Philip K. Howard, the author of *The Death of Common Sense,* points out, lawsuits are springing up for past employers who give references. Howard notes that, "References are quickly becoming a thing of the past. Employers rarely give them any longer, because there is a potential lawsuit in any message—"* A good credit report becomes more important every day.

After you dig your way out of the debt trenches, go with a *debit card*. (You know these commercials, some guy named Nigel is standing in his underwear guarding Windsor Castle, "Dry cleaners wouldn't take a check again, eh Nigel?") A debit card lets you spend only money you already have, yet it is accepted as widely as a credit card. It's like a checkbook in the form of a card. When you swipe the

---

* Howard, Phillip K., *The Death of Common Sense*, page 135.

debit card, the amount you spend is automatically deducted from your checking account. You can also get a *charge card*, which is a credit card that requires you pay off your balance in full every month. Just be careful of the annual fees with these cards. If you do want to keep your regular credit card, you can call the company and ask them to lower your credit limit to a level that won't allow you to wreak financial havoc on yourself.

Secret #12 in a Nutshell

Your financial actions are kept track of on your credit report. Pay on time and you get a good report. Pay late, and it's not so good. You should get a copy of your report to make sure everything is in order. If something is incorrect, be sure to fix it or attach a statement explaining the error. If you already have high-interest debt, do *everything* you can to pay it off, because chances are your other investments aren't paying as much as you're losing. Bankruptcy remains a last-resort option, but first talk to a qualified and honest attorney, which is a hard thing to find. Try the following ad:

WANTED: Qualified, honest, attorney. Must be all one person. Call 555-1234.

become a savvy shopper

A penny saved is—impossible.

OGDEN NASH

Why It Works

Many people feel that saving money will restrict their lifestyle. Not true. You just have to know how the game is played. Veteran bargain hunters end up paying less and getting more. They know the tricks of the retail world and how to avoid them. When you are a savvy shopper, you'll have the same lifestyle, but you'll leave the store with more money in your pocket. This secret will alert you to some of the schemes retailers use to get you to buy stuff you don't need and how you can get around them.

How It Works

Here are the ten best tips to becoming a savvy shopper:

Tip #1—Often the most overpriced items are always the easiest to find. Stores will often hide their bargains. In a grocery store, for instance, the bargain foods will be on the bottom and top shelves, while the pricey products will be within easy reach at eye level. Every store disguises its bargains in its own way. In a casino, for example, the hardest thing to find is an exit door. The only exception to this secret occurs when stores are trying to unload inventory and put their best deals in plain sight. When you enter a store, be sure to look around. Those bargains may be hard to find.

Tip #2—Join the club. *What club?* Any club! These days, every store has some sort of discount club you can sign up for. Rent ten videos, get the eleventh one free. Buy six footlong sandwiches, get the seventh one free. Get a free wedding cake on your third marriage. So long as it's free, why the hell not join?

One of my favorite clubs is a wholesale club. These clubs, like Costco, B.J.'s, or Sam's Club can cut 10% to 40% off your grocery bill. Plus, when you buy in bulk, you save time and money by making fewer trips to the store. If the club asks you to pay an annual membership fee, pay it. You'll easily save the fee in bargains. Some clubs may require that you be part of an organization. Don't let this hassle deter you. You're probably a member of some organization, like a church, business, or student group. If not, you can simply shop with someone who is.

 Tip #3—Go generic. *Generic? Hey Pete, you told me I didn't have to change my lifestyle! What's this generic crap?* Actually going generic doesn't change your life, just your labels. Many times, the generic store brand is the *exact same product* as the advertised label brand. I mean this literally. At times, the brand name company is making the store brand's products. Generic can erase 50% or more from your shopping bill. Which products should you buy generic? Look at your I-don't-care Lists from Secret #9 for ideas.

Tip #4—Beware of upselling. This trick has been pulled on you countless times, and you may not even know it. Immediately after you buy something, salespeople will ask you if you want to buy something else: "Would you like a coffee to go with that donut?" "Can I super-size those fries for just another 39 cents?" "How about a shirt to go with that sweater?" That's upselling. These days everybody's doing it. I was recently upsold at the post office. I sent a little certified mail, and the slicker behind the counter hit me with a roll of stamps. Damn, they're good! We're coaxed into buying more every day, but when you know it is being done to you, you're less likely to cave in. A nice defense for upselling is to make a shopping list; if it's not on the list, don't buy it.*

The brother of upselling is lead pricing. Lead pricing is the art of lowering one item to a rock-bottom rate with the idea that you'll buy other items related to the cheap item. For instance, you may see a stereo on sale for what appears to be a steal. But who is the real crook? Maybe the store suckered you in with the cheap stereo but got you to pay extra for speakers and cables. You thought you had them, but they had you.

> *"Can I super-size those fries for just another 39 cents?" "How about a shirt to go with that sweater?" That's upselling. These days everybody's doing it.*

---

* For more information on upselling, check out the book *How to Never Be Upsold*. For just $10 more, the author will send you a video.

Tip #5—Understand chain-reaction shopping. This is a big-picture idea. Chain-reaction shopping is the theory that one expense affects the price of other subsequent expenses. These subsequent expenses will follow the same trend as the first purchase. Imagine you are apartment shopping and you've narrowed your choices down to two places. One place is $1,000 per month, while the other is $1,100 a month. You choose the $1,100-a-month apartment because you're thinking, "Hey, it's only an extra $100 a month." Not so fast there, Speedracer. Since the apartment is more expensive, you can bet the restaurants, the parking garages, and all the shops will have higher prices as well. Chain-reaction shopping can really screw up a budget. Many people increase only the one item at hand, such as the apartment, but they don't figure that all the other items in their budget—food, entertainment, and parking—will go up in price as the apartment goes up in price. Chain-reaction shopping will remind you that spending more on one item will force you to spend more on others.

The good news is that just like Sharon Stone's character in *Basic Instinct*, chain-reaction shopping goes both ways. Choose the cheaper apartment for instance and you'll enjoy cheaper parking, better bargains in the shops, and less expensive restaurants.

Tip #6—Laugh. No joke. This will save you hundreds of dollars in wasted purchases. If you can find something that can make you laugh when you're in the middle of an impulse buy, you're less likely to make that impulse buy. What I do is picture an old comedy routine by Chris Rock in which he denounces every price as "Good Lord, that's a lotta money!" Remember this statement whenever you go shopping. Okay. I'm half-joking here. But to cut back on impulse purchases, you do have to change your mental state. Find something that will turn you from a drooling consumer into an objective buyer. When I'm about to overspend, I visualize Chris Rock's performance, and it cracks me up. I suddenly snap out of the glazed-eye look of my materialistic mode and regain that savvy-shopper look in my eye. Do what works for you. Take a walk, sleep on it, dress in drag, and dance the hula. Anything that helps you avoid buying something you really don't need.

Tip #7—If you're new in town, drive around. In order to enjoy life's free lunches, you have to know where they are being served. When you're new to an area, spend some time actively looking for bargains. Which movie theaters have student discounts? Which restaurants have the early bird specials? What bar has two-for-one night?

My friend Carolyn taught me this secret. In college, I noticed she was always going out to eat, while I was stuck munching down on a ramen noodle sandwich. Since we worked the same sweatshop-wage job, I asked her how she could afford her lifestyle. She proceeded to outline for me every bargain that existed in the city of Miami. She knew it all. I soon found myself frequenting the same places she did. And boy, did I save. Simply by switching to a less expensive video store, I saved $151 a year in video rentals. (One rents a lot of videos in college.) And that was just videos. In my current neighborhood, one gas station sells gas for $1.35 per gallon. Two blocks down the street, gas goes for $1.40. Saving 5 cents a gallon on ten gallons a week for fifty-two weeks is $26 a year. Get paid $26 to drive two blocks? Fine by me. By driving around, I save hundreds in meals, drinks, and movies. You can too, if you see what's out there.

I'm not saying you have to sell out to the thrift shops. But you'll know where they are if you need them. And don't take my word for it. Wasn't it the Economist Formally Known as Prince who said, "She wore a raspberry beret, the kind you find in a secondhand store?"

Tip #8—Preshop. Preshopping is the art of shopping without buying in order to find the best bargains. In the past, this trick was a real pain in the ass, due to the sheer amount of time it required, but now the internet makes it easy. Rather than spending a day going store to store, you can spend a few minutes online to see who has the lowest prices. Most of the major retailers have their prices and products online, so it's easy to compare. Check out the websites I recommend at the end of this secret.

Tip #9—Put your life on the line. This tip is not as bad as it sounds. Actually, I take that back. This tip *is* as bad as it sounds, and that's the point. Before you buy something, think about how many hours of your life you worked to get it. Let's say you make $10 an hour as the cashier in a bowling alley. For some time now you've had your eye on a $300 sweater by some Italian designer who strangely enough was born in Detroit. To buy that sweater will take thirty hours of your life—sweeping the lanes, polishing the pins, and spraying deodorizer into the bowling shoes. Is it worth it? Simply think about how many hours of your life a particular product will consume, and you're less likely to make an unnecessary purchase.

Tip #10—Always remember that a penny saved is two pennies earned. I came across this when I read *The Only Investment Guide You'll Ever Need*, by Andrew Tobias. He compares savings to earnings for a convincing argument.

Pretend you are in the 28% tax bracket. For every $100 you earn, the government gets $28* (ouch!). Let's say you earn a dreamy $100 an hour. Now imagine you want to take your dreamy spouse out to a dreamy dinner that will end up costing $100 (food, drinks, gas, parking, tip, and two Hard Rock Café T-shirts). The dinner cost you one hour's worth of work, right?

Nope. Remember, you are paid $100 per hour, but you keep only $72. You have to work an hour and a half just to

---

* Actually, because our tax rate is marginal, this is not exact. To be super precise, I'd need to use what's known as the *effective tax rate*, which is a pain in the ass to calculate. Using the marginal tax rate is close enough for this example. If you must know more about tax rates, flip to Secret #16.

get that dinner. If you stayed home and ate what was already in the fridge, you would have saved $100. But to *earn* that $100, you would actually have to earn $150, because of taxes. So saving a penny is like earning two pennies. If you don't like to save, you better like your job.

Secret #13 at Work

Too much penny pinching? What's the harm in blowing a few bucks here and there on impulse purchases? When you think of the future value of your money, the harm becomes more apparent.

Investors know when they sink their money into one thing they can't put it anywhere else. In the world of economics, this is known as *opportunity cost*. Before investors sink their cash into something, they look at the alternatives.

What happens if you invest that dollar instead of spending it? The following table shows what one dollar invested at 15% will be worth in the future.

In ten years, your invested dollar is worth **$4.06**.

In twenty years, your invested dollar is worth **$16.37**.

In thirty years, your invested dollar is worth **$66.21**.

In forty years, your invested dollar is worth **$267.86**.

In fifty years, your invested dollar is worth **$1,083.66**.

Feel free to cut out this section of the book and carry it in your wallet or purse. Next time you don't feel like making the effort to save a few dollars, whip out this chart. Remember how I saved $151 by switching video stores? I'm glad I did, because that money will be worth over $35,000 when I retire.*

Secret #13 in a Nutshell

Buy what you want and buy what you need, but don't buy what you don't want or don't need. Keep your eyes open when you shop to see if the store is up to any tricks. If you must have an item, quickly change your state of mind by doing something crazy and then go back and see if you still want that item.

---

* $151 dollars, invested at 15% interest over forty years is $35,171.65.

Websites for Savvy Shoppers

There are thousands of websites out there to help you save. Here are a few of my favorites:

 www.coolsavings.com Check this site out for free coupons, free samples, and great savings.

www.priceline.com You've heard William Shatner talk about this site, and he's right. Name your own price on hundreds of items, from airfares to gasoline.

www.mysimon.com Comparison shop for thousands of different products without leaving your home. Mysimon is a great site for preshopping.

www.bestdeal.com This is also a great comparison site for preshopping. I recently bought a camcorder that would've cost $2,000—had I not gone to bestdeal.com. I logged off that website with the same camcorder coming to me in the mail for $1,600.

www.lowermybills.com Hey, what more could you want? This site helps you find the best discounts in your area. Just type in your zip code.

get celebrity status—form a consumer buying pool

Possunt quia posse videntur (*They can because they think they can*).

VIRGIL

Why It Works

Hell, if it works for Wal-Mart, it'll work for you. Why are prices so low at Wal-Mart? Because they're nice people? Because they don't mind losing money? Because they're really a front for Tony Soprano? No! Prices are low at Wal-Mart for one reason: it buys in bulk. No matter what you buy, be it stocks, shocks, socks, or rocks, the more you buy, the better the discount.

Or think about celebrities. Why do celebrities get comped at restaurants? Why are they always getting special treatment? One reason: celebrities create more business. The trouble is, while many of us wouldn't mind getting a fat discount, most of us aren't celebrities. But you can get treated like a celebrity if you form a CBP.

So what's a CBP? CBP stands for consumer buying pool. A consumer buying pool is just like a car pool. You form a car pool because everyone has the same need (to get somewhere). yet, by forming a pool, the process of getting somewhere makes it cheaper for everyone.

In a CBP, everyone has the same need (to buy stuff), but by forming a pool, each member of the pool can buy stuff cheaper.

Why do celebrities get comped at restaurants? Why are they always getting special treatment? One reason: celebrities create more business.

How It Works

Imagine Buck, the hero of *Getting Loaded,* trying to buy his first car:

- When Buck was a sophomore in high school, he turned sixteen and he got his driver's license.
- He wanted to buy a Ford as his first car.
- Buck's high school class had a hundred students in it.
- Of those hundred students, fifty of them turned sixteen the same time as Buck.
- Of those fifty that turned sixteen, twenty-five wanted to buy a car just like Buck.
- Of those twenty-five, eight of them wanted to buy a Ford just like Buck.

Buck used these stats to his advantage. He put up a sign on his school's bulletin board that said, "Want to save hundreds, even thousands, on the purchase of a Ford? Call me, Buck, at 555-2376."

By the end of the week, Buck had received twelve phone calls. Eight were from sophomores and three from seniors. Even one teacher responded. That weekend, Buck and his newly formed CBP headed to their local Ford dealership.

The ending of this story is as predictable as a Stallone film. You can imagine the deal Buck and his CBP got when they showed up at the dealership, picked one salesperson, and said, "Hi, I'm Buck and I'm the head of the Buck CBP. We're here to buy some Fords. Give us a good deal, and we'll buy *twelve* cars from you today."

You can see the power of a CBP. What car salesperson is dumb enough to lose twelve sales in one afternoon? You can use CBPs to grow Wal-Martesque muscles. And you'll get celebrity status, because businesses know that you will bring more business.

Here's what you do. When you're about to make a major purchase, announce it. Maybe you could put up a sign, at your school, college, or office. Or shoot out an email. When it comes to CBPs, the more, the better. So contact everyone.

 Pete, I'm not sure where you come from, but if I put up a sign like that at my school, I'd get only one thing—beaten up! None of my friends are going to go for this! My goal with this book is that you take the basic concepts of each secret and make them work for you. Maybe this secret wouldn't go over so well in your circle of friends. But circles change and so do friends, so at least you have it in the back of your head.

 But I hope that you will at least try it. The technique actually works best for younger people—those still in school—because you're surrounded by people your age. Everyone's going to get their driver's licenses at the same time, everyone is going to have to furnish a college dorm room at the same time, everyone is going to go to the prom at the same time (Why pay full price for your powder blue tux?). A friend of mine was in a fraternity that worked out a deal with a tuxedo shop, where the tailor actually came and took all the measurements in the fraternity house. Plus the tailor gave them a discount on all the tuxedos.

Secret #14 at Work

Here are some examples of how you can use your CBP:

- Airlines are suckers for CBPs. The reason is that a plane must fly even if it hasn't sold all of its seats. So if there is room in first class, wouldn't they want to wine and dine the head of a consumer buying pool by offering a free upgrade?

    This works. In high school, I went on a student tour to Australia. Our tour leader used this technique to get our group four free upgrades to business class. That was like a $40,000 value to us, but it made almost no difference to the airline, except that they got to provide great service to a huge potential customer.

- Here's another one. Do you get coffee on your way into work? I'll bet you've never asked the coffee shop to give your whole office a discount. Same thing with your sorority and your sorority's favorite bar. Or your CBP's favorite clothing store, car wash, or gas station. If you can save 25 cents a day from coffee, that's $91 a year. Not a fortune, but how hard did you have to work to get it?

- Let's take it even further. Suppose twenty people in your CBP plan to shop at the Gap for holiday gifts. Suppose they figure that they'll each spend about $300. You, as the head of the CBP, could approach the manager of Gap and say, "Tell you what, this Sunday night you keep the store open for one extra hour exclusively for my CBP, and we'll guarantee to spend at least $6,000 in your store." You could have your own private shopping experience. This may not work at every store, but I'd hate to be the Gap store manager who had to tell his regional manager that he turned down a guaranteed $6,000 in one hour simply so he could go home early to watch *E!* What's the worst thing that could happen? The manager says no. Big deal.

 I can't possibly list all the creative ways to use your CBP, so you'll have to use your own creativity to take full advantage of bulk buying. The technique works best when there is a living, breathing salesperson involved, preferably one who works on commission. And I do encourage you to be the head of your CBP, because often the organizer will get his or her product or service for nothing. *"If I bring by ten people to get an oil change, will you give me my oil change for free?"*

And if this all seems like penny pinching, don't do it. Or maybe only do it on the big-ticket items, like cars and airline tickets. However you use a CBP, it can be an effortless way to save thousands of dollars.

Secret #14 in a Nutshell

An easy way to save on your purchases is to buy in groups. A simple mass email sent to everyone you know or a conspicuously placed sign can set this up. Whenever someone in your group wants to buy something, they simply email the group and travel to the store in packs.

negotiate

It's not what you say. It's what they hear.

SIGN IN AN ADVERTISING OFFICE

Why It Works

Leonardo DiCaprio was paid twenty million dollars to star in the movie *The Beach*. In the course of a year, he was paid roughly $10,000 an hour. Jealous? Don't be. You can earn that kind of money, too. But you must know how to effectively negotiate. By learning the ten rules of negotiation, you can save hundreds, even thousands of dollars in just a few minutes. While it's nice to be a movie star, it's not the only way to earn titanic hourly wages. Just be a good negotiator.

How It Works

If you're going to become a superstar negotiator, you must first learn the ten rules of negotiation:

> **Rule #1—Everything is negotiable.** Yes, everything. Maybe it's not worth half an hour of your time to get 10% off

a 25-cent pack of LifeSavers, but everything is negotiable.
Don't ever be afraid to negotiate when buying or selling
anything. I'm not saying you should nickel and dime every
purchase. That's just a flat-out waste of time. But if you are
short on cash, you can always bargain.*

**Rule #2—The person with more information will come
out better.** Find out as much as you can about the person
you're negotiating with. Why are they buying/selling? How
much can they afford? Are they on a time limit?
The subclause to this rule is that the person with
the least information usually fares worse. Another
way to say it is that the person who does more of
the listening and less of the talking usually comes
out better. I know this is starting to sound like an
excerpt from *Men Are from Mars, Women Are from
Venus*, but it happens to apply to negotiating as
well as it does to relationships. I believe the saying
is, "Knowledge is power."

> *Don't ever be
> afraid to
> negotiate when
> buying or
> selling
> anything.*

Rule #3—Be honest. Being caught in a lie hurts.
While you don't have to tell your opponent every
little detail about yourself, you must be honest when asked
a question.

If you're caught in one lie, people assume you've been
lying about everything. Just ask almost any former U.S.
president. If you get a reputation as a dishonest negotiator,
no one will ever want to negotiate with you. It is crucial
that people trust you and feel comfortable with you during
negotiations. Otherwise, they won't budge.

Rule #4—Chill. In a negotiation, the person with the most
amount of time usually fares better. You don't always have
control over the time, but planning ahead can make it
easier. A time crunch can hurt your negotiation by forcing
you to accept what would otherwise be an unacceptable offer. If you know your opponent is watching the clock, you

* And this isn't just about money. You can use these ten rules to negotiate anything—speeding tickets, dishwashing duty, anything.

can use that knowledge to your advantage. Simply wait until they are forced to accept your offer.

Look at your list of written goals. Is there anything coming up you should be preparing for? If you wanted to buy a new car for an upcoming road trip, start looking today. If you wait until the day before your 3,000-mile road trip, then your back will be against the wall and you'll be forced to pay whatever price is given to you. Plan ahead so you never get cornered in a negotiation.

A time crunch can hurt your negotiation by forcing you to accept what would otherwise be an unacceptable offer.

Rule #5—Never fall in love with what you are buying or selling. Fall in love with things that can't be bought or sold, like people, sunsets, or fresh air. But never get attached to anything material. If you do, plan to lose the negotiation.

Rule #6—Ask. How do you get a date with that special someone? Telepathy? Smoke signals? Kidnapping? No, you ask! If you want something, you have to ask for it. Ask whomever you are buying from if you qualify for a discount. If the seller says no, then feed them suggestions. Ask them who does qualify for a discount: teachers, students, senior citizens, AAA members, members of nonprofit organizations, young children, families, repeat customers—I don't know. Suggest anything that could possibly shave some green off the price.

If you want something, you have to ask for it.

Rule #7—In every negotiation, there is more than one thing to negotiate. People always focus on price, when in fact price is usually where your opponent will move the least. In fact, the more things there are to negotiate, the better the chances for creating a win-win negotiation. Imagine you're trying to buy a $150,000 house. If the price is firm, negotiate something else. You could negotiate the payment terms: offer to pay $1800 a month for the next hundred months. What about telling the seller to drop $5,000 off the price of the house if you agree to help her move? Tell her you'll pay $150,000, but she has to give you all the furniture. You can use this technique in any negotiation. If you're buying a suit, ask if they will throw in a free alteration. If you're buying a stereo, ask if they will add another year on to the warranty. How can it hurt?

Before you begin a negotiation, draft a list of everything that's negotiable. Price, payment terms, delivery, whatever. Size matters here! The bigger the list, the easier the negotiation will be. The trick is to find out what on the list your opponent wants and match it with something you are happy to give away. I care about the price of your house. You care about your prize-winning rose bushes. So I agree to let you dig up the rose bushes and take them with you, if I get the right price for the house. You win, I win.

Rule #8—Greed is good. We can all learn from Gordon Gekko's adage in the movie *Wall Street*. A little greed is good. The majority of negotiations unfold the same way. Picture an argument between Batman and Robin. Typically, the crime-fighting duo gets along, but not when it comes to gas for the Batmobile. True it's Batman's car, but he thinks Robin should cough up some gas money. Batman suggests a hundred bucks, to which Robin says, "Holy California oil prices Batman! How about $80?" The Dark Knight comes back at $95, while Boy Wonder ups to $85. Within moments, they agree at $90. So end most of the world's negotiations. One person will name a price, the other person will counteroffer, and the majority of the time they will end up agreeing in the middle. So make the middle a little bigger! If Batman wanted $100, he should've started at $120. That way, Robin feels good he knocked Batman down by $20.

Obvious? Sure, but few people do it. They're afraid of being too high or too low. Always remember that if you start greedy, you can always become more generous. But start generous and you cannot become greedier.

> *Before you begin a negotiation, draft a list of everything that's negotiable.*

Rule #9—Be a Gump, not a Trump. How would you act if Donald Trump showed up at your house looking to buy your used car? You'd probably think, "Hey, I know this guy has mad cash, and I know he's one of the best negotiators in the country, so I'm going to take him for everything he's got, because I know he's trying to do the same thing to me."

On the other hand, suppose Forrest Gump drops by to buy that same car. (How'd he get a license?) How would you react? You'd notice that he doesn't have much money, plus he's a few fries short of a Happy Meal. I mean, honestly, could you rip off a guy who opened negotiations with, "A car is like a box of chocolates, you never know what you're going to get?"

The point is, if you appear super smart or super rich, your opponents will use those appearances against you. So leave the Armani wardrobe at home when you go to a negotiation. Dress down, act a little naive, and if you're buying a car, don't show up in your Mercedes, show up on your bike. It will make your opponents relax and probably mention something they otherwise wouldn't have. So be a Gump, not a Trump.

Rule #10—Watch the right movies. Be sure to watch *Dog Day Afternoon* starring Al Pacino, *The Godfather* starring Marlon Brando and Al Pacino, *The Negotiator* (how'd you know I'd pick that one?) starring Kevin Spacey and Samuel L. Jackson, and *A Civil Action* starring John Travolta. All these movies are enjoyable, but each one involves serious negotiations. Also read the play *The Price*, by Arthur Miller. It is a wonderful play about a couple trying to sell their furniture to a furniture dealer who will never quote them a price for their furniture. He just keeps wearing down their patience, finding out more information. Pay close attention and see if the characters in any of these stories use any of the nine rules in their negotiations.

Secret #15 at Work

People always ask me if there is a way to make easy money. There is—negotiate for it. If you go to buy a car for $15,000, and it takes you an hour to buy that car and negotiate the price down to $14,000, you just made $1,000 an hour.

I've used the ten rules to negotiate everything from my rent to my report card. I'm not a movie star, so the only time in my life when I've made more than $1,000 an hour is when I negotiated. Remember, the final price is anything but final. The way to get more for less is to ask for it.

 ### Secret #15 in a Nutshell

Everything is negotiable. Don't focus on price. Make a list of everything that can be traded and decide what is important to you and what isn't. Don't get cocky, and don't get emotional. Don't be afraid to ask for a little more; you can always come down. Learn from the films you watch.

---

look for the happy hours

You're through Part Deux. You now know how the credit card and retail industries work. To fight back, you got a card with a rewards program and you formed a consumer buying pool. This weekend, you're going to rent some Pacino flicks to brush up on your negotiation skills.

In Part III, we're going to talk about saving money. But I'm not going to tell you to reuse teabags and clip coupons. It'll be cool saving. Cool saving happens when you get more money in your pocket without changing your lifestyle.

Sound impossible? Read on.

axe the tax

"What's two plus two?" the CEO asked his accountant.
"Hmm," replied the accountant, "what kind of a number did you have in mind?"

OLD ACCOUNTING JOKE

Why It Works

Probably the best description of the Federal Tax System I've ever heard was from Gene Hackman in the movie *The Firm*. He says (to Tom Cruise), "It's a game [taxes], we teach the rich how to play it, so they can stay rich. The IRS keeps changing the rules so we can keep getting rich teaching them. It's a game." I think Hackman is right on here. Taxes are just one large and confusing game.

Basically, society works like this: we realized a long while ago that we can't do everything on our own. I couldn't afford to hire my own personal police force, and neither could you, so you and I and everyone else who couldn't afford to hire their own police force got together and formed a society. We each chipped in a little bit of money to a group we called the government, and the money we all coughed up we called taxes. The government uses this money to benefit the people that forked over the cash in the first place.

The government can use its money to benefit society in two

ways. It can spend more money in areas that would benefit society, like the military, health care, education or covering up that whole Roswell thing. Or the government can ease the tax bill on those individuals and entities that benefit society.

There's the key to the tax code. If you're doing something that benefits society, the government says, "Hey thanks," by offering you a tax break.

For instance, you get a tax break for donating to charity because donating to charity is considered a good thing for society.

There's the key to the tax code. If you're doing something that benefits society, the government says, "Hey thanks," by offering you a tax break.

How It Works

There are only two types of tax breaks, *tax deductions* and *tax credits*. The best way to explain deductions and credits is by going through the process you use to calculate how much money you owe in taxes. To calculate your tax bill, the first number you need to come up with is your *total income.* This is all the money you made from all your jobs, plus any money you made from investments—bank account interest, stock sales, even profits from your own business. Add all these up and you have your total income. But you're not taxed on your total income, you're only taxed on your *taxable income* which is always smaller than your total income. The path from total income to taxable income is paved with tax deductions. A tax deduction is simply an amount you can subtract from your total income. Once the deductions are subtracted you come up with your taxable income.

Imagine you earned $35,000 last year as an administrative assistant. You also made a $3,000 profit from selling stock in Yahoo! Your total income then is $38,000 ($35,000 from your job plus $3,000 from Yahoo!) Now let's say you had a $2,000 tax deduction. You subtract $2,000 (your tax deduction) from $38,000 (your total income), to arrive at $36,000, your taxable income. This number ($36,000) is what you will pay taxes on.

Let's say the taxes on $36,000 come to $6,251. This amount ($6,251) is the amount of money you would owe the government, *unless* you qualify for any tax credits. A tax credit is an amount you can subtract directly from the taxes you owe, In this case you have a tax bill of $6,251. If you qualified for a $200 tax credit, then you could subtract $200 directly from your tax bill of $6,251, reducing the taxes you owe to $6,051.

The amount of taxes you pay depends on your particular *tax bracket*. The easiest way to understand tax brackets is to use the handy dandy chart below. Grab six quarters, which will represent your salary. (Times sure are tough!) Imagine this year you only earned 25 cents. Put one quarter in the 10% box. Because you only earned 25 cents you only pay 10% of that 25 cents in taxes. Next year however things get a little better and you earn 50 cents. Now put one quarter in the 10% box and one in the 15% box. On the first 25 cents you made, you're still only taxed 10%. But on the *next* 25 cents you made, you're taxed 15%. Make another 25 cents and *that* 25 cents is taxed at 28%.

Any money in this box is taxed at 10%	Any money in this box is taxed at 15%	Any money in this box is taxed at 28%	Any money in this box is taxed at 31%	Any money in this box is taxed at 36%	Any money in this box is taxed at 39%. Any additional money is also taxed at 39%

What are we learning here? As you make more money, a higher percentage of that money will go to taxes.

The danger is for young people who fall into the 15% and 28% tax brackets. Between these two brackets the tax rate almost doubles. Someone who normally makes $27,000 a year would expect to pay about 15% of that in taxes. But then all of a sudden this person gets a new job paying $32,000 a year. Thinking they have an extra $5,000 in spending money, this person upgrades to a nicer apartment. A dangerous move, because this extra $5,000 falls into a new tax bracket, the 28% tax bracket. For many people, it is not until tax time that they realize 28%, not 15% of this extra $5,000 will go to taxes. This is of course, after they have spent it.

It's tax brackets that make tax deductions so precious. The real tax bite comes from the final dollars you earn. A deduction will help you lower your income, thereby lowering the tax bite.

Suppose you make $50,000 a year selling your patented hair replacement system. Business is good (because hey, you're not only the president you're also a client), so you decide to give $1,000 to charity. While the charity you choose gets the entire $1,000 of your money, it really only costs you $720 to give them $1,000. This is because you would have had to pay $280 in taxes on that last $1,000 of your income. (28% × $1,000=$280) But you were able to deduct that $1,000 donation so your taxable income was lowered to $49,000. If you get enough deductions, you may be able to slide out of a high tax bracket altogether.

Let's go through a year in the life of an average taxpayer. Whenever you start a new job, your employer always asks you to fill out a W-4 form (you can remember this because a W-4 form is the form you fill out be*FOUR* you start working). The W-4 form tells your employer how much money to take out of your paycheck each week to pay for taxes. Why would someone have less money taken out of their paycheck for taxes than someone else? The primary reason is dependents. People with children qualify for a lot of tax breaks so they're not going to pay as much in taxes as a single person with no children. These people with children need their paychecks to be as big as possible, because they have more than one mouth to feed.

The W-4 form asks you to determine how many people are dependent on your paycheck. If you're a single mom with one child you would claim "two" on your W-4. That means you're telling your employer you support two people with this paycheck, yourself and your child. If you are a single guy, then your W-4 would read "one." It's also possible to put down "zero" on your W-4 form, which just tells your employer to withhold the maximum amount of money. People do this because they like to get a fat refund check at tax time, but this is the absolute worst way to save, because the government does not pay you any interest. Claiming zero is really only a good idea if you A) have additional income from things like stocks and bank account interest where taxes are not normally withheld or B) if you have several small jobs that add up to a large salary. If you work

three jobs, each paying an annual salary of $10,000 each job as-
sumes they're the only job you have, so each job withholds money
assuming you're in a low tax bracket. But when you add up all the
jobs you're actually in the 28% tax bracket.

If your brain is fried from reading this, just remember: *The W-4
form asks for the number of people you support on that paycheck*. If you
really get lost just ask whoever handed you the W-4 form—your
boss or the guy from human resources—for help.

Every January, you start receiving tax forms for the previous
year (you fill out 2002 tax forms in the winter of 2003, 2003 tax
forms are filled out in the winter of 2004 and so on). The most
common tax form people receive is the W-2 form. This form sum-
marizes how much money you made in wages and how much you
paid in taxes over the year.

You use the information from the W-2 and other tax documents to fill out a *tax return*. A tax return is filled out on one of
three tax forms. Tax forms vary by their degree of complexity. The
simplest tax form is appropriately named the 1040EZ. The 1040A is
a bit more complicated, while the 1040 is the most complicated tax
form.*

If after filling out an entire tax return you determine that you
paid in more money over the year than you actually owe, then you
get a *refund* which means the government will be sending you back
some of the money you paid in over the year. If on the other hand
your tax bill totals more than you paid in, then you have a *balance
due* which means you'll need to send the government the additional
money you owe. One thing I want to stress here is that if you do get
a refund, the government isn't giving you any money, they're giving
you *back your money*. If you have a large refund, like $1,200, that
means you lent the government $1,200 for the whole year and they
didn't pay you any interest. How do you fix this? Ask your boss for a
new W-4 form and claim a higher number so less money will be

---

* See the IRS was on the right track here but they blew it. I'm talking about the
names of the forms. 1040EZ is a great name because it's the easiest form. But the
other two names don't give you any clue as to what you're in for. My suggestion?
How about the 1040EZ, the 1040 OK and the 1040 ONO?

taken out of each paycheck. If you've been claiming zero, try claiming one.

There are only two ways to fill out your tax return. You can either take the *standard deduction*, or you can *itemize* your deductions. Remember a deduction is an amount you're allowed to subtract from your total income. But rather than let every person count every little deduction, the government set a floor for deductions and they called that floor the standard deduction. Everyone is eligible for the standard deduction. If all your deductions add up to more than the standard deduction, then you should itemize. If not, just take the standard deduction.

Let's pretend the standard deduction is $5,000 this year. Let's also pretend you gave $3,000 to charity. Donating to charity is of course a deduction, because you're doing something that benefits society. However, if this $3,000 charity donation is your only deduction, then it's not worth you itemizing, because the $5,000 standard deduction would result in much greater savings. The smart move would be to "bunch" your charity contributions in one year. If you give $3,000 a year to charity better to give three years' worth in one year and take the bigger deduction than give $3,000 each year and not qualify for the deduction.

It's this catch, that the total of your itemized deductions must exceed the standard deduction, that gets people upset. I've had tax clients donate $1,000 to charity thinking they'll get some sort of tax break for it. But if they don't have enough other deductions to exceed the standard deduction, then that charity donation will not help ease your tax bill. The good news is that some tax deductions do not fall under the itemize umbrella. You can take them regardless of their amount.

Secret #16 at Work

I have a fairly complex tax return but I still get away with using one folder for all my tax stuff. At the beginning of every year I label a new folder with that year. Throughout the year I throw in all the stuff I feel might relate to my tax return. If I donate $25 to the United Way

I put a photocopy of the check in this folder. And when in January of the next year I begin receiving tax forms for the previous year I stuff them all into the folder until I'm ready (last minute) to sit down and start doing (cramming) my taxes.

Some of the more common tax forms readers in the age range of this book will receive are:

- **The W-2 form** This form outlines how much money you made in wages as an employee of a company as well as the total amount of money that was withheld from your paychecks for taxes.
- **The 1099 INT** This form tells how much money you made in taxable interest perhaps from a bank account or Certificate of Deposit.
- **The 1099 DIV** This form indicates how much money you made from dividends from any stocks you own. (What are dividends? Read Secret #32.)
- **The 1099 B** If you sold stock during the year your stockbroker will send you one of these forms during tax season indicating what you sold and how much you sold it for.
- **The 1098 E** If you're paying back student loans with interest, that interest is a tax deduction. The 1098 E form tells you how much you paid throughout the year in tax deductible student loan interest.
- **The 1098 T** If you paid (or your parents paid) tuition for the year you *might* get one of these forms—not every school will send you one. Tuition payments may qualify as a tax credit. Note that "tuition" doesn't necessarily have to be for a college education. There are tax breaks for tuition you pay to attend a two hour seminar on how to negotiate. Whenever you take a class, always get a receipt. It may not qualify, but if it does, you'll be glad you have a receipt.

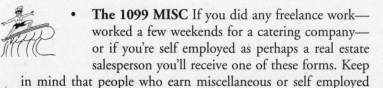

- **The 1099 MISC** If you did any freelance work— worked a few weekends for a catering company— or if you're self employed as perhaps a real estate salesperson you'll receive one of these forms. Keep in mind that people who earn miscellaneous or self employed income are responsible for paying their own taxes. Taxes usually aren't withheld for you. You can pay estimated taxes on your own by filling out a simple 1040 ES form and sending in a check to the IRS once every quarter. You can send in any amount, but each payment should be one fourth of what you will most likely owe in taxes. You can download form 1040 ES from the website of the Internal Revenue Service at www.irs.gov. If you have any questions about estimated taxes, just ask your tax advisor for help. The form is pathetically easy and they probably won't even charge you for it.

- **The 1098** If you own a home, look out for this one. This is the form that will tell you how much you paid in tax deductible mortgage interest

You'll receive most of these forms in January and February, but accounting departments make mistakes too (and lately more than a few mistakes), so double check to make sure you have everything. When you have gathered all your tax information you have two basic options. Doing it yourself or have someone else do it. Doing it yourself might mean using a computer or doing the old pencil/calculator routine. If you're the computer type, I recommend using the programs Turbo Tax or Kiplinger's Tax Cut. If you're the pencil/calculator type I recommend Pentech Pencils and Casio Calculators.

Having someone else do your taxes may consist of your uncle who is an accountant, or the accounting major you know from French class, or it may entail hiring a professional tax preparer. A professional might cost between $75 and $150 depending on how complex your taxes are.

 So, Pete, whatdya think? Hire a pro or no? Overall, I think personal finance is a relatively simple world. I won't kid you though, taxes are the exception. They can be very complex. I'm a big fan of meeting a tax advisor at least once to create a *tax strategy*. People spend all their time on tax preparation—filling in the blanks—but few people develop a strategy to actually reduce their taxes. You may think your taxes are simple, but that may be because you are doing something wrong. I knew a couple that had fairly simple taxes, but in chatting with them I discovered they were about to rent out the apartment in their attic. I told them they must go see a tax advisor, because he could help them minimize the taxes on the rent they collect. You may have a similar situation. Another advantage of having a professional do your taxes the first time is that you'll have a form to work off of, should you decide to go it alone in the future.

 If you do want help creating a tax strategy you have a few options. The most expensive option is to use a Certified Public Accountant (CPA). If you own your own business or have a complex financial life, a CPA might be able to save you even more than he costs. It will however be cheaper to use a tax preparer or Enrolled Agent (EA) than a CPA. Your company may offer free tax preparation as a perk. No luck? Most college campuses have accounting majors eager to practice on tax returns for *free*. Try to find a graduate student who has spent some time in the professional world. If you do take my advice and seek out a tax professional, ask if they will go through the tax return with you. You'll get to see where your total income, your taxable income, and all your deductions and credits fit in. Ask a lot of questions. You paid to have your taxes done. Now squeeze a quick educational session out of them.

Whether you opt for a computer program, the old pad and pencil or hiring a professional let's take a minute to learn about some of the more common tax breaks that apply to young people.

Below are some common tax deductions that you can take *even if you don't itemize*. You may still have to meet certain requirements to take these deductions, the most annoying requirement being that your income must be below a certain level.

• The most common tax deduction is known as the *personal exemption*. This is an amount you can subtract from your total income so long as you support yourself. If you have children or people you support *you* get to take *their* personal exemptions. If your parents support you, then they will take your personal exemption. See it's all about who supports who. If you live off your parents, why should you get a tax break? You shouldn't. (Or so argues the IRS.) So your parents (if they're married) will take three personal exemptions, one for your mom, one for your dad and one for you. Personal exemptions seem pretty straightforward and they are, except that whoever claims the personal exemption is often the person entitled to all the other tax breaks. In other words, if your mom claims your personal exemption, then she is entitled to the education tax breaks that arise from you being a full time student. It's the ever inescapable "let's get the family together and figure out our financial lives" theme again. The exemption question is especially important for college students because many of them are both eligible for education credits and being supported by their parents. If you're a college student supported by your parents ask if they will be claiming you on their tax return. If and when they say, "Yeah, why do you ask?" suggest you consider talking to a tax advisor to see if that is the smartest course of action. Ask them to ask their tax advisor for help. Or ask your tax advisor for help. I know this seems confusing but the worst thing that could happen is that your parents will be impressed you're talkin' tax strategies.

- Contributions to an employer sponsored retirement plan reduce your total income. If you make $43,000 a year and contribute $3,000 to your plan, you're now only taxed on $40,000. Secret #31 covers these employer-sponsored retirement plans in detail.

- Another tax deduction that you should *not* take but is nonetheless available is to contribute to an Individual Retirement Account or IRA. We'll talk more about IRAs in Secret #28. When we do, you'll find that I don't like the tax deductible version of the IRA. There is, believe it or not, a better kind.

 - You can deduct up to $2,500 in interest on your student loans. This perk got much better in 2002. Before you could only deduct interest payments for the first 60 months of the loan. That window has been broken. You may now deduct interest payments for as long as you pay interest. The company that loaned you your money will send you form 1098-E which tells you the amount of student loan interest. For more information on deducting student loan interest check out IRS Publication 970—Tax Benefits For Higher Education. To get this (and any other tax form) just call the IRS at 1-800-TAX-FORM or go to www.irs.gov.

- If you are required by a divorce agreement to pay alimony the amount you pay in alimony is deductible. There are of course restrictions. First you must make the payments in cash. If you buy a George Foreman Grill for $100 and never use it you can't give it to your ex-husband and deduct that $100 grill as an alimony payment. Send him a check for $100, let him get his own grill, while you take a nice tax deduction. Speaking of sending checks, if you're the one *receiving* alimony, that amount is taxable income, so plan ahead. Finally the answer to the most frequently asked tax divorce question is no. Child support is *not* deductible.

- *Capital Losses* are deductible. For the overwhelming majority of us the term capital loss will refer to when we buy a stock or a bond at one price and sell it a lower price. All of your gains and all of your losses get combined and losses cancel out gains. If you have more gains than losses, then this profit is taxed as income. If on the other hand (my dot com friends), you have more losses than gains you are stuck with what is known as a *net capital loss*. This loss is a tax deduction, up to $3,000 dollars. If you lost more than $3,000 in one year (my dot com friends) you can carry forward the remainder of the loss into next year, and can keep doing so until you've completely accounted for the loss. If you had a net capital loss of say $8,000 (my dot com—okay, okay I'll shut up) then you could deduct $3,000 this year, $3,000 next year and $2,000 the following year. If you own your own business and that loses money the amount lost is a deduction as well. However, if you own your own business I do recommend seeing a tax advisor. They may be able to help your business "lose" more than you thought it lost thereby making the deduction bigger. And do it legally.

- Moving expenses are deductible so long as the distance between your new job location and your old house is at least fifty miles more than the distance between your old job location and your old house. Confused? Just write down the number of miles from your old home to your new job. Under it write down the number of miles from your old home to your old job. Subtract the bottom number from the top number. If the answer's more than fifty, you win a moving expense deduction. For more information on moving expenses check out IRS Publication 521.

 Hey Pete, when it comes to calculating the distance test for moving expenses, why don't I just take "the long way" wink wink? Do that and you can look forward to your new prison roommate. Wink wink.

- There are more, a lot more, tax deductions available to the self employed. If this is your first time through the tax maze as a self employed person, go see a tax advisor. Or at the very least use a tax program like Tax Cut or Turbo Tax.

The following are some tax credits that typically apply to young people (mainly because our incomes are at a lifetime low). Remember that these are credits, which means they are amounts you can subtract directly from the taxes you owe.

- If you make a low income, you may be eligible for the *Earned Income Credit*. Unless you have children you must be at least twenty-five years old to take the credit. If you have children the credit does not have an age limit, so long as you are not claimed as an exemption on someone else's return. If the above description seems to fit you, check out IRS Publication 596 to see if you qualify for the Earned Income Credit.
- If you have children, you can take the *Child Tax Credit* and the *Child Care Tax Credit* if you pay someone to take care of your children. For more information on Child Care Credits, check out IRS Publication 503 and for more information on the Child Tax Credit, check out IRS Publication 972.
- If you are in school, check out the *Hope Scholarship Credit* and the *Lifetime Learning Credit* (discussed in Secret #19) by reading IRS Publication 970. The important thing to remember here is that while the Hope Scholarship Credit can only be taken in

your first two years of higher education, the Lifetime Learning Credit can be taken for just about any educational course that helps you acquire new job skills or improve current job skills. Once your income hits a certain level you're no longer eligible for this credit, but always get a receipt, just in case.

Below are some tax deductions you can take if and only if you itemize:

- A word about itemizing. It's a tough thing to do unless you own a home or make close to $90,000 a year, while living in a state that has a state income tax. Paying a large state income tax which is deductible or paying a large amount of home mortgage interest, which is also deductible, are typically the only two ways people can cross over the standard deduction line, thus making itemizing worthwhile. The reason is because most itemized deductions are subject to a floor. In other words, a particular itemized deduction may not count, unless it exceeds a certain percentage of your adjusted gross income. For instance, unreimbursed medical expenses are one of the itemized deductions, but only those medical expenses that exceed 7.5% of your gross income count. So if you make $30,000 a year, only medical expenses that exceed $2,250 (which is 7.5% of $30,000) will count.
- You can deduct contributions to a charity so always get a receipt. If you donate stuff to charity—clothes, furniture—you can deduct the fair market value of what you donate. Keep good records and try to get receipts for these donated items.
- State and local income taxes are deductible from your federal income tax. This can mean big money as well as big revenge on those who live in income-tax-free states. (Listen up Manhattan readers.)
- You can deduct property taxes and interest on your mortgage for a primary residence. (One of the many advantages of buying your own home.)
- Work-related expenses are deductible if you are not reimbursed for them. These work related expenses are subject to a 2% floor, which makes them tough to deduct.

- Consider bunching deductions into one year making itemizing worthwhile. We talked about this with charity donations, remember? Give three years worth of donations in one year to qualify for itemizing, rather than an equal amount each year.
- If you have any control over when you receive your income (perhaps you're self-employed and enjoy a little control as to when you get paid) you may want to take on more income one year and less income another year. What does this matter? Well think about it. If your bonus was $1,000 would you rather take that bonus when you were in the 28% tax bracket or the 15% tax bracket? In the 15% tax bracket you'd get to keep $850 of that $1,000 bonus. If you were in the 28% bracket, you'd keep only $720. If you see yourself switching tax brackets, and you can control when you receive your income investigate the best time to receive that money.

 ### Secret #16 in a Nutshell

Sorry to take so many pages on such a boring subject but since taxes are probably your single biggest expense, it pays to try and reduce them. Think about it, if you find after forty-five minutes of research you're eligible for a $500 tax break, you just made $500 in forty-five minutes. Does your regular job pay that much? So in a nutshell the key to the tax game is taking advantage of deductions, which allow you to lower your taxable income, and credits, which allow you to subtract from the money you owe. One can either itemize or take the standard deduction. If your finances are the least bit complicated, it may make sense to develop a strategy with a tax advisor.

---

cover your ass

Shit happens.

BUMPER STICKER

Why It Works

Insurance is tricky. Not only are you buying a product you cannot see, feel, taste, smell, or listen to, but you're buying a product that, if all goes well, you will never use. Because of the peculiar nature of insurance, people tend to either buy too much or too little. The purpose of this secret is to find out (just as Goldilocks did) what is just right for you.

How It Works

The primary purpose of insurance is *to protect what you already have.* I wish it were as simple as needing $100,000 worth of insurance to cover $100,000 worth of damages. But it's not. For this complexity (and nearly every other one in your life), you can thank the lawyers. We're living in an age in which lawsuits are as common as a neighborhood McDonald's. Don't believe me? Next time you're in said neighborhood of McDonald's, you can see how outrageous lawsuits have become. Glance at the temperature warning printed on your next cup of hot (excuse me, *extremely* hot) coffee from your favorite national franchise. That warning is there because people successfully sued Mickey D's for having hot coffee that was, well, hot. It's sad, but any one of us can be sued at any time for any thing.

Your best protection (besides three years of law school) is insurance. You need to purchase the right insurance, from the right place, with the right coverage for you. Before we get into the specific types of insurance, let's talk more generally:

Your best

protection

(besides three

years of law

school) is

insurance.

- There are two parts to any insurance policy: the *premium* and the *coverage*. The premium is what you pay; the coverage is what you get. You get what you pay for. That's why when you compare policies, you can't just look at price or premium. You must also compare coverage. A possible third part of an insurance policy may be a *rider*. A rider is extra coverage. In some cases, you may need it (you may add an expensive piece of jewelry to your home-owner's policy); in other cases, it's just fat (like insuring your left hand for $1.6 million*). Often, the standard policies are all you need.

- When purchasing any insurance, be sure the company is reputable and will not be going out of business. You want to find out what happens to your policy should your insurance company go belly-up. In some cases, you could lose your policy. A good rule of thumb is to purchase insurance from the biggest, oldest, most well-known insurance company you can find.

- In general, with any insurance policy, money can be saved by taking a higher *deductible*. A deductible is the amount you are willing to pay before the insurance policy kicks in. For instance, if you have a $500 deductible on your car insurance policy and you crash, you will pay the first $500 in damages. Once the $500 is used up, the policy will cover the rest. The higher the deductible, the less risk there is for the insurance company, so your

---

* As Rolling Stones' guitarist Keith Richards has done.

payments will be lower. Ask your insurance company for a bunch of different quotes with different deductibles. There may be a point when taking on a higher deductible no longer makes financial sense. Needless to say, be sure you have enough cash to cover yourself before your policy kicks in.

- Besides the deductible, there are countless other ways to lower your insurance policy. Nonsmokers will enjoy up to a 10% discount on their home and auto insurance, maybe more on life insurance. Installing an alarm system in your home or car, or a sprinkler system in your home, can create additional discounts. Be sure to ask the insurance company what you can do to lower your premiums.

- Another way to save money is to buy an insurance package. You may be able to get your home and auto insurance in a package from one company, which could mean 10% in savings.

- Do you belong to any organizations that offer discount insurance? Check with your employer, or your professional organization, to see if they have any discount policies. Even your college, perhaps through its alumni association, may offer discounts on insurance. It can't hurt to check.*

- The easiest and best (and most boring) way to save on insurance is to lead a wholesome lifestyle. Being healthy, being a good driver, being a nonsmoker, and giving up BMX jousting will add up to thousands of dollars saved on your insurance premiums.

Here are the types of insurance most people should have:

- **Auto insurance.** Auto has three parts. First and most expensive is *auto liability*. Imagine you drive into someone's living room. Auto liability will help pay to repair the living room and it will help pay to repair the people sitting in the living room. Next is *medical*. If you or anyone in your car was hurt when you drove into that living room, medical covers those bills. Finally, we have

---

* Well, there is the chance that when you call your alumni association they'll hit you up for a donation. No big deal, just get the info you need and mail them a fivesky. It'll be worth it.

collision. Again, we're back in the living room, and collision will pay for the repairs done to your car. There's also *comprehensive coverage*, which protects against things like floods, fires, and thefts. It's impossible to duck auto liability. You may be able to forgo medical coverage, but even if your state allows you to skip it, medical is still probably a good idea. Collision and comprehensive are almost unnecessary if your car is a piece of junk. If you have a nice car, or bought one with a loan, you'll need comprehensive and collision. (But more about the benefits of buying a clunker in the next secret.) Your auto insurance premium is based primarily on five criteria: 1) your age 2) the use of the car 3) the value of the car 4) where it is garaged every night (is it in a high-accident or low-accident area?) and 5) of course, your driving record. Discounts are also given for having good grades. Women will often pay less, as will married couples. *"Dearly beloved, we are gathered here today to cut down on our premiums."*

> *Your stuff might be a little old and worn out, but how much would it cost to replace it?*

- **Renter's insurance.** Renter's insurance is easy. Get it. Renter's insurance is one of the best deals in Insurance Town. For less than $200 a year, you can get all the coverage you'll need. Most renter's policies protect your valuables from being stolen, burned in a fire, or destroyed by some new and creative way I haven't thought of. And don't give me the "I don't have any really valuable stuff" routine. Your stuff might be a little old and worn out, but how much would it cost to replace it? Renter's also protects you from liability. Unfortunately, if you have a party in your apartment and your drunken friend falls down the stairs and breaks his neck, he can sue you. So blow the $200 (or less) on renter's insurance. If and when Johnny Cochran does come a knockin', your insurance policy will pay for your own legal defense. *"Now where did I put that number for Alan Dershowitz?"*

- **Homeowner's insurance.** If you borrow money to buy your house (and who doesn't?), you'll be forced to get this. Like auto, homeowner's has three main parts. There's the insurance that replaces the structure of your home if, for instance, it burns in a fire. Then there's the insurance to replace the contents of your home, if said contents also burn in said fire. Then there's liability, which protects you if people are hurt while in your home (perhaps in a fire). Homeowner's also protects you if you hurt someone outside your home. If you hit someone in the head with a zinger golf ball, your homeowner's should cover this.* A good idea may be to have your stuff insured for *guaranteed replacement*. This simply means the company will cut you a check large enough to replace the items you lost should disaster strike. If you bought a computer with a processor equal to that of an Atari 2600, it's probably worth less than a buck today, but to replace that computer would cost over $1,000. Guaranteed replacement means you get a check for $1,000.

Another part of homeowner's insurance is a rider for disasters like earthquakes and floods. These disasters usually aren't covered in a normal policy and are worth looking into (even if you don't live in California). Remember, you can always take a high deductible to lower costs.

- **Disability insurance.** Disability insurance is perhaps the most overlooked and most important insurance. Young people like you and me are four times more likely to become disabled than we are to die, so it makes sense to insure yourself should you become unable to work. Your employer probably provides some sort of disability coverage, but it may not be enough and most likely only protects you if you are hurt while on the job. If you're hurt demonstrating the latest WWE move in your living room, your employer's policy won't cover you, and neither will Vince McMahon. When shopping for disability insurance, you should ask the insurance company five questions:

1) *How soon after my accident will I start getting checks?* The sooner you get the checks the higher the premiums. In other words if you can wait a whole year to start receiving disability payments, your premiums will be lower than a policy that kicks in after six months.

---

* If not, sue your golf pro.

Why? Because during that year you're waiting for the checks from the insurance company, you might get well again, and no longer need the policy. As a rule of thumb, anything that reduces the risk for the insurance company will in turn reduce your premiums. If you can afford to wait six months to receive your checks as opposed to only thirty days you can reduce your monthly premiums by half.

2) *What requirements must be met for my policy to kick in?* Are you covered if you can't do *your* job, or are you only covered if you can't do *any* job? If you're a fireman and you break your leg but you can still type, some policies won't pay you because you can still work as a typist. A policy that pays you only if you can't do any job is known as an "any occ" (any occupation) policy. A policy that pays you only if you can't do *your* job is known as an "owner's occ" policy.

3) *Is the policy **guaranteed renewable**?* We are looking for a "yes" here. This means that the company won't require you to continually pass a physical exam to qualify.

4) *Is the policy **cancelable**?* The answer should be "no." Some policies can be canceled if your health worsens. You want a policy that cannot be canceled as long as you pay your premiums on time.

5) *How long will I get these checks?* Hmmm. This is a tough one. Ideally I'd like to say you should get these checks as long as you are disabled. It's quite possible that you could be disabled for many years. If you assign a year time limit to the payments you're just delaying the problem. Instead of going bankrupt today you'll live off the insurance for a year, and then go bankrupt. Putting a time limit on your disability policy is like scheduling a bankruptcy. *"Honey, are we going bankrupt on the tenth or the eighteenth?" "The eighteenth dear, the tenth is dinner with the Andersons."*

But a policy that protects you for as long as you are disabled will be expensive, like over $100 a month for a nonsmoking twenty-five-year-old. A limited policy, one that lasts for two years and pays $2,000 a month with a six-month waiting period might only cost $15 a month. So a few things to consider would be: could a family member support me if I became disabled? Could my spouse? How long could I live without my income? A parental pow wow may be in order here because these questions aren't easy to answer. The bottom line is that you're better off with some coverage, even if it's for only two years. In that time you may recover or at worst, it would give those who will be caring for you time to organize their lives.

It's best to buy disability insurance through your employer. Many companies work out a group plan, which makes it cheap (or cheaper, rather) for everyone. If you have one of those cafeteria benefits plans at work, where you get a set amount of money to spend as you choose—on life insurance, on disability insurance, on health insurance, maybe even on retirement or child care—you may opt to put less into services like child care, retirement, and life insurance and put more into health and disability. If your employer has no such program, go through an insurance agent. Disability is one type of insurance where you literally need to comb through the policy, looking for unnecessary riders.

Another cost-cutting technique may be buying a *gradual payment disability policy*. This policy allows you to pay less when you're younger—when you're more likely to recover quickly from an injury.

I realize that people don't want to think about becoming disabled, let alone buying insurance for it. I also realize many people will read this section thinking, "I should look into that," and then intentionally forget about it. It's this line of thinking that brings me to: *the scariest thought in the book*. No matter how strong you are financially, you will soon be wiped out if you become disabled and you don't have disability insurance. I've never been disabled, but I have taken time off to write. During this time I would live off my savings. When no new money is coming in, you would not believe how quickly your savings fade away. It's tough enough to budget *with* an income—imagine budgeting without one. My dream is that you'll take action right now, perhaps hop on the internet and look at some prices, or pick up the phone and call your parents and tell them you need to talk about this. At the very least, I hope my words disturb you, like an annoying rock in your hiking boot, that after enough time, you'll have to take a moment to sit down and do something about it.

- **Health insurance.** Your employer may provide you with health insurance. If not, you must get a policy of your own. Like disability, your policy should be *guaranteed renewable*. If you're on your own, it's best to choose a large company that's been around and will continue to be around for a while. Despite all the jokes we hear in movies, HMOs (health maintenance organizations) are solid yet relatively inexpensive health plans (especially for healthy young people).

  It may be tough to find an HMO that will sell you an individual plan but look around. About a quarter of HMOs will do this. You could also consider buying through an association which in most instances will be cheaper. If health insurance is going to break your budget (and it is expensive—for individuals we're talking $150 plus per month, and more if you smoke) you may want to consider catastrophic coverage, which is exactly what you think it is—you're only covered for the worst. This may work well for a recent graduate trying to get a job and get on their feet or even for someone who chooses to take a year off for some self-enlightenment. The deductibles on catastrophic policies are *very* high, but the premiums will be quite low.

- **Umbrella policy.** Another overlooked bargain in the insurance world is an umbrella policy. This policy kicks in when your other policies run out. For instance, if you have a $500,000 policy on your car and you cause an accident involving five people who each sue you for $120,000, your policy will be out of money. You may be personally liable. That's when the umbrella policy kicks in. If you have anything to show for yourself in assets, like a home or investments, you should consider an umbrella policy. They're cheap; you should be able to get a million dollar policy for less than $200 a year. Umbrellas are usually a better deal than buying more auto or home insurance. If, however, you have no significant assets, no need for the umbrella. Can't squeeze blood from a stone.

- **Insurance to Forget.** Once you get the big stuff out of the way, it rarely makes sense to buy insurance for the little stuff. What often ends up happening is that the little policies overlap the coverage from one of the big policies. I'd skip *credit protection insurance* which pays your credit card bills if you die or become disabled. If you die, your creditors can seize your assets to pay your debts. Let *them* find a buyer for your *Harry Potter* books. If you become disabled you still need to pay your bills, but a regular disability policy offers more flexibility than credit protection insurance. Also forget about flight insurance, which is a life insurance policy that kicks in if you die in a plane crash. First of all, many young people do not need life insurance (Read Secret #49 for further argument). Second, this is an expensive way to buy it and it's very inflexible (it only works if you die on the plane. There's no coverage for the *real* danger—the Boston cab drivers). We tend to think flying is unsafe, but statistically speaking it is the safest way to travel. You have a much better chance of breaking your neck as you struggle down the airport escalator with your luggage—especially with the way *you* pack. One little policy you might want to look into is *car rental liability* which insures you if you do some damage to other people and their property while in a rental car. If you have your own car insurance, it may bleed over to cover rental liability. But if you don't have any car insurance it may make sense to purchase rental liability at the rental counter.

Secret #17 at Work

Insurance can either be bought through an *agent* or a *direct underwriter*. A direct underwriter is a company that sells its own insurance policies. Geico would be an example of a direct underwriter. An agent sells policies from many different insurance companies and tries to find you the best deal. The direct underwriter will be cheaper, but because of the low price, you may not get as much counseling and your options may be limited. With an agent, you will pay more (and perhaps way more if he tries to add on unnecessary insurance), but you will get a variety of options, you will be dealing with an actual person, and you will get your hand held through the process.

If you use an agent, find an honest one (duh). Ask your friends and family who they use. You can interview several agents before you give one your business.

With an agent, you will pay more (and perhaps way more if he tries to add on unnecessary insurance), but you will get a variety of options, you will be dealing with an actual person, and you will get your hand held through the process.

If you decide to buy direct or over the internet, no one is going to hold your hand. The internet will quote you a price, but it won't make comments on the quote you requested. Unlike that calculus homework you once copied, you must do your own research.

You can, of course, consult a qualified financial advisor for insurance advice (provided she works 100% on hourly fees and earns no commissions from the policies she recommends).

What I would do first is visit the websites recommended below for each type of insurance you are looking to buy. Get an idea of premiums and coverage. Try to get at least five quotes for each type of insurance, either on the web or by calling names in your phonebook. From there, you may feel comfortable enough to buy on your own, or you may decide you want to go through an agent. Either way, you'll be much more informed and less likely to overpay or underinsure.

Websites for Auto Insurance:
Geico: www.geico.com (800) 841-3000
Amica: www.amica.com (800) 242-6422

Websites for Homeowner's Insurance
Insweb: www.insweb.com
Amica: www.amica.com (800) 242-6422

Websites for Disability Insurance
Unum: (who came up with that name?)
www.unum.com (800) 227-8138

Northwestern Mutual Life: (now there's a good-sounding insurance name) www.northwesternmutual.com (800) 672-4341

Websites for Health Insurance
Insweb: www.insweb.com
Quotesmith: www.quotesmith.com (800) 556-9393

 ### Secret #17 in a Nutshell

With an insurance policy, the premiums are your payments, the coverage is what you get if something goes wrong. Since suing someone is the easiest way to get loaded in America, it pays to properly insure yourself. Take a higher deductible. Even though it requires you to pay more money before the policy kicks in, it will lower your payments. You can either buy insurance direct and enjoy lower rates, or go through an agent and enjoy some hand holding. Whatever you do, first hop on the internet to familiarize yourself with the going rates.

---

cut car costs

I'm living so far beyond my income that we may almost be said to be living apart.

—E. E. CUMMINGS

Why It Works

The purchase of one car probably won't be the single biggest expense in your life, but add up *all* the cars you'll buy, and the expense is an enormous one. Over your lifetime, you may easily spend more than $100,000 on car purchases. What's worse is that every car is a *purchase*. The money you spend on a car, as opposed to the money you spend on your house or a college education, will never come back to you. So you might as well learn a few quick ways to lower the price of your next set of wheels.

How It Works

For the majority of people, only two things should influence the purchase of a car: safety and price—in that order. Sure if you're married with seven kids, you gotta go with the minivan. Or if you live deep in *Deliverance* country (where Jeff Foxworthy's redneck jokes are no longer funny), you may need four-wheel drive.

But other than that, you simply need to ask, "Do I feel safe in this car?" and "Can I afford it?"

I said it before and I'll say it again: every car is a purchase. The moment you buy it, you'll start losing money, because the car is going down in value every day you own it. So all the add-ons, like the CD player, moon roof, leather seats, or the words "Pimp Daddy" stenciled on the side, only mean you'll lose more money. That's because everything you add on also goes down in value as the car goes down in value.

Some general rules about buying a car:

- **Don't buy a new car.** Just too much money down the drain. What's the price difference between buying a new car, driving it for four years then selling it versus buying a four-year-old car, driving it for four years then selling it? Well, factoring in repairs, financing, and maintenance, the consulting firm of Runzheimer International found that the new-car option cost almost *double* the used-car option. So buy a used car and drive it until it dies. (Another used-car savings is the insurance. If your car is a clunker, you may be able to avoid collision insurance and comprehensive insurance*.)
- **Don't lease.** When you lease, you end up spending money you don't have. "Can't afford to buy it? Why not lease it?" asks the pearly toothed salesman. But when you lease, instead of the financial pain coming all at once in the form of a down payment, you spread this burden over many, many, many months. And at the end of those many, many, many months, ya got nothin' to show for all those payments. Even though every car depreciates in value, at least a car you own can be sold for *something*. A leased car is a total loss. Plus, there are stiff penalties for violating the rules of the lease (like driving over the yearly mileage limit). Leases, like VCR instructions, are often so confusing it makes it impossible to determine if you got a good deal.
- **Pay cash for the car.** *What!* I know, I know. All I'm saying is that if you can pay cash for the car, do it. If you can't, consider

---

* See Secret #17 for more info on insurance.

buying a cheaper car. Car loans often carry interest rates that would make most credit cards jealous. If you do have bulletproof credit (as I know you now do), you may be able to get a rock-bottom rate that would be lower than what your investments pay. In that case, it makes sense to finance. For example, the interest rate on my car loan (nope I couldn't come up with the cash either) is less than 1%. Since my bank account earns more than that interest rate, it did not make sense for me to pay cash.

- **Remember that when you negotiate, there is more than just price.** People are too fixed on price when they buy something. Equally the salesperson becomes fixed on price, so that no one budges. What about better service? A better warranty? A better interest rate on the loan? Plus, there are all the extras. If the salesperson won't come down in price, now's the time to talk about the free CD player and complimentary leather seats. Will he throw in any of those at no extra charge?

Leases, like VCR instructions, are often so confusing it makes it impossible to determine if you got a good deal.

- **Forget the fluff.** Rust proofing, paint sealant, fabric protection, and undercoating are all unnecessary add-ons. Also forget credit life insurance, which helps pay your loan bills if you die. Better to purchase term life insurance, which I talk about in Secret #49. Don't bother with extended warranties (which rarely pay out as much as they cost).

- **All else being equal, buy at the end of the month.** Car salespeople are tied to quotas—minimum sales requirements they are required to meet each month. If you hit up a salesperson that hasn't yet hit the quota, he'll be pretty motivated to cut you a deal. All else being equal, buy on a Tuesday, Wednesday, or Thursday, typically slow days in the car-selling industry.

- **Develop a personal relationship.** In the generation before ours, the sales industry was focused on the sale. That is to say, salespeople wanted you to buy no matter what. Today, the sales industry is smarter and so focuses on building relationships. The industry realized that if it told its customers lies like, "They're gonna lock me in jail for giving you a deal this good, but I'm gonna do it anyway," it would make one sale and lose a customer for life. When you buy a car, the salesman doesn't want you to buy just one car from him, he wants you to buy every car for the rest of your life from him. So coax that relationship. Don't say, "I'm looking to buy a car," say, "I hope this will be more than just a car purchase, I'm looking to establish a relationship with a dealership and advisor I can trust." I admit I'm laying the cheese on pretty thick here, but it works. If you make it look as though you'll only buy one car, the salesman is going to treat you like you'll only buy one car; he'll try to squeeze every last dime out of you. If, on the other hand, you make it appear that you'll come back, he'll try to give you the best deal to make sure you will come back.

- **Pretend you're more than one person.** This is taking the cheesy relationship thing one step further. I'm not saying go schitzo' on the car salesman, just tell him that if he gives you a good deal, you'll refer your friends his way. That way, he'll treat you as if you're actually more than one person. Mind you, this may not work, but what have you got to lose?

Secret #18 at Work

To find a car, the best place to start is on the web. Try www.edmunds.com, which is the website for Edmund's Car Guides. The site offers information about used cars, such as price, reliability, and safety ratings. Another site for the lowdown on cars is www.kbb.com, which is the site for Kelly Blue Book. *Consumer Reports* also offers solid information on new and used cars. Check to see if your local library has a subscription.

Unless you can secure a sweet deal on financing (a rate that costs less than what your investments pay out), make the biggest down payment you can afford. If you do need a loan, try Bankrate, at www.bankrate.com,

Lending Tree, at www.lendingtree.com, or RateNet, at www.rate.net. You may not actually get your loan online, but you'll at least have something to compare to the dealership's offer.

You can buy a car from one of four places:

- **A new car dealership.** In general, dealers will offer the best service but the highest price. If you do buy new, keep in mind that the dealer typically pays 10% to 20% less than the sticker price. That's your negotiating room. He may be willing to come down if he knows he can make money off you in other ways, such as service visits and sales referrals. Trying wetting his beak with both.

- **A car superstore.** These are places like AutoNation and CarMax. Prices here will tend to be a bit lower than a dealership, and the selection will be much larger. Not a bad place for a used car. Check out www.carmax.com or www.autonation.com to get started with a used-car superstore.

Unless you can secure a sweet deal on financing (a rate that costs less than what your investments pay out), make the biggest down payment you can afford.

- **A used-car dealer.** Here's that stereotype. But despite the stereotype, reputable used-car dealers can save you hundreds. The trouble is that reputable used-car dealers may not come by the hundreds. Ask friends and family who they used.

- **A former owner.** Scouring the newspaper can offer the greatest savings. You may find, buried in a cavern of classifieds, someone who *must* sell and will take any price. However, we're talking zero service and high risk. If you buy from a dealership and there's a problem, you can always take the car back to a physical place. But that shady guy who sold you his old car may be hiding out in South America. *Hablas espanol?* Also, you can file a complaint with your local Chamber of Commerce or Better Business Bureau office if a dealer cons you. Dealerships don't like to have such scars on their business records. But the already dishonest individual who sold you his old metallic pea-colored Griswold family wagon couldn't care less what other people thought of him.

One good way to protect yourself from buying a lemon is to use a service called Carfax at www.carfax.com. For only $12.50, Carfax will give you a complete history of your car. You can find out all the dirty details, like if the car was in an accident, or if it ever had fire damage. All the Carfax crew needs is the vehicle identification number or VIN.

So you've been online. You know the prices. You know the rates. It's time to buy. I think you're crazy if you don't slap together a quick consumer buying pool before you approach the car dealer. There must be *someone* you know who is also looking for a car. If you're in high school or college, you're surrounded by people your age, people who need cars at the same time you do. Without a doubt, you can form a CBP. (I have *eight* friends who own Volkswagens. They all bought within a three-year period, yet not one of them contacted another for a better deal.)

If you are short in the friends department, put up a flyer somewhere—anywhere. Tack one to your office bulletin board or at your local library. Something like, "Thinking of buying a Ford? Me too. Call me. We'll go to the dealership together and get the best deal." You don't have to know the people in your CBP; you can even meet for the first time right at the dealership.

But when you go as a group, the salesman will realize that he will lose multiple sales if he doesn't come up with a significant price break. Forming a CBP eliminates the need for negotiating. You'll call the shots.

Secret #18 in a Nutshell

Buy a used car and drive it until it dies. Don't lease and don't pay for a car by borrowing, unless the rate is lower than what your investments pay out. Use the internet to get an idea of prices before you go out kicking tires. Form a consumer buying pool before buying a car to save big bucks.

---

cut college costs

If you think education is expensive, try ig-
norance.

DEREK BOK

Why It Works

The cost of a college education is one of the largest investments you
will make in your life, second only to the investment in a home.
And since education is an investment like any other, it should be approached the same way you approach any other investment. You're
trying to get the highest value for the smallest amount of money.
Here's how.

How It Works

Let's assume you are only one of five types of people: 1) those who
don't care about college, 2) those who haven't gone to college but are
trying to go, 3) those who are in college, 4) those who are out of college, or 5) those who think a "college" is a bunch of pictures pasted
together. I have some tips for each, save for those unfortunate souls
in group five.

For those who don't care about college, think again. Education is the only investment you can *never* lose. While it is difficult to measure the reward of an educational investment in dollars and cents, according to the book *Investing for Life* published by the National Association of Investors Corporation (www.betterinvesting.org), on average college graduates earn $1,245 more each month than those with just a high school diploma. That's over a half million bucks over a lifetime.

What's more, some employers won't even consider your application unless you have a college degree. In addition, college is fun! It's a great place to meet people, a great place to network, a great place to hang out with people you would never have hung out with before, a great opportunity to live in a different part of the country, and a great place to wake up naked in a shopping cart wearing nothing but a pair of shorts (on your head), only to come home for Thanksgiving and have everyone tell you how proud they are of you. Priceless!

For those of you trying to go to college, it's expensive, but in most cases, worth it. Here are some ways to shrink the costs:

> **College graduates earn $1,245 more each month than those with just a high school diploma. That's over a half million bucks over a lifetime.**

- When it comes to financial aid, the best advice is to apply. Don't give me any "Oh, I wouldn't qualify" crap. You might. It can't hurt to call (800-433-3243) and fill out the Free Application for Federal Student Aid. While college costs are on the rise, so is the amount of money being given out. See if you qualify for this educational free lunch.
- There are four types of financial aid:

    - Scholarships: This is free money given away based on merit.
    - Grants: This is free money given away based on need.
    - Loans: This is money that you have to pay back.
    - Work-study: This is a guaranteed job while you're in college.

Ideally, you want to subsidize your whole education with grants and scholarships. But for those of us who live in reality, we'll probably need to take out some loans, which is not necessarily a bad thing. Student loans don't look nearly as bad on a credit report as high-interest credit card debt. Having student loans means you're trying to brighten your future with additional education. Having credit card debt means you're trying to brighten your living room with additional lava lamps.

Many educational loans do not start charging you interest until after you graduate. If you head to grad school right after college, you may be able to defer loan payments even longer.

I have three words of advice when it comes to scholarships: apply, apply, apply. There are scholarships that reward nearly everything, from your ability to dance to the fact that you're left-handed.* So find one for you. Don't think you're not good enough. For some scholarships, especially those offered by small local organizations, you might be the only one applying! You should always be looking for scholarships even if you're already in college. Who knows?

 Hey Pete, I knew a guy who knew a guy who told him scholarships were taxable. Is that true?
Yes and no. Yes scholarships are taxable if they are used to pay for things like room and board. No they are not taxable if they are used to pay for tuition and fees, assuming you are working toward a degree.

Grants are the tricky part. When a school looks at your finances to determine how much need-based aid you should get, some things count and some things don't. The fact is that if you save $10,000 for your college education, and the girl down the street (we'll call her Darcy) spent all her money amassing the most impressive Armani wardrobe the world has ever seen, she's going to get more money (all other things being equal). For you to get any money, the college is going to ask you to first cough up some of your ten grand.

---

* No, I'm serious. The Frederick and Mary F. Beckly Scholarship is a $1,000 scholarship for left-handed students attending Juniata College in Pennsylvania. Go for it, Lefty!

Look at the situation from the college's prospective. Both you and Darcy are asking for money. They look at your finances and see you have $10,000 in your bank account. Darcy has nothing in her bank account. True, Darcy may have a $10,000 wardrobe in her closet, but colleges don't look in closets. They won't ask Darcy to sell her clothes to pay for school. But they will ask you to put up some of your hard-earned $10,000. This is a sad situation, because it re-wards the people who don't save and punishes the people who do.

I'm not suggesting you spend your college savings on blouses and button-downs just to qualify for more financial aid. You may not get any aid. Or worse, you may not get any compliments on your outfits. The real trick is to stash the cash in places where colleges don't look. This way, you'll appear desperate when in reality your money is yours. As a rule of thumb, the year before you go to college is the year you and your parents want to have the lowest income possible.

The real trick is to stash the cash in places where colleges don't look.

So, where are these hiding places? Well, first and foremost, pay off consumer debt. Paying off credit cards and high-interest car loans is always good financial advice, college or not. The next best place is your retirement accounts. Either an IRA or 401k (more on these ac-counts in Secrets #27 and #28). Max out these accounts because the cash within them won't be considered when determining financial aid. Tell your parents, if they're helping you out with the bill, to do the same.

Remember the big-picture idea that no one is a finan-cial island. Perhaps this is never truer than with fi-nancial aid. Some parents (fueled by the completely innocent desire to create a solid future for their chil-dren) save money in an account in their child's name. At times, this account was created the day the child was born, so by the time the college years roll around, there is an im-pressive chunk of change in the account. This is a mistake. When money is in the student's name, the college expects the student to cough up about five times more money than the parent. Unless a family is so wealthy it simply doesn't know where else to put the money, that money in the child's name would have been much better off in a retirement account.

Here's what I mean. If you have $1,000 in a bank account and you apply for financial aid, your college will ask you to put about $350 of that money toward your education. However, if that money was in your parent's account, the school might ask them to put only $60 of that toward your tuition. Why do they do this? Well think about it. If your mom has $1,000 in her bank account, the college isn't sure how much of that money is going to be used for your college education and how much is going to be used for other important family expenses, like clothing, rent, and Cheerios. But if you have that $1,000 in your bank account, the college assumes you don't have too many other expenses in your life besides tuition, so they're gonna ask you to pay more.

 As a rule of thumb, families who will be applying for financial aid should save money in the parent's, not the student's name. And before any college savings accounts are opened up, everyone should save money in a retirement plan.

It may also make sense to buy expensive items now. If you need a computer for school, buy it *before* you apply for financial aid. If you have $2,000 in your bank account, the college will count that as money you could apply toward tuition. But if you buy a $2,000 computer with that money, the college won't ask you to sell the Dell.

So that's how you can increase your chances of getting financial aid. Here are some ways to help pay for college.

 • **Tax credits.** Remember, these are *credits* not deductions. Credits allow you to subtract an amount *directly* from the taxes you owe, whereas deductions reduce your taxable income. If the folks are helping you pay the college bill, tell them to look into the Hope

Scholarship, which allows them to take a credit of up to $1,500 each year for the first two years while you're in college. After those two years, your parents can use the Lifetime Learning Tax Credit, which is a credit of up to $1,000 each year. If your parents do not claim you as a dependent on their tax return then *you* can take these credits even if they pay your tuition. If someone else, like your grandfather or your rich uncle, pays your college tuition you can still take these credits as long as no one claims you as a dependent. The bad news is you can't use both at the same time. The good news is the Lifetime Learning Credit can be used throughout your life. Even after you graduate, you can use it to reduce the cost of courses taken to improve job skills. Let me say that a little louder. *As long as your income remains below a certain level, you can take the Lifetime Learning Credit for almost any class that helps you improve job skills or acquire new ones for the rest of your life.* So please be sure to get a receipt every time you take a class. Check out IRS Publication 970 (found on www.irs.gov) for more information on how these credits work.

- **Employer help.** If you're working full or even part time, your employer may be able to help you out with tuition. I like to think of employer-sponsored tuition as a salary increase. If you make $30,000 a year, but also managed to get a $100,000 college education fully paid for in four years, you really made $55,000 a year. You got $30,000 a year from your salary, plus $25,000 a year in free tuition. Your employer can pay as much as $5,250 in education expenses for you before it becomes a taxable fringe benefit for you. In other words, the government will tax as part of your income any amount over $5,250 in tuition assistance from your employer. Just be sure to find out what stipulations come with your employer-sponsored tuition. You may, for instance, have to stay at the company for a few years after you get the degree.

- **Consider the two-and-two program.** Most colleges will grant you a degree provided you earn at least half of your credits at their colleges. One way to drastically reduce the tuition bill is to spend your first two years at a state school or community college, and your last two at the college of your choice. With private college tuition averaging more than five times that of a public school the two-and-two program really makes sense for those who are private college bound. In the first two years of college, you'll be doing mainly general education classes anyway. (*In other words, don't worry about sleeping late.*) Just be sure to speak with the college you're thinking of transferring to before you embark on the two-and-two program to see what specific requirements they have and to be sure they accept the credits.

- *Hey Pete, what's the best way to save for college?* You're in luck! You've got a new weapon in the fight to pay for college, and it's called a 529 College Savings Plan. These are state-sponsored plans that offer a tax-friendly way to save for college. When you put money in the plan, it's invested by a professional money management company. The earnings from your investments grow tax deferred until you withdraw the money and use it to pay for qualified education expenses. The money can be used to pay for the typical college stuff—tuition, room, and board—but if you use the money to buy something other than an education, you will be slapped with a penalty. Here's what else is cool about these plans (the first thing being that they're tax friendly):

Your parents, aunts, even your local barber can name you as the beneficiary of their 529 account. You can even name yourself as a beneficiary.

- When you open a plan, you get to name a *beneficiary*. A beneficiary is the person who will be receiving the money from the plan. It can be whomever you want. Your parents, aunts, even your local barber can name you as the beneficiary of their account. You can even name yourself as a beneficiary.
- Whoever opens the plan retains control of it. This is what's cool. Your grandfather can open a plan and name you as the beneficiary. But Grandpa still has control of the money in

the plan. Even though you're the beneficiary, you can't just take the money whenever you want. That's up to Grandpa. Of course before you get the money, you will have to listen to the story of how "When I was a boy I had to walk thirteen miles to school uphill both ways during a snowstorm in July."

- It's easy to change the beneficiary. You could open an account for yourself, then if and when you have a child, you could switch the account over to the child. This flexibility is a really great feature, just don't piss off Grandpa or he'll make cousin Earl the new beneficiary.

- The money in these plans can be used at *any college in the country*—maybe even some foreign schools. Many people believe that if they open up a Massachusetts 529 plan, they'll have to go to college in Massachusetts. Not true! (I mean, come on now, name one good college in Massachusetts.) The money in the plan can be used at any college in the country, regardless of which state handles the administration of the plan.

When it comes to 529 plans, the financial aid question is still a bit unclear. Do expect some loss in financial aid eligibility because of these plans. Still, I'd rather bet on a sure thing—like savings in a 529 plan—than bet on an unsure thing—like financial aid. Also don't worry about 529 plans until the retirement accounts are funded.

The biggest problem with these plans is picking one. I mentioned these were state-sponsored plans, which basically means each state offers a slightly different variation of the plan. As I write this, forty-one states offer plans, and the numbers are rising. My advice would be to first decide what it is you're looking for in a plan and then try to find a state that offers a plan like the one you want. For instance, some states do not allow you to name yourself as the beneficiary and some states do have residency requirements to participate in their plans.

A great website for 529 plans is www.savingforcollege.com. The site gives an overview of every state's plan, so it's easy to research which plan will work for you. It may make sense to contact a qualified financial advisor before starting a plan.

How about a free lunch to go along with that 529 plan? Check out the website www.upromise.com. Upromise offers a sort of frequent-flyer-mile program for college savings. When you spend money on certain brand-name products, like cars from General Motors, or at certain brand-name stores, like Toys "R" Us and Staples, a portion of the money you spend will be contributed to your Upromise account. These contributions in your Upromise account are periodically transferred into your 529 account.

Let's say you spend $100 at Toys "R" Us. This toy titan has agreed to contribute 2% of the money you spend into your Upromise account. So when you shell out $100 for "Retirement Plan Barbie," $2 of that money goes toward your college savings. I admit it's not a lot of money, but it will add up over the years—$2 from Toys "R" Us, $3 from Exxon Mobile, $1 from AT&T. And come on now, how hard did you have to work to get it? Please check out Upromise. It's one of those rare free lunches out there.

Hold up, Pete. I'm a senior in high school. These 529 plans and Upromise stuff, should I worry about that? I mean I'm going to college in like ten months. The reward points from Upromise and the tax free savings of 529 accounts probably won't do much for someone just about to enter college. In your case you want to consider opening a retirement account such as a Roth IRA (explained in detail in Secret #28) and transferring some of that money you have in your savings account into the Roth IRA. Not only are you saving for retirement at an impressively early age—which is a great topic to bring up just before your parents are about to ground you—but you've also moved money into a place where financial aid offices won't look. But now that you read this secret, the idea of 529 plans and Upromise is in your head. Why not open a

Upromise account for *your* kids *before* they're born? (Scary thought I know, but even if you don't take that turn in life, remember it's easy to switch beneficiaries.)

For those of you who are now in college, for one, get a work-study job. If you look, you should be able to find a work-study job that pays you to do your homework. All over college campuses, people are needed to sit on their butts and monitor their fellow students. Monitor the dorm lobby, monitor the study room, and monitor the computer lab. Get a job like this. You don't get paid much, but since you have to study anyway, and you can do a slacker job without getting fired, why not? Be sure to look for a work-study job the moment you get on campus. Otherwise, you'll be the person who has to sand the scuff marks off the racquetball court.*

Be sure to look for a work-study job the moment you get on campus.

Be sure to keep applying for scholarships, and if your finances change drastically, be sure the financial aid office knows this.

If you can, live off campus. Depending on your school, this may or may not be the cool thing to do, but unless you're attending college in a big city like New York or Boston, off-campus housing will probably be cheaper.

And speaking of living, do you live in-state? If you're going to a state school, but you're an out-of-state resident, find out what it takes to transfer your residency. In some cases, it's not much work, clearly worth the several thousand dollars your new tuition bill will save you. In my home state of New Hampshire, in-state tuition for the university is $7,693, while out-of-staters get socked for $17,113. The school's financial aid office should have information about transferring your residency.

Also consider going to school over the summer. This worked out very advantageously for me. I went to school fifteen hundred miles from my home, so it was very expensive to move back and

---

* At my school, I actually met this unfortunate gentleman. Look for a work-study job the second you get to campus. That way you'll be sure to find a cushy one. Otherwise you might be forced to take a work-study job where you'll actually have to . . . work.

forth. In addition, all the leases on the local apartments were for twelve months, so if I left in the summer, I would have lost three months worth of rent. A final factor was that in taking summer classes, I was able to complete school in three years instead of four, which saved a whole year of living expenses. Please note that financial aid usually can't be applied to summer sessions. The other drawback to summer sessions is that they may impede your ability to get an internship. If you're in class all day, will you still have time to dress up in that pirate suit and greet all the Landlubbers who come into the Peg Leg Pub? I'll leave this time management question up to you, but I've seen many students do the summer class/job thing—myself being one of them.

For those of you out of college, well, first of all congratulations! You made it. Companies may offer you the chance to consolidate all your loans, from car loans, student loans, and credit cards into one loan. Their brochures claim that you will save money. But be sure to read the interest rates. My college loans carry an 8.25% interest rate. The consolidation loan I was offered carried an interest rate of 12%. So much for savings. Also remember the interest on your student loans is tax deductible.

Secret #19 at Work

Some websites that may be helpful:

Scholarships:

www.fastweb.com
www.college-scholarships.com

Financial Aid
www.debtfreegrad.com
www.fafsa.ed.gov (Free application for federal student aid)
www.cashforcollege.com

529 Accounts
www.savingforcollege.com
www.upromise.com

Secret #19 in a Nutshell

Education is the one investment that is impossible to lose. Get loans that delay interest accrual until graduation. Apply for every scholarship you can. You and your parents should fund retirement accounts. Your parents should hold money in their name, not yours. Take advantage of the Lifetime Learning and Hope Scholarship Tax Credits. Consider doing your first two years at a state school or community college. Consider summer sessions. Ask your employer for help. 529 plans offer a flexible, tax-friendly way to save for school. Check out Upromise.com to get free money for college.

---

rent right

A great man can come from a cabin.

SENECA

Why It Works

Unfortunately, renting is a necessary step in life. It would be great if the moment we moved out of our parents' homes, we could move straight into a home of our own, but unless your last name is Rockefeller, this probably isn't happening. What's worse, after watching *Friends*, *Frasier*, and *Seinfeld*, we're conned into thinking a top-floor apartment with a balcony can be had on the earnings of a coffee-bar waitress. Adding to this puzzling conundrum of how the food service industry can subsidize a penthouse is MTV's *Real World*. My first apartment had less room than the *Road Rules* RV.

Your rent is a purchase. On the other hand, when you buy a home, that's an investment. If you rent for a year, at the end of the year, you have nothing to show for it. If you buy a home with a thirty-year mortgage and live in it for a year, you're one-thirtieth of the way toward owning that home. In both instances, you paid for a place to live, but in the latter, you're also saving money. In the former, you lost it.

This chapter will take you through the rental process, so you can get an affordable but admirable place. It's actually not that complicated. The hard part is getting over your TV sitcom fantasies.

How It Works

I divide all renters into two categories: urbanites and country folk. Urbanites will enjoy higher rents, smaller rooms, and unpleasant real estate agents. Country folk will enjoy, well . . . the country. Regardless of where you fall, the tips for saving money remain the same.

- As I said above, the most important thing to remember about renting a place is that it is a purchase. Ideally, you should find the cheapest apartment you feel safe and comfortable in and live there. The money you save should be invested (see part IV of this book) so you can eventually buy your own place.
- Take on roommates. The more roommates you have, the lower the cost per room. In other words, a two-bedroom apartment will be cheaper per bedroom than a one-bedroom apartment. In a five-bedroom, you'll pay less per room than in a two-bedroom. Not only will your costs per room lower, your phone, electric, heat, and cable bills will head south because they will be shared by more people.
- Every roommate must be on the lease. In terms of bills, I thought I had a good arrangement with my first roommates. I put the phone bill in my name, one put the electric bill in his name, and another put the water and sewer bill in his name. Our idea was to set up a brinkmanship situation—if you don't pay the bills in our name, we won't pay the bills in yours. Trouble is, my roommate sublet his room to a guy from South America. Next semester, when I was studying overseas, these credit collectors were hounding my parents saying that I owe the phone company for $2,000 worth of calls to South America! *Aye Caramba!* So try to get everyone's name on all the bills or get your own phone line. If not, you'd better talk to your phone company about their South American calling plans.

- That leads me to *subletting*. Subletting is the art of renting a place and then rerenting it to someone else, perhaps because you are going away for the summer. If you live alone, subletting is not a problem. If you have roommates (which I hope you do), then how do you prevent your roommates from subletting to the "cable guy"? The problem may already be solved for you, because many *leases* (the legal agreement between landlord and tenant) don't allow subletting. If it is permitted, you and your roommates need to sit down and work out how you're going to deal with subletting. Perhaps the whole apartment has to approve the sublettor. Or the sublettor has to pay a little more to compensate everyone else. Work something out, just work it out before the issue comes up.

Take some pictures when you move in and when you move out. This will prove that you didn't damage anything.

- Take some pictures when you move in and when you move out. This will prove that you didn't damage anything. If you did damage something, then, er . . . I guess you'll want to skip this picture idea.
- You can also do a walk-through with the landlord. You both walk through the place before you move in to be sure everything is in working order.
- If the landlord promises to do something (like wear pants to the lease signing), get it in writing. Often on most leases, there is a space where you can write additional provisions. If the landlord agrees to allow your dog Snuffy to live with you, be sure that's written in the lease.
- And speaking of leases—read 'em. They're about four pages and they're pretty standard, but you do want to know exactly what you signed. The lease might say you can't have any water-filled furniture, like a waterbed or fish tank. If you add this aquatic accoutrement to your room and it leaks, you could be on the hook for the damage.
- This damage won't be so bad if you bought renter's insurance. It's one of the best insurance deals around; for less than $200, you should be able to get all the coverage you need. Renter's insurance not only protects your stuff, it also pro-

tects you from lawsuits that may arise, if, for instance, you have someone over and they slip on the water leaking out of your waterbed.

- Rent is negotiable in any market. I rented an apartment in Boston, a city where people scramble for apartments the way they scramble for Dave Matthews tickets. Even as all the little ants were marching the city for places to live, I still convinced the landlord to drop the price by $100 per month. The unit was going for $1,100, and my roommate and I were looking to cap our expenses at $1,000. So I turned to the real estate agent and said, "If the landlord will take $1,000 a month, we'll rent this unit today." The agent called the landlord on her cell, and she accepted. Will this work every time? Absolutely not. But what did I have to lose? Remember that even in the hottest markets, some units just don't rent that quickly. Landlords get weary. They may negotiate, but only if you ask. I saved $100. Try getting that out of Dave Matthews. Not to preen too much, but think about what $50 a month (my share) adds up to over time. That's $600 for the year. Invest that at 12% for twenty years and you'll have $5,787.78.

Secret #20 at Work

When you rent, you can either find the property on your own or use a real estate agent or realtor. The landlord will pay for the real estate agent's fee the majority of the time. If, however, you're an urbanite searching for housing in Boston or New York or one of their worthy equivalents, the tenant (that's you) will most likely pay the agent's fee. This fee may be equal to one month's rent, but in some cases, it can get as high as 15% of the year's rent. Don't forget the agent's fee when figuring out how much you can afford to spend on rent. If you set a rental budget of $1,200 a month and pay the agent a fee of $1,200, your rental budget just went up by $100 a month.

If the landlord pays the agent's fee, then use one. If you have to pay the fee, it may or may not be worth it. When you work with an agent, he'll call you when a new apartment hits the market and set up all the appointments for you. All you need to do is show up.

Otherwise, you'll have to look in the paper and on the web yourself, and set up your own appointments. After a few weekends of doing this, you may find it easier to just eat the fee and use a real estate agent. On the web, try www.apartments.com.

Real estate agent or no real estate agent, be prepared to cough up some cash. If you use a real estate agent, you might have to put down a deposit for the first month, last month, one month's security, and a one-month realtor fee. If your rent is $1,000 a month, that's $4,000 even before you move in! It won't be this bad in every city, but in the hot cities, like San Francisco, New York, and Boston, deposits this large are not uncommon.

Real estate agent or no real estate agent, be prepared to cough up some cash.

Finally, you found a place. You've gone from the dorm to a domicile of your own, even though it's still small and the food still lousy. You did a walk-through and plunked down some serious green. After your third try, you got through reading the entire lease and you realize now you'll have to sell your waterbed. My closing advice is that you change your moving day to a weekday. Everybody moves on weekends, and rates can be drastically higher. So skip class or take a sick day and save some money on the move.

Secret #20 in a Nutshell

Rent is a purchase. Try to cut costs and save up for a place you can one day call your own. Take on roommates, but set up some ground rules regarding subletting and bill payment. Buy renter's insurance. It can't hurt to try and negotiate the rent. If the landlord pays for a realtor, use one. If not, you'll have to decide how much of a pain it will be to find your own place. Get everything in writing.

---

reap the benefits

Things may come to those who wait but only the things left by those who hustle.

ABRAHAM LINCOLN

Why It Works

 You already know from the Victoria's Secret example that there is such a thing as a free lunch. If you are already employed, your company may offer a score of free services. If you're in college, your school probably offers just as many, if not more, although in college, it's not exactly free, it's just already paid for. Still, whether something is free or already paid for, you might as well take advantage of it.

How It Works

This is easy. If you're employed, jog down to your human resources department. Find out who is in charge of employee benefits. Set up an appointment with that person to find out every benefit you are entitled to as an employee. They may even have some brochures for you to take. That's it. If you don't have an HR department, ask your boss what benefits you are entitled to. If you don't have a boss, then you're probably in college so skip to the next paragraph. Many people don't do this and lose hundreds, even thousands, of dollars in free money. Some employers, for example, allow you to buy health insurance on a pre-tax basis, which reduces your taxable income. If you make $40,000 a year and you buy $2,000 worth of pre-tax medical insurance, your taxable income now is only $38,000. That's more than $600 in your pocket.

If you're in school, find your college's student-service center or student-resource center or whatever it is called on your campus. Ask them to tell you every service your school offers for free. This may take some searching, as the person working the student center desk may be a first year who knows less than you.

Secret #21 at Work

Here are some of the benefits your school or corporation may offer. Take *Getting Loaded* with you when you do this secret and just read off the list, asking if your school or company offers these benefits.

Company Benefits

Discounted/pre-tax Health Insurance

Discounted/pre-tax Disability Insurance

Life Insurance

On-Site Medical Care

Career Planning

Free Seminars

Free Tax Preparation

Resume Review

Corporate Discounts at Local Retailers

Free Health Club Membership

Free Financial Planning

Employer-Sponsored Tuition

School Benefits

Discounted Health Insurance

Discounted Disability Insurance

On-Campus Medical Care

Career Planning

Free Seminars

Free Tax Preparation

Resume Review

Student Discounts at Local Retailers

Free Health Club Membership

Interviewing Practice

Free Legal Services

If you worked for a dot com company, your benefits probably included things like Back Rub Day, Foot Massage Day, Free Lunch Day, Barefoot Day, Razor Scooter Day, Coffee's On Us Day. Needless to say, those days are over.

When job searching, be sure and find out what benefits companies offer their employees. And before you accept a job, you should do a quick budget. This is really the only way to accurately compare job offers. One company may offer you a salary of $25,000 but offer $6,000 in tax-free fringe benefits, while another offers $28,000, with only $2,000 in fringe benefits.*

Remember that you can work for your money, but you can also *fight* for your money. If you work for a small company with few benefits, it may make sense for you to talk to your boss about setting up a win-win situation. For instance, you could tell him that the average employee will spend ten hours doing their taxes. They'll get frustrated and maybe even lose sleep. In short, they'll be less productive workers. So ask your boss to hire a tax expert to come in and do everyone's taxes. Your boss gets to deduct the cost of this tax expert, plus he gets more productive employees. You get free tax help. Everyone wins.

When job searching, be sure and find out what benefits companies offer their employees.

Secret #21 in a Nutshell

Your school or company may have free programs you're not aware of. Go to the human resources department of your company and ask what they offer for benefits. If you're in school, find your student-resource center and ask what they offer to students. If you don't find the benefits you're looking for, suggest a win-win situation to get the benefits you want.

---

* A recruiter friend of mine warned me to warn you that you should never talk about benefits during a job interview. It's as taboo as talking about salary. But there are other ways to find out what the company offers in term of benefits—perhaps they have a brochure for you to take, or if you use a recruiting firm, ask them for help.

go for the green

To affect the quality of the day, that is the
highest of the arts.

—HENRY DAVID THOREAU

Why It Works

If you're truly committed to creating a healthy financial life, or if
you have a seriously unhealthy financial life, this secret is for you.
Much money can be saved by paying some attention to the environment, because waste is expensive. It used to be cool to fill in landfills, waste energy, and burn dirty fossil fuels (you know what they
say about the size of a man's smoke stack?). But now consumers as
well as corporations can save a boatload of cash simply by being a
little nicer to Mother Nature. On the surface, these tricks may seem
like nitpicky endeavors. But a closer examination will reveal that
they result in significant savings and cause almost zero disturbance
to your lifestyle.

How It Works

Contrary to popular belief, it is possible to get money out of thin air.

- Lightbulbs. Switch to compact fluorescents. The initial up-front cost is more, but they last thirteen times longer than traditional incandescent. In addition, they use only a third of the electricity that a regular lightbulb uses! You can find compact fluorescents at your local hardware store.

- A low-flow shower head cuts water use by 50% and pays for itself in less than a year. The other way to save 50% on your water bills is to shower with someone else, but this line has yet to work for me.

Start a change jar.

- And now that you got me talking hot water, your water heater should be set at 130 degrees. Most Americans keep their heaters at 140. Turning down the heater just 10 degrees can result in a 6% savings. You should also wrap the heater in a pre-fab blanket (careful—don't block any vents). This blanket can be bought at your local hardware store. Count on 8%+ in savings. Why the hell not do this? Would you rather pay $8 on a heating bill, or use the $8 you save to go see a movie?

Remember that the worst place to invest your money is in the folds of your couch.

- A heating system tune-up can save about 6% in heating bills. If your heating bill is $100/month, next month hire a heating technician (maybe $100) to fix the system and save about 6% risk free, tax free. Is your bank account paying 6% in interest? I doubt it. By the way, for every degree you lower on your thermostat, you cut 2% off your fuel bill. Use the money you save to buy a new sweater.

- Start a change jar. This one has nothing to do with the environment, but you'd be surprised how much you lose in loose change. After my first year of college, I had to clean out my dorm room. It took me about two hours, but I was delighted when I found $87 in loose change scattered around the room.

Now, all my change goes straight from my pocket into my change jar. I collect about $11 a month in loose change. Remember that the worst place to invest your money is in the folds of your couch.

- Dam up that toilet! Simply by placing a brick inside the tank, you block off part of the tank, so the toilet uses less water. This brick, which costs nothing and lasts forever, can save up to 2,500 gallons per person per year.

- Carpooling. Not only will you save on gas, but you'll spend less money on oil changes, tire rotations, general wear, and even insurance. (Plus, by having other people in the car, you'll never get caught singing to yourself, "And I would walk 500 miles and I would walk 500 more . . .") Keep tires properly inflated and rotate every 6,000 to 8,000 miles for a fuel savings of 5%. A well-tuned car is 9% more fuel-efficient. (By the way, Peter Lynch, who was making several million dollars a year managing the multibillion dollar Magellan Fund, used to carpool to work—and he rode in the back seat!) No friends? Consider a more fuel-efficient car (and consider rereading Secret #18 for more info on car buying).

- Go solar. Solar's too expensive on a large scale, but on a small scale, like using solar water heaters (for my Arizona and Florida readers), painting the pool black, (for my readers who somehow managed to afford a pool), or buying solar outdoor lights, soaking up rays can make sense. You know the old saying, "Make solar energy while the sun shines." Or maybe that was hay . . .

- Call your power company and request an energy audit. This is where a guy from the energy company comes to your house or apartment and tells you how to make your pad more efficient. There may or may not be a charge for this, but it's probably going to be worth it either way. Contrary to popular belief, energy companies don't necessarily make more money when you use more power. They should be happy to help you cut your bills. And here's a free lunch. If you rent, and your utilities are already included in that rent, get an audit. The audit may prove to your landlord that he can cut costs by buying a more efficient refrigerator. He saves money, you get a new fridge.

- Pay now, save later. If you've got old appliances, like a refrigerator that looks like a set piece from the *Brady Bunch*, it might make more sense to trade it in for a new one and cut your electric bill way down. Same with an air conditioning unit and windows. Ask the guy who does your energy audit what he thinks.

- Have an annual yard sale. Instead of throwing your stuff away, thereby enlarging the world's landfills, why not sell it? This is the environmental cash cow. I made $625 on my last yard sale and not one item was priced over $20. And I've made as much as $1,300 in a day. Not bad for a day's work. Remember that the best day is Saturday, because flea markets are on Sundays. Well-displayed items are easier to sell so spend some time on arrangement. Use price tags, since some people feel uncomfortable asking for prices. If you live in an apartment or condo that doesn't permit a yard sale, look at the classified ads to see if you can join someone else's. Or hock your stuff on Ebay. And yard sales aren't that much work, when you consider that you'd have to haul the stuff to the dump anyway.*

- Don't smoke. It's a costly habit—and not just those rising pack

> *Have an annual yard sale. Instead of throwing your stuff away, thereby enlarging the world's landfills, why not sell it? This is the environmental cash cow.*

---

* I don't want to hear anyone knockin' yard sales either. They're for everyone. As I write this, Jefri Bolkiah, the Prince of the oil-rich country of Brunei, just wrapped up a pseudo yard sale. The Prince actually had an auction, selling personal items to help pay back some of the $600 million he spent over the years on essentials like gold-plated toilet bowl brushes and a twelve-foot-tall rocking horse (ya know—just in case). And while you'll never see gold-plated toilet bowl brushes at my yard sales (I'd never part with mine), the message is clear. We could all use a little extra cash, and yard sales can be a great way to get it.

prices. Plan on paying more for life insurance, more for health insurance, and more on medical bills and cough syrup. Smokers can also enjoy legal discrimination—landlords don't have to rent to you, politicians are more than happy to tax you, bosses won't promote you (it happens)—and you'll have a tougher time selling your home or car because nonsmokers don't want to buy goods that smell like an ashtray. Oh, I almost forgot. There's one other drawback to smoking—it will kill you.

Secret #22 at Work

Let's have some fun with numbers:

- If every American replaced just one regular incandescent lightbulb with a compact fluorescent, we would save the energy equivalent of the yearly output of an entire nuclear power plant.
- If every American added one person to their car pool, the country would save forty million gallons of gas a *day*.

- Would you stop smoking for a million bucks? Three bucks a pack. A pack a day. 365 days a year. $43,800 over forty years. A lot to pay for nasty breath. Invest the $1,095 you spend a year on smokes, and after forty years, you've got $1,948,103.
- We can't control the effects of inflation, but we can control the effects of tire inflation. If every American did the proper pumping up, this country would save two billion gallons of gas a year.

Here's a realistic assumption of what you can save:

Compact Fluorescents	$3 per month
Loose Change	$10 per month
Pre-fab Blanket/Water Heater	$3 per month
Proper Tire Inflation	$5 per month

Car Pool	$65 per month
Yard Sale (averaged monthly)	$45 per month
Heating System Tune-up	$3 per month

TOTAL SAVINGS **$134 per month**

Some will save more, some less, but how hard did you have to work to get this money?

I'd like you to try following the suggestions in this secret. Take a look at this month's heating/electric/water/gasoline bill and compare it to next month's heating/electric/water/gasoline bill. The difference in savings is yours to do with as you please. Start a fund. Call it the "You Fund" and use it to do something creative and exciting. Use it to take a trip, start a business, or buy a new computer. Whatever you want. Even though you didn't have to work too hard to get it, it's still your money.

If you're having trouble getting started on a savings program, just get some friends together and make a competition out of it. See who can save the most money. Perhaps the winner gets a free lunch, and the loser has to read a book by Paul Reiser.

 ### Secret #22 in a Nutshell

Helping the environment will save you money and will have little effect on your lifestyle. With the money you save, start a fund that finances a fun or creative activity.

sock it away

"Why do you rob banks?" was asked of the famous bank robber Willy Sutton. His response: "Because that's where the money is."

Why It Works

The sad thing is that Willy Sutton was right. Banks are where a lot of the money is. Most people have either a savings or checking account, when in reality it is relatively pointless to have either. Secret #28 is going to show you how you can shift some cash to investments that work just like banks, only better.

How It Works

 Before I get on my apple box about how I don't like traditional bank accounts, let me first say that bank selection won't make you or lose you a fortune. When it comes to your bank account, or one of its equivalents, the big-picture idea is that you should keep three months worth of living expenses in this account. This is your disaster fund. If you get laid off, fired, or somehow become victim to some horrible accident, like you get trapped in an elevator playing nothing but Debbie Gibson, this money will carry you through the tough times. So if you learn nothing else about the world of banks, just remember that you need to keep three months' worth of living expenses in a safe liquid account.

Now where's that apple box?

We're probably drawn to banks because we know that at banks our money is insured by the U.S. Federal Government.* So we can sleep easy at night because our money is safe from the Willy Suttons of the world. We know it's impossible for us to lose our money.

This is a mistake.

The big-picture idea is that you should keep three months' worth of living expenses in this account.

 By socking away a lot of cash in a bank account, you are likely to lose money. The reason is because of *inflation*. Inflation is a rise in the cost of goods and services. Stuff's getting more expensive, to the tune of maybe a 4% increase every year (more on inflation in Secret #25). Your checking account is probably paying nothing in interest. You dump $100 into your checking account and at the end of the year that $100, because of inflation, can only buy $96 worth of stuff. You just lost $4 in this perfectly safe bank. If you have a savings account, you're probably still losing money, only not as quickly. Many traditional bank savings accounts pay less than 3% in interest. Inflation is going to beat down the returns of any investment, but in order to preserve your money, you have to at least match the inflation rate. I mention this not to coax every reader into abandoning your local bank, but to warn those super savers that the thousands of dollars they have sitting in a savings account is often losing, not making money.

* The Federal Deposit Insurance Corporation (FDIC) is the federal agency responsible for insuring the funds on deposit at its member banks.

Hey Pete, where do I stash the cash? Put your money in the mattress of the investment world—the *money market.*

The money market is a market just like any other, it's a place where stuff gets bought and sold. But in the money market, the only thing traded is short-term debt. Here's what I mean. Governments and companies always need to borrow cash quickly. You and I have cash. Governments and corporations say, "Give us your cash." You and I say, "What's in it for us?" Governments and corporations say, "We'll pay you interest." You and I say, "Who cares? Our savings accounts pay us interest." Governments and corporations say, "Tell ya what. We'll pay you *more* interest than your bank *and* we'll let you write checks against the cash you give us."*

The thousands of dollars they have sitting in a savings account is often losing, not making money.

Everything is quick and short term in the money market. When you deposit money in the money market, you and every other investor depositing into the money market are essentially loaning your money to governments and corporations. It's easy for you to get your money, and it's easy for governments and corporations to borrow money. But to draw people away from traditional bank accounts, the money market has to be a sweeter deal than your local bank, so the money market typically allows people to write checks on the money they deposit and also pays a higher interest rate than your local bank. In short, having a money market account is like having a checking account that pays more interest than your savings account. Not bad.

There is one catch that's not really a catch. The Federal Deposit Insurance Corporation insures your bank account. Not so in a money market account. But don't let this deter you. When you place your money in the money market, your money is invested in only the safest of investments. Plus, unlike a bank, a money market is impossible to rob. To put it in perspective, your money market account

---

* Please note that there may be some restrictions on check writing for money market accounts. But some accounts are as flexible as a regular checking account.

will go belly-up the day Sir Mix-A-Lot's "Baby Got Back" becomes your school song.*

Where can you open your money market account? Just about anywhere, but I think the best place to have a money market account is with your brokerage company or mutual fund company because these places most often pay the highest interest rates. A money market account with a brokerage firm is often referred to as a cash management account or CMA. When you sell a stock, the cash from the sale automatically gets swept into the CMA. With a mutual fund company, your cash from sales gets swept into a money market mutual fund. When you set up a money market account at a brokerage firm or mutual fund company, your money is always earning interest. You don't have to wait for a check to come in the mail—everything is instant. Plus, these money market accounts often allow you to write checks against the money in your account. (Don't have a brokerage account or an account with a mutual fund company? Don't worry, by the end of this book, you will.)

 The ideal money market account? Well, it should:

- Credit interest daily.
- Have no penalty for not carrying a minimum balance.
- Have unlimited check writing.
- Have no minimum amount per check written.
- Have the highest interest rate and lowest annual expenses you can find.

It's okay if your money market account doesn't meet all these criteria. In fact, once you choose a brokerage firm in Secret #34, the money market account will simply fall into place. I think the important

* *Come on Pete, the money market sounds too good to be true. Can't they fail?* In theory, they can, but the parent company wouldn't let that happen because it would put the parent company in serious jeopardy. Should the investments in a money market fund go sour, the parent company that oversees the fund would infuse it with cash.

things are that the money market account has unlimited check writing, no minimum amount per check with low annual expenses. Most money market accounts will demand that you open the account with at least $1,000 but many don't care if you drop below that amount once the account is open.

Hey Pete, if money market accounts are so great, why do people still use bank accounts? For the same reason that over a million personal bankruptcies are filed every year. Or that an average household has $8,000 in credit card debt. Or that over 100 million Americans don't own any stock. *They don't know any better.* We were taught either by our parents or our schools to keep it simple. Checking accounts were for paying bills. Savings accounts were for savings. Both are bad advice, because in a money market account you'll save more money and still be able to write checks.

Checking accounts were for paying bills. Savings accounts were for savings. Both are bad advice, because in a money market account you'll earn more money and still be able to write checks.

Secret #23 at Work

We'll talk about opening up a brokerage account with a cash management account in Secret #34. First, you have to know what you use your money market account for.

The money market account is a safe place to store cash and it pays an interest rate that's above, or at least equal to, inflation. Keep three months' worth of living expenses in cash in your money market account. I know that's a lot to save up for, but it's important. That's your emergency fund. Hey, shit happens, and this is the money that's going to save you. So, before stocks, bonds, mutual funds, real estate, or even a new pair of Maui Jams, stash three months' worth of living expenses in the money market account and don't dip into it unless you have an emergency. And once you're out of that emergency, be sure to restash the cash.

Pete, you have got to be kidding me. Do you know how long it is going to take to save up three months worth of living expenses? It'll probably take well over a year to do this. Financially speaking it is better to start this fund than it is an investment fund, because if disaster strikes you'll be forced to sell those investments, quite possibly at a significant loss. The stock market crashes, you get laid off, you can't find work, so you sell some of the stocks that just crashed. I do however realize that saving for an emergency fund, hell saving for anything, is difficult. You might want to put $50 a week into this fund. I know that'll hurt but here's the good news. Once you save the emergency cushion, you're done—*forever*. What's more you may already have a good portion of this money. Did your grandmother buy you a $25 savings bond every birthday since you were born? That's money that could be used. Did your dad purchase a cash value life insurance policy for you? You can borrow against that fairly cheaply. Look at your asset and liability sheets again. You may be further along than you think. And if you want to start an investment fund while you're still building up the cushion, then why not? Who am I to lecture someone so eager to save and invest?

Besides your emergency cash fund, you can use your money market account as a checking account. Deposit your paycheck in it and pay your bills from it. You may be able to replace your regular bank checking account altogether. However you may still need a regular bank account for ATM purposes.

I encourage you to open a money market account. You won't make a fortune, but at least you won't lose any more money in a traditional bank account. Check out www.bankrate.com and www.fool.com for help with your bank selection.

And again, don't spend too much time in the quest for the perfect bank. In 1999, the Gramm Leach Bliley Act was passed, and the financial industry is now enjoying deregulation. Financial institutions are becoming financial Wal-Marts. Banks are now able to sell stocks and mutual funds, and stock brokerage firms and mutual fund companies are now offering the services of banks. This trend toward one-stop shopping is likely to continue, making it much easier for you and me to centralize our finances. As I write this, my stock, mutual fund, and money market account, as well as my interest-paying checking account are all held with the same online firm. It is very easy for me to transfer my money around, because there is one company handling everything. But again, the best advice I can give you is not to worry too much. The whole key here is to build up that emergency fund until it has three months of living expenses. Pick a place to set up shop and be done with it.

Secret #23 in a Nutshell

Money market accounts are a better alternative to bank savings and checking accounts. They pay more in interest and let you write checks. You can easily centralize your finances by having a high-interest cash management account that lets you write an unlimited number of checks for any amount, and a brokerage account that lets you buy a variety of investments, like stocks, bonds, and mutual funds. A money market account is a great place to store your three months of emergency living expenses.

---

skip the bank cds

For a country, everything will become lost
when the jobs of an economist and a banker
become highly respected professions.

MONTESQUIEU

Why It Works

As a nation, we really put a lot of trust in the local bank. That's the
only reason I can see why bank certificates of deposit (CDs) are so
popular. On their own they don't seem like such a bad investment.
But when you compare them to the alternatives, they're a pretty
lousy deal. That's why you should skip them.

How It Works

When you buy a bank CD, you loan a specific amount of money to
the bank for a specific amount of time, and they pay you a predetermined amount of interest. If you buy a $1,000 one year CD paying
5% in interest, you can expect to have your $1,000 principal plus
$50 in interest back by the end of the year.

Here's why people buy CDs:

- They can be bought at a local bank. When it comes to personal finance, anything that's "local" seems to sell quite well.
- They're completely safe. CDs are insured by the Federal Deposit Insurance Corporation.

But here's why people should *not* buy CDs:

- They are fully taxed. Treasury securities (which we'll talk about in Secret #36) are exempt from state and local taxes.
- Your money is not liquid. True, you can get your money out of a CD early, but you will pay a severe penalty for doing so. You could easily end up losing half a year's worth of interest. Treasury securities trade actively in the open market. You can sell a Treasury security whenever you want to, maybe even for more than you bought it for. With a bank CD, you will always pay a penalty.
- Interest on Treasury bills is just about the same as the interest on CDs. But remember Treasuries are exempt from state and local taxes.

Secret #24 at Work

I took a whole secret to preach against CDs because they're so popular and many people reading this book may already have them. They are certainly not a place for emergency cash, because emergencies happen just when we don't want them to, not on the date our CDs mature.

 ## Secret #24 in a Nutshell

When it comes to CDs, remember Kenny Rogers' advice from the song, "The Gambler": hold 'em (until they mature), then fold 'em (when they mature). Your money is better off in a money market fund for emergencies or Treasuries for tax-friendly interest.

---

put it on ice

By now you've tossed a brick in your toilet and kicked back a few cold ones with your energy auditor. You've trimmed your taxes under compact fluorescent lighting, while sipping discounted coffee purchased at a shop that now has an agreement with your consumer buying pool.

One final word about saving: you can take all my suggestions or none of them. If it crimps your style, don't do it. But at least you have some options. You know how to pull some money out of thin air. If you don't like the idea of carpooling, that's cool, but at least you know the advantages of carpooling if you want some extra cash in Cancún. The more options you have, the easier it is to live life on your own terms.

So you have a small mound of money (hopefully). What do you do with it?

So you have a small mound of money (hopefully). What do you do with it?

The same thing you do with a beverage before you drink it. You put it in a place where it can stay cool.

We need to do the same thing with your money. We need to move it into accounts that will protect it from the "heat" of the financial world, namely taxes and inflation. Read on to find out what I mean.

save—
don't be an idiot

When the well's dry, we know the worth of the water.

BENJAMIN FRANKLIN

Why It Works

Getting your first paycheck is an instant high followed by an instant low. It's a high because hey, it's your first paycheck. You know that sealed in that envelope is your reward for all the hard work you've done—mowing lawns, serving cappuccinos, and answering phones. But the moment you tear open this treasure, you're a little disappointed because you see that the government has already taken its share. A paycheck, for most people, is often their first introduction to the inevitable truth about taxes—you gotta pay 'em. But part of this chunk of change that the government takes out goes toward Social Security. You've heard about this. The government withholds a portion of every paycheck, then, way, way, *way* into the future, the government gives you back this money. That's something to be happy about.

Well . . .

Social Security was a good idea at its inception. In theory, it remains a good idea. But Social Security will not serve as a comfortable retirement cushion. It won't even serve as a rough and splintery retirement bench. Don't be an idiot and rely on Social Security. Even if it is still around when most of us reach our golden years, our annual Social Security checks wouldn't even put us above the poverty line. I hope, by explaining how the system works and why its future appears ominous, that I will inspire you to invest more time into creating your own financial security.

How It Works

Social Security will not serve as a comfortable retirement cushion. It won't even serve as a rough and splintery retirement bench.

(More like how it doesn't work.) The long-term future for Social Security does not look bright. A more proper name would be Social Insecurity. With government overspending and longer life expectancies, it appears that Social Security's days are numbered.

At its original inception in 1935, Social Security paid out an income for people over the age of sixty-five. At that time, the average life expectancy was less than sixty-five years. Very few people lived long enough to collect their checks, and those who did typically did not collect for very long.

Today, the average life expectancy is above seventy-five years. Now, the number of people taking money out is much closer to the number of people putting money in. Someday in the future, when we're all commuting to work in our spaceships,* the number of people taking out will equal or even outnumber the number of people putting money in. When that happens, the system goes the way of the *Chevy Chase Show*.**

---

* Speaking of spaceships, did you know that more people under the age of thirty believe in UFOs than believe they'll get any money from Social Security?
** *Hey Pete, I didn't know Chevy Chase had a show.* My point exactly.

Hey Pete, can't the government fix this problem? Not without difficulty. The government has several options to attempt to correct this problem, and all of the solutions are as about as plausible as James Bond becoming a housewife. This becomes apparent when you look at the options. The government could:

- Cut back on spending and put more money into Social Security. (The government? Cut back on spending? Sure. Them and Ivana Trump.)
- Raise the age when people can begin receiving Social Security, say, to maybe age eighty-five. (Who wants to work until they are eighty-five years old?)
- Tax all benefits paid out. (In other words, less money to you.)
- Make the cost of living increases smaller. (Again a more complex way of saying, "Less money to you.")
- It can invest part of the money in riskier investments that pay a higher return. But if these risky investments lose money, then what happens?

You know our country has an enormous debt. And you've heard that the money Social Security takes out of your paycheck is safe from this enormous debt. But it's not. The government finances this debt by selling bonds, which pay interest. The government sells these bonds to raise money and agrees to pay off the bonds with interest at a later date. The problem is that our government has oversold . . . oh, I don't know, a TRILLION or so too many bonds, and now we have more debt than we can handle. Contrary to popular belief, Social Security is not entirely protected from this growing debt. Social Security funds can only be invested in, you guessed it, government bonds! So the money being taken out of your paycheck is safe as long as the government is able to effectively pay off over a trillion dollars in debt. Sure, that'll happen as soon as Hugh Hefner is elected to head the National Organization of Women. (Okay fine, that last sentence was an exaggeration. I just want you to realize Social Security isn't as safe as many believe.)

I guess now is a good time to prep you for the other big disappointment in the financial world—*inflation*. Perhaps you first heard about the concept of inflation from the renowned economist Young MC. In his 1989 essay "Bust a Move," he argues, "A movie's showin', so you're goin'/ Could care less about the five you're blowin'."

The problem is that our government has oversold . . . oh, I don't know, a TRILLION or so too many bonds, and now we have more debt than we can handle. Contrary to popular belief, Social Security is not entirely protected from this growing debt.

A five for a movie? Sure, when the song came out, but now we're crossing the $10 mark. That's *inflation* working its evil magic. Inflation is simply the rise in the price of goods. Young MC paid $5 for his movie (or twice his reported income in the year 2001). You and I pay $10. Our children will pay $20 because of inflation.

 What really gets me is that people use inflation as an excuse *not* to save. When I tell them that by investing a few dollars a day, they'll have a million dollars, they come back with, "Yeah, but a million dollars won't be worth as much in the future." Garbage! Inflation is all the more reason to save. Don't you want to be prepared for the day when a movie costs $20?

Why inflation happens is another book and a boring one at that. It's just important to know that products do get more expensive (well, not everything gets more expensive—Young MC's albums, for example). The best way to protect yourself against $20 movies is to start investing today.*

---

* You also ran into inflation in the first Austin Powers movie. Dr. Evil, being a little out of the loop (due to the fact that he was cryogenically frozen), suggests to his minions that they ask for one *million* dollars in ransom. Number 2 (played by the cycloptical Robert Wagner) quickly explains to his boss the effects of inflation. Dr. Evil soon ups his ransom to 100 *billion* dollars.

Secret #25 at Work

Wanna know how much moohla you will be getting from Social Security? Simply call the Social Security Administration at 800-772-1213 (www.ssa.gov) and request your report showing the estimated size of your benefits. This is a good exercise because chances are you will be disappointed by the report and, thus, more eager and willing to invest. Not that I want to spoil the surprise, but the average yearly Social Security check currently floats around $12,000. That's just not enough money.

Anything's possible. Social Security could go the way of (insert your favorite one-hit wonder band here) so you need to look after your own finances.

How much will inflation cut into your cash? Will the *Getting Loaded* plan be enough? Well, it certainly won't hurt. Forty years from now, a million dollars in the bank won't be worth what it is today. Only zero dollars in the bank will. If inflation averages around 4% per year, that means that by this time next year, $100 will only buy $96 worth of stuff. And if inflation continues to be 4% per year, then every eighteen years the price of goods will double in value. All the more reason to start getting loaded.

Secret #25 in a Nutshell
Don't count on Social Security. Even if the payments are still there when you retire, the benefits aren't enough to live on. Even worse is inflation—the rising cost of goods—because it erodes the purchasing power of your money. Lack of Social Security and the effects of inflation are only more reason to pay attention to your finances, so you can have the life you want.

screw the cable company—pay yourself first

Look and you will find it. What is unsought will go undetected.

SOPHOCLES

Why It Works

I don't mean screw the cable company literally (that's a different book). I mean *pay yourself first*. You should invest the first few dollars of your paycheck in a fund that will help you reach your dreams and use the remaining dollars to pay your bills. Most people pay all their bills first, then invest whatever's left over. The trouble is, after the bills are square, nothing's left over.

When I first read about paying yourself, it didn't make sense to me. I thought, What if I didn't have enough money to pay my bills? What will my creditors do? Won't the cable company charge me a late fee? I'll pay! Just don't take away the Bowling Channel!

Then I came across the book *Rich Dad, Poor Dad*. Its author,

Robert Kiyosaki, argues that if you pay yourself first, you'll only work harder and budget better to be sure your other bills are paid. If, however, you pay your bills first, and there is no money left over, you'll just be content that your bills are paid. You'll never end up saving anything for yourself.

Remember this book is about living life on your own terms. If you pay your bills first and yourself last, you are basically living your life on the cable company's terms. You have to pay yourself first; you are your most important bill and your most important creditor. Screw the cable company.

I'm not telling you to be irresponsible and go into debt. Chances are if you pay yourself first, that won't happen anyway. And if you're late once or twice with a bill, who cares? Pay the late fee and get it in on time next month. After a month or two, you'll realize that you can still make things work out by paying yourself first. Think about why you are reading this book. Is it for you or the cable company?

If you pay your bills first and yourself last, you are basically living your life on the cable company's terms.

How It Works

I'm not here to give orders, only advice. How much money you save depends on your goals and how you want to live your life. If your goal is to retire in ten years, you're going to have to do some balls-to-the-wall saving. If you love your job, you may never want to retire. You may not need to be so aggressive. How much you save is based on your goals.

But save *something* and make it your first priority. This is the one time in your life when it's okay to be selfish! If you don't save first for yourself, I guarantee you will never save anything.

Hey Pete, what's the best way to save money?

The easiest way to do it is to save money you never had. Here's what I mean. Let's say you're going to save the first 10% of your paycheck. Let's say you make $1,000 a month. So you've got $1,000 and now you have to invest

10% or $100 of that. But that's tough to do when you have the check sitting in your hands. You can probably think of a million things more fun to do with $100 than invest it.

What you can do is arrange to have a certain amount of money automatically deducted from your paycheck and invested in an account. Your paychecks will now be $900 a month. Even though you've invested $100, you'll act as though you never had it. By having money immediately withdrawn from your paycheck, you take the discipline of investing right out of your hands. It's a painless way to save.

> **By having money immediately withdrawn from your paycheck, you take the discipline of investing right out of your hands. It's a painless way to save.**

Talk to your employer to find out if he/she will withhold money from your paycheck. Most likely your company already sponsors a retirement plan with an automatic withdrawal program. We'll talk about these in the next secret. If your employer won't withhold money, then you can arrange to have your brokerage account withdraw a certain amount of money from your bank account on the same day every month. You can arrange to have $50 withdrawn each month and invested in the mutual fund of your choice. I'll explain how to do all this in the upcoming secrets. For now just realize that the easiest way to save is to invest your money *before* it's actually in your hands.

Secret #26 at Work

Still unsure as to how much you should save? I have a few benchmarks to help you:

- The more you save now, the less you need to save later. Remember, with compound interest you make the majority of your money in the few final years of your investment career. Imagine Jerry Seinfeld and George Costanza want to start investing. Jerry decides to invest $1,000 a year. But five years go by and after the final episode, money's tight, so he stops and doesn't invest another penny. George doesn't start right away. He actually waits ten years and then begins investing $1,000 a year for the next twenty years. Jerry put in $1,000 a year for five years, a total of $5,000. George invested $20,000. After thirty years, Jerry has $221,952.13, while George is still living at home with his parents with only $118,810.12. Remember it's not about money; it's about time. Sacrifices made now are going to pay off later.

- According to *The Millionaire Next Door*, by Thomas Stanley and William Danko, the average millionaire saves 15% of their income. I admit that's a big chunk of change, but how do you think they get to be millionaires?

- Remember inflation floats around 4%, so about every eighteen years, the price of stuff doubles. Not every product will go up in value at this rate, but overall, eighteen years from now, your income needs to be at least double what it is today—just to maintain your current lifestyle.

- A nice saving trick I learned is once you pay off your loans, pretend you're still in debt. Since you are used to not having that money, why not just invest it? You probably have loans of some sort—college loans, car loans, credit card balances. When you pretend you're still in debt, you pay the amount of your loan payments to your investment account after your loans are paid off. Imagine your college loan payments were $160 a month. After you pay off your college loan, pretend that you still owe that money, only now pay it to yourself. Invest $160 a month in your retirement fund. You'll find this easy to do, because you have been doing it anyway. So the moment you get out of debt, pretend you're still in debt and pay yourself.

Remember it's not about money; it's about time. Sacrifices made now are going to pay off later.

A widely held rule of thumb in the investment community is that you should invest the first 10% of every paycheck for the rest of your life. Sounds harsh I know, but after two or three paychecks, believe me, you won't even miss it. Ten percent right off the top makes budgeting easy—what's leftover is yours. Every few months glance at your net worth and see it rise. Life gets easier as your fortune increases. I've heard this fortune referred to as a "go-to-hell fund," which basically means you can tell people, like your tyrannical boss or your annoying coworker, to go to hell because now you've stockpiled a financial arsenal.

After you pay off your college loan, pretend that you still owe that money, only now pay it to yourself.

As your salary increases over the years, still take 10% right off the top. As your lifestyle gets better, you'll have to save more to preserve that lifestyle.

Secret #26 in a Nutshell

If you don't set aside the first dollars of your paycheck for yourself, you will never have anything. Pay yourself first and your bills second. An easy way to do this is to have money invested from your paycheck *before* you get it. A good benchmark amount to invest is 10% of every paycheck. By doing this, you may even be able to duck taxes by reducing your taxable income.

come on and take a free ride

Man must choose whether to be rich in things, or in the freedom to use them.

IVAN ILLICH

Why It Works

 If you're a full-time student, skip this chapter and go on to the next one. If you are employed, even though the coffee sucks, the commute is horrible, and the fax machine always jams up, I do have some good news. Your employer is looking out for you in one distinct way—your employer-sponsored retirement plan. We just talked about paying yourself first, and this is the way to do it. Your employer-sponsored retirement plan is not only the best way to reduce your tax bill, it's also the best way to save for retirement, and it's *the biggest free lunch in the book.*

Some companies offer matching funds. This means that when you contribute money to the plan, your company will also contribute money to your plan—FO' FREE.

The employer-sponsored retirement plan free lunch makes all

the other free lunches in this book look like Happy Meals. Consistently contributing to your employer-sponsored retirement plan will earn you hundreds of thousands of dollars, in tax savings, accrued interest, and matching contributions.

How It Works

Basically there are two types of retirement plans, *defined benefit plans* and *defined contribution plans*. A defined benefit plan is often referred to as a *pension plan*. Two cool things about defined benefit plans are that the money you would receive at retirement is defined and these plans are funded by your employer. All you had to do was show up to work and not get caught sleeping during the sales meeting. Today, pension plans are rare. Now people switch jobs much more often than they used to, and companies don't want to take on the risk of offering a defined benefit plan.

The employer-sponsored retirement plan free lunch makes all the other free lunches in this book look like Happy Meals.

Most retirement plans are now defined contribution plans. As the name states, the amount you can contribute is defined, but the amount of the benefit is not. There is no guarantee as to how much money you will get when you retire.

The most popular employer-sponsored retirement plan is the 401k. If you work for a big private corporation, you're probably entitled to join one of these plans. If you work for a nonprofit company, like a college, you'll have a 403b plan instead of the 401k. These plans are nearly the same, so from now on when I refer to 401k, I'm also talking 403b.

The government has set a limit on the maximum contribution one can make, but it's up to you to get your butt down to your company's human resources (HR) department and fill out the paperwork. You'll be able to tell HR how much money you want them to take out of your paycheck and put into your plan. You'll also be able to tell the HR crew how you want to invest that money, in stocks, bonds, mutual funds, or a little of each.

Here are the benefits of investing in a 401k:

- Tax savings. You can deduct contributions to the plan, thereby reducing your taxable income. Imagine you make $50,000 a year and you're in the 28% tax bracket. Normally you would pay about $10,376 in taxes. But if you contribute $5,000 to your 401k, the government now only taxes you on $45,000, which is a tax bill of $9,001. You just saved $1,375 in taxes! The more you contribute, the more money you will save.

- Your money in the retirement plan grows tax-free. You only pay taxes on the money when you withdraw it. Who cares about tax-deferred growth? If you're in the 28% tax bracket and you invested $2,000 annually in a tax-deferred account, after forty years you'd have $559,562 (assuming an 8% annual interest rate). If, however, you invested that money *outside* a tax-deferred account, you'd have only $308,252. You lost a quarter mil in taxes. Ouch.

- Going bankrupt? Hopefully not, but if you do, creditors cannot touch the money in retirement accounts. Plus colleges don't count the money in retirement accounts when considering you for financial aid. They won't count the money in your parents' accounts either.

- You can borrow against the money in the plan to, for instance, pay off debt. Don't get into the habit of borrowing against your plan, but it does remain an option.

- Your employer may offer a matching funds program. Here's that free lunch. For instance, your employer may contribute 50 cents for every dollar you put into the plan. You put in $5,000, and the boss kicks in another $2,500, *fo' free*. If your company offers a matching funds program, and you don't contribute, you should be tied to a chair and forced to watch *Spice World* until you cave in. In fact these matching contributions are so powerful that I would put them above all else—even paying off credit card debt. If your employer matches 50 cents for every dollar you contribute that's a risk free 50% return. Even the worst credit cards don't charge much more than 20% in interest. So even though you're losing 20% to your credit cards, you're gaining 50% in your retirement plan. The choice is obvious.

The 401k has but one drawback. You can't get the money out right away. If you take out the money before you reach the age of fifty-nine and six months, you will be slapped with a 10% penalty, *and* it will be taxed as regular income. Don't let this scare you. This is "don't touch" money anyway. Plus, you have your three months of emergency living expenses in your money market account. You can borrow against the plan at any time. (But don't!) In the unlikely event you do have to withdraw and pay the penalty, chances are the tax deductions and the tax-deferred growth will still make contributing a smart move.

If your company offers a matching funds program, and you don't contribute, you should be tied to a chair and forced to watch Spice World until you cave in.

If you work for a small company, your company may have a Savings Incentive Match Plan for Employees (or SIMPLE). SIMPLEs allow annual contributions of up to $7,000 (this number will increase with inflation). SIMPLEs aren't exactly 401ks, but, for the most part, they are similar.

If you're self-employed, you won't have a 401k, but there are other retirement plans available to you. The two most common plans are the Keogh and SEP. The Keogh allows you to save the most money, but it requires a good deal of paperwork. The SEP or Simplified Employee Pension is easier to set up, but you may not be able to save as much as the Keogh. If you have employees, both plans require you to include your employees in the plan. This caveat may make it sensible for a business owner *not* to set up a plan at all. Since each plan has their ups and downs, and affects not only you but also your entire business, it is best to speak with a tax advisor before starting one.

You may not have any employee-sponsored retirement plan. That's okay, just max out your Individual Retirement Account or

IRA, which is a tax-friendly account available to just about anyone. We'll talk IRAs in the next secret.

Secret #27 at Work

Retirement plans vary from company to company, so it's worth a trek down to your human resources department. Please do this trek soon, as in tomorrow. Remember, the earlier you start, the more money you'll wind up with. When you enter the cubicle maze of the human resources department, the person you're looking for is the *plan administrator*. The plan administrator knows all about your company's plan. She may be an actual employee of your company or, if you work for a small company, the plan administrator probably works for an outside firm that handles retirement accounts. Either way, HR will know where the plan administrator hangs out.

If you're under twenty-one, you'll have to wait until you can buy alcohol before contributing to a 401k.

Here are some good questions to throw at the plan administrator:

- *How much can I contribute to the plan?* Amounts vary from company to company and can depend on your salary. The maximum annual contribution however is set by the government and is currently $11,000 for 401ks and $7,000 for SIMPLEs. The feds are likely to change that amount to stay hip with inflation. So be sure to ask.
- *When can I start contributing?* Some companies may want you to work for them for a little while before taking advantage of the plan. If you're under twenty-one, you'll have to wait until you can buy alcohol before contributing to a 401k.
- *What type of investments can I invest in?* A typical 401k should allow you to invest in just about anything you want, like stocks, bonds, and mutual funds. However, I've seen more than a few 401k plans that have a very limited choice of investments. We'll talk about the ideal investments in Secret #44. If your plan doesn't

offer these, just get as close as you can. You can always quietly complain to your company's top dogs to either swap the current plan administrator for one with more choices or suggest the current administrator increase their selection.

- *Do you offer matching contributions?* Hopefully the answer is yes. If not, a 401k plan is still a great deal.
- *What is the speed velocity of a swallow?* This will depend on whether or not it is an African or Australian swallow.
- *What happens if I am fired or if I leave the company?* This is important. Sometimes you can leave your 401k with that company and just let it grow on its own. This may be a good idea, especially if your new employer's plan doesn't have a good selection of investments. What's a good selection of investments? See Secret #44 for help. Other times you can transfer it into a new 401k at your new company or into an Individual Retirement Account using a *direct rollover*. A rollover is both a) the one trick you could never get your dog to do and b) how you move money from one retirement account to another. The word *direct* means that you do not take possession of the money before moving it into the new account. Don't take possession of the money, because if you do, you'll pay taxes and perhaps penalties.

So you went to HR and did the paperwork for your 401k. Now you need to decide what to invest in. The 401k is a retirement account, so we're looking long term here. That means don't be a wuss. Be aggressive. Most of the money (if not all) should be in equity investments, like stocks or stock mutual funds. In Secret #44, I give some specific recommendations.

And don't be lured into purchasing your own company's stock just because you work for them. The rule is that you should spread your risks. You already risk your paycheck on the firm, why your retirement, too? A much better choice would be an index mutual fund, which we'll talk about in Secret #35.

The big picture here is these retirement accounts offer tax-deferred growth, deductible contributions, and even matching funds. Even a simple example proves how beneficial these accounts are.

Imagine Bobby and Cindy Brady both get jobs at Brady-Mart, a clothing store dedicated to the fashion needs of *Brady Bunch* fans. Both are earning $30,000 a year. Bobby hates his job. He feels like he went from bell bottoms to rock bottom. But he decides to do something about it. He starts to sink $1,000 a year into his company's 401k plan, which offers a 50% matching program.

Cindy, the wild child that she is, says, "I live for the moment, so I want every dime I can get in my wallet every month." Our pig-tailed princess doesn't put anything into her 401k plan.

Simply by contributing to the plan, Bobby cuts his taxable income by $1,000, saving $280 a year in taxes. Then he earned an instant $500 because for every $1 he put into his 401k, his employer contributed 50 cents. His $1,500 investment ($1,000 from Bobby, $500 from his employer) grew to $1,680 by the end of the year. Total all this up ($280 in tax savings, $500 from employer contributions and $180 in earned interest) and Bobby made $960 simply by contributing to his retirement plan. If he continues to contribute $1,000 a year for forty years, he can expect to earn a total of $20,000 just from employer contributions, another $11,200 from tax savings and a whopping $1.15 million thanks to compound interest. More than enough money to rehire Alice as his housekeeper.

After forty years, how much will Cindy have? Well, let me see, that's two plus the—wait what am I doing? Cindy has *nothing*. Even though she spent several years on the small screen, she missed the big picture.

Secret #27 in a Nutshell

Employer-sponsored retirement plans are often the best way to invest for retirement because they allow you to reduce your taxable income, your boss may match some of the money you contribute, and the money in these accounts is protected from taxes and is not taxed until it is taken out of the account. The catch is that the money must stay in the accounts until you reach age fifty-nine and six months, otherwise you'll be slapped with a penalty. Major corporations and nonprofits offer 401k and 403b plans respectively. Smaller companies offer the SIMPLE plan, and the self-employed should look into (with the help of a tax professional) the possibility of setting up a Keogh or SEP plan.

open an ira

The power to tax involves the power to destroy.

—JOHN MARSHALL,
U.S. SUPREME COURT, 1819

Why It Works

Every time you sell an investment at a profit the government takes a piece of it. Or if your investments are paying income, the government still gets a piece of this income. It's tough to build up money when someone else is always taking it away from you. But there is a way around these taxes—you can open an Individual Retirement Account (IRA). If you have investments that are inside an IRA, then any income or profits these investments produce is protected from taxes.

How It Works

Forget about the IRA until you have made the full contributions allowable to your employer-sponsored plan. Your employer-sponsored plan is the better deal. IRAs are for people with no such employer plans or for those dedicated savers who are looking to sock even more away.

IRAs have many of the characteristics that employer-sponsored retirement plans have. Both are accounts that allow you to invest in a variety of investments, like stocks, bonds, and mutual funds. Both offer some sort of tax-favored investment growth in exchange for your promise to put your money in the account and leave it there until you hit age fifty-nine and six months. Make no mistake though; IRAs are completely separate from your employer-sponsored plan. Employer-sponsored plans were created because your company doesn't want to take care of you when you retire. The IRA was created because the government doesn't want to take care of you when you retire. I'm telling you about these plans because I don't want to take care of you when you retire.

I'm telling you about these plans because I don't want to take care of you when you retire.

Basically, you trade the immediate use of your money for tax-free growth. The government, realizing the shortcomings of the Social Security System, created the IRA to let individuals save for themselves. But they figured if they let us take out money any time we wanted to, we'd never save for retirement, we'd simply spend it all on Ferraris and Tae Bo tapes. Sorry I don't write the rules, I just write about them.

Here's how an IRA works. You put *cash* into the account (you can't put stocks and bonds into the account. All investments going into an IRA or coming out of an IRA must first be sold and converted to cash). Once your cash is inside the IRA *then* you can use that cash to buy investments. If you make any profit off those investments you are not taxed on those profits. And if you sell those investments for a loss you can't deduct that either. Currently you can put up to $3,000 a year into an IRA. The only catch is that the money must remain in the account until you reach age fifty-nine and six months. Take it out early and you'll pay a penalty.

There are two types of IRAs, the *Traditional IRA* and the *Roth IRA*. The selling point of the Traditional IRA is that your contributions to it may be tax deductible, based on your situation. But with a Traditional IRA, the earnings and deducted contributions you withdraw after age fifty-nine and six months is taxed as regular income. With a Roth IRA there are no tax deductions for putting money in, but when you withdraw the money after age fifty-nine and six months you will pay no taxes on the money you withdraw. The difference becomes apparent when we throw in some numbers.

Imagine at age twenty you put $2,000 into a Roth IRA. Your twin sister Wanda puts $2,000 into a traditional IRA. Because Wanda did that she gets an immediate tax deduction of $300 (Why? Because Wanda like many twenty-year-olds is in the 15% tax bracket. Her $2,000 contribution is deductible. 15% × $2,000 equals a $300 tax deduction). Let's pretend both you and Wanda buy the same investment. When you both turn age sixty, both your investments are worth about $186,000. If you want to get your hands on that money, then you can call your IRA account administrator and tell him to cut you a check for $186,000. It's all yours because the Roth IRA does not tax withdrawals after age fifty-nine and six months. Wanda on the other hand would be looking at a minimum tax bill of $27,900 (if she took a little bit each year) and most likely her tax bill would be much higher because she's in a higher tax bracket. Even if Wanda had invested the $300 she saved as an original tax deduction it wouldn't matter, because whatever investment that $300 bought would be taxed *every* year.

For young investors like you and me the Roth IRA is probably going to be the better bet.

If this is confusing, just remember that for young investors like you and me the Roth IRA is probably going to be the better bet for two main reasons. The first reason is that we're all broke. Our incomes are at a lifetime low so we're all in low tax brackets now. That means that the money we save with a deductible IRA doesn't amount to much. The second reason the Roth is better is because we're ambitious. If you made it this far in the book that means you've given considerable thought to your retirement at a young age. It's quite conceivable that when you retire you will have several million dollars in your IRA. Then you *will* be in a high tax bracket, but if those millions are in the Roth, it doesn't matter.

Here are some other advantages of the Roth IRA:

- You can take out the *contributions* anytime without paying any penalties or taxes. Be careful, I said contributions, not earned interest. Imagine you deposit $1,000 one year and earn $100 in interest. Then you need cash. You can take out the $1,000, which is your contribution, but the $100, your earned interest, must stay in the account until age fifty-nine and six months. After that, you can withdraw everything tax and penalty free.
- In the event of your death, the Roth IRA provides a much more favorable tax angle. Your beneficiaries get the money tax-free.
- Retirement accounts are usually protected from bankruptcy. Should you ever file (I hope not), most likely your creditors will not be able to get the money inside your retirement accounts.
- Some of the money in your Roth IRA can be taken out, tax-free and penalty-free if it is applied toward the purchase of your first home.

Secret #28 at Work

Time for some Q&A.

- *Who can open a Roth IRA?* Anyone that makes an income. The only people that may be excluded from making the full contribution to a Roth IRA are those folks who are making salaries above $95,000 a year (or $150,000 for couples).
- *So how much money do you have to make?* Doesn't matter. The only rule is that you can only contribute up to 100% of your salary or $3,000 whichever is less. So if you're raking in $500 a year baby-sitting, you can only contribute $500 to your IRA. If you make $65,000 a year selling socks made out of hemp, you can contribute up to $3,000.
- *Cool. So where do I open a Roth IRA?* Your stockbroker will be able to open a Roth IRA account for you. Just ask him for an application.

- *Ummm . . . Pete, I don't have a stockbroker.* Don't worry, we'll get to that in Secret #34.
- *What type of investments should I buy in my Roth IRA?* Well remember that it is a retirement account. You'll be putting the money in, and you won't be taking it out for many years. (Again don't wuss out on me here. Be aggressive.) Stocks and, even more preferably, stock mutual funds are the way to go. Obviously you shouldn't put any tax-exempt investments in a retirement account, because taxes on these are nil anyway. We'll get to specific investments in upcoming chapters.

- *What if I already have a Traditional IRA. Can I switch the money in that to a Roth IRA?* Yes you can, but it may not make sense, unless the amount of money you have is really small. The reason is because they hit you with a tax. You can just let your Traditional IRA be, and just open a Roth IRA and start contributing to that instead.

- *I'm still in school and I don't make much money. Should I still contribute?* If you can swing it, most definitely. And yes, a minor can open a Roth IRA so long as the minor has earned income (an allowance doesn't count). If you're a minor who makes $1,200 a year at Saul's Frozen Soup On A Stick Stand, you can contribute $1,200 (or 100% of your income) to a Roth IRA. What's cool is that it's legal for your parents to give you $1,200 to spend on things you *really* need, like clothes and CDs. If you are a minor reading this book, I'm proud of you. So proud that I'll share with you some of the best investment advice I've ever come across. Tell your parents you want to start saving for retirement. (That alone should get you the car keys this Friday.) Tell them you want to put $1,200 (or whatever) into a Roth IRA, but if you do that you won't have any spending money. Ask if they will supplement your spending money, if you put all your earned income into a Roth. This puts your parents in a difficult situation. On the one hand they're *giving* you money. But they're only giving you this money because you, at age seventeen, have put all your money into a retirement account. My guess is they'll agree for the bragging rights alone.

Secret #28 in a Nutshell

An IRA is an Individual Retirement Account. It allows anyone with an income to put up to $3,000 a year in a tax-favored account. The Traditional IRA may or may not allow you to deduct your contributions from your taxes. This privilege will depend on your income and whether you have a retirement plan at work. Regardless, the money inside a traditional IRA grows tax-free and is taxed only when you begin withdrawing it at age fifty-nine and six months. The Roth IRA allows no deductions but withdrawals made after age fifty-nine and six months are not taxed at all. This makes the Roth a better choice for young investors who will reap years of fruitful compound interest earnings. Your broker can give you the application for an IRA.

PART FIVE

get loaded

You've been to human resources. You have all the retirement plan info. And when you called to find out how much money you'd get from Social Security, you were only on hold for a week and a half.

Now we get to investing, what to do with all the money you saved. In the fifth act of this six-act financial comedy, you'll learn how the stock market works. I'll show you the investment traps people fall into and how to get out of them. When you turn the last page of the fifth section, you'll have an investment plan that not only fits your needs, but also your budget.

On to investing.

know thy investment

Knowledge is power.

—FRANCIS BACON

Why It Works

Over your lifetime, you will be bombarded by investment schemes just as you are bombarded with commercials telling you that you can get a twenty-minute phone call for only 99 cents. Very few of them will actually be worth your time. The reason you know this is because the investments that are worth your time don't require mail, e-mail and telephone bombardment to get you to buy them. By understanding the components of investing, you will be able to do a general analysis of any investment proposal that lands in your lap. Since investing is just as much, if not more, about avoiding the losers as it is about picking the winners, knowing the components of an investment will lead to a bottom-line savings of thousands of dollars in your lifetime.

How It Works

You invest in something to achieve one of your goals. You may invest in your relationship to improve it.* You may invest in a driver's education class to get your license. You may invest in a lawyer after you lose your license. When it comes to the investment world, you invest your money to make more money. That's why you invest, and that's the easy part.

The tough part is where to invest? When to invest? How much to invest? Before I get into specific recommendations, I want to build for you a foundation of investment knowledge. Since there are thousands of investments available today, the only way to reasonably evaluate them is to learn the basics.

As a rule of thumb, you can evaluate just about every investment on the following five characteristics:

Risk
Reward
Control
Minimum Investment/Cost of Investment
Liquidity

Let me break this down:

Risk: Risk is simply the likelihood that you'll get all your money back. The higher the risk, the more likely you are to wind up empty-handed.

Reward: Reward is the reason high-risk investments even exist. A fundamental principle of investing is *the higher the risk, the higher the reward.* Could it be any other way? Why take on more risk for less reward?

Control: Control of an investment is defined as your ability to exercise an advantage. If you own shares of Microsoft and Bill Gates announces that he will design an operating system for Communist countries called MS Dos

---

* Or we invest in a relationship because the market is down.

Kapital, you're helpless in convincing him this is a bad idea. But if you own your own computer company, you can control how much of your marketing budget will go toward attracting the Marxists. Or suppose I hear from the patrons of my lemonade stand that I'm using too much sugar. No problem. I simply make an instant decision to reduce sugar in the next batch. As a small investor in a multibillion-dollar corporation, though, I don't have the power to make such bold decisions. If I did have such power, there never would have been New Coke.

Minimum Investment/Cost of Investment: Minimum investment is like the cover charge at a club—how much does it cost to get in? You need to keep in mind that money put "here" can't be put "there." Large minimum investments will force you to ask yourself, "What else would I do with this money?" "Will I need it in the near future?" Typically, the larger the minimum investment, the larger the reward. You may have noticed this with your bank; the more money you have in your account, the higher the interest rate is on that account. Or perhaps, once you deposit a certain amount, they'll waive some administrative fees.

Investments also have costs—fees or commissions built into the purchase price. If, for instance, you buy a $1,000 investment with a 5% commission, you only bought $950 worth of the investment and paid $50 in commission charges. Keep a close eye on fees and commissions. Often in the investment world, the same investment is for sale with and without the fee—it all depends on where you buy it. Be sure to find out what commissions and fees are built into the cost of the investment and see if you can buy the investment elsewhere without the fee. Taxes of course are another cost of investment, some investments being fully taxable, others being completely free from taxes.

Liquidity: Liquidity is a measure of how quickly you can get your cash back. An investment that is liquid means that you can get your cash very easily. For instance, if you sock $200 away into a bank savings account, that money is liquid because you can get it at any time. If, on the other hand, you invest $100,000 in a home, it may take you several months to sell it and get your cash. In general, the more liquid an investment, the lower the return. Think about it—why would you tie your money up longer than you have to unless you're going to be compensated with a higher return?

Okay Pete, so ideally I want a high-reward, low-risk, low-minimum liquid investment that I have complete control over. Is there such a thing?

Yep. Save money and pay down high-interest consumer debt.

Be sure to find out what commissions and fees are built into the cost of the investment and see if you can buy the investment elsewhere without the fee.

I know that's not the answer you wanted to hear. But look at it this way. Imagine you had $100 to invest. You could put it in the bank where it would be safe but earn crap for interest—about 3%. You could invest in a stock, where you might make more money (say 12%), but you could lose everything. Or you could truck down to your local hardware store, which has a no-questions-asked 100%-money-back guarantee on all its products. You could buy ten compact fluorescent lightbulbs, which provide over 30% in energy savings. You have complete control over where you buy the bulbs and where you put them, and the money you invested in these bulbs is 100% safe because, if they don't work, you can take them back. Show me an investment that can beat that.

Or, if you have a credit card balance with an APR of 20% and you pay it off, you've now stopped yourself from losing 20% a year. Paying off high-interest debt is risk-free—you can't lose any money because you're already losing it! What's more, it's tax-free, so the return you save from paying off debt is actually higher than the return you would earn on a taxable investment paying 20%.

Many people spend a lot of time searching for the hottest stock (cough! dot coms), or some slick-sounding oil-drilling operation that's going to make them millions. The truth, however boring, is that many of the best investments aren't found on Wall Street; they're found on Main Street. Don't even bother investing if you have high-interest consumer debt. And before you sink too much money into stocks, a trip to your local hardware store is in order.

Now you know the components of an investment. So when a glossy brochure lands in your mailbox to invest $25,000 to mine the Midwest for oil, you'll know, just by reading the highlights, that it's not for you. Big minimum investment. High risk (How do you know you'll find anything? And with so many people switching to compact fluorescents, isn't the demand for oil going down?). Zero control (unless you're actually working on the rig). Lousy liquidity (do you know how long it takes to find a site, get the rights to drill it, drill it, pump it, refine it, and sell it?*).

Secret #29 at Work

The world of money is a simple place, because there are only two kinds of money. There is the money you own, and the money you owe. Money you own has many names, like *assets* and *equity*, just as money you owe has many names, like *liabilities* and *debts*.

Just like money, all investments can be divided up into two categories: *investments where you own* (a.k.a. equity investments) and *investments where you loan* (a.k.a. lending investments). When you buy a stock, you own that stock and you hope to share in the company's profits. While you are guaranteed nothing when you buy that stock, the amount of money you can make is unlimited. When you buy a bond (which is an IOU), you are loaning your money to an entity, such as a government or corporation, that agrees to pay you interest on the money you loan them. While you are guaranteed a fixed amount of interest, your profits are limited to the amount of your interest payments.

---

* I don't either, but I bet it's a long time.

Hey Pete, what is better—equity investments or lending investments? Well both have their place in the financial world. Equity investments are sometimes referred to as *growth investments*, while lending investments are sometimes referred to as *income investments*. Remember that equity investments can, at times, pay out income, and it is possible to buy a lending investment and have it grow in value.

But for right now, it's growth we're looking for. Think of your investing as planting an apple orchard.

Imagine you're an apple picker who works for an apple orchard. This apple-picking gig is just a temp thing though, because one day you want to own your own apple orchard. The trouble is that buying your own apple orchard with fully grown apple trees would be too expensive, so for now you just buy the seeds, which cost almost nothing. You work in someone else's orchard every year, but you continue to buy seeds and plant a few more trees. You're investing in apple seeds, which, if you'll forgive the pun, are a growth investment. Year after year you do this. Some years are bad—no rain, and the price of seeds is high—while some years are great—plenty of rain and lots of growth. Finally the day comes when you're too tired to work. But now you have an entire apple orchard with fully grown trees that produce apples. Fully grown trees are income investments because they produce a fixed amount of delicious apples. How do you like them apples?

Most of us are not farmers, but the strategy in my Taoist tale should be used in the investment world. When you're young, you can work to produce an income. When you're old, you'll need income from your investments. So, as young investors, we need growth with the idea that one day our fortunes will grow large enough that we can switch purely to income investments. The earlier we start investing, the sooner we can live off the income. We can't start off with income investments because they just don't pay enough. The unlimited growth potential that comes with equity investments is the only way to build up our fortunes enough so that one day we can live off our fortune's income.

Income investments have their place in a young investor's portfolio, but for now, most of your seeds (or cents) will be in growth investments. But how do you plant? Read on.

 ### Secret #29 in a Nutshell

You invest in something to achieve one of your goals. The five components for evaluating an investment are risk, reward, control, minimum investment, and liquidity. Saving and paying down high-interest debt are the two best investments you can make. As young investors, our plan should be to invest the bulk of our money in equity investments for the purpose of growth, and then once our fortunes are big enough, we can switch our money to lending investments and live off the income.

The earlier we start investing, the sooner we can live off the income.

---

match investments to goals

The nighttime-sniffling-sneezing-coughing-
aching-stuffy-head-fever-so-you-can-rest
medicine.

—NYQUIL COMMERCIAL

Why It Works

If you invest based on your goals, you need to know what investments complement what goals.

How It Works

 Hey Pete, what's up with the NyQuil quote? Some investment books tell you that what you invest in depends
on how well you want to sleep at night. The purpose of
investing is to help you get your goals, not your Zs. If
you have trouble sleeping at night, the answer isn't bonds or bank
accounts, it's NyQuil. That's why I gave them a free plug.

Yes, some investments are risky, but by investing solely in the super-safe investments, you don't avoid the problem of getting a good night's sleep, you just delay it. After twenty years of putting your money in the ultra-safe bank savings account, you'll find that after taxes and inflation, you hardly have enough to get by. In fact, you probably spent that last twenty years losing money! Remember movies used to cost $5. Now they cost $10. Someday they'll cost $20. "Come on guys," the savings account investor will quibble, "can't we just rent a movie instead?" Even this won't work because a video rental will be $8. "Come on guys, let's just play charades." That's one hell of a nightmare to wake up to. Believe me—I've actually played charades.

My point is that every investment you make should be for a specific goal. To get loaded, you have to get smart about money, but you also have to get tough about money. Here's what often happens to investors who invest to get a good night's sleep. Let's call our hypothetical investor "Stu." Stu hears around the office that technology stocks are hot. For many months, he just listens. But the buzz about tech stocks doesn't go away. Stu starts to feel like he's missing something. So without reading a personal finance book (I mean honestly, what good would that do?), he moves some money out of his bank savings account and buys a few of the stocks he's been hearing so much about. In three months, Stu's stocks start to take off. He buys a little more, because Stu now knows he's got an eye for this kind of thing. Then, all of a sudden, the market crashes. Stu loses $3,000 in one day. Better get out while I still can he says to himself. He sells all his stocks at a $3,000 loss and plunks it back into the savings account, where it is nice and safe. Nice and safe, nice and safe. Then after four years of niceness and safeness, the air around the water cooler begins to buzz again. For many months, Stu just listens . . .

And the cycle repeats itself.

Yes, some investments are risky, but by investing solely in the super-safe investments, you don't avoid the problem of getting a good night's sleep, you just delay it.

Pete, leave poor Stu alone. Who wouldn't be bummed at losing $3,000 in a day? A person with written goals, that's who. Yes, it's not easy seeing your money shrink in value so quickly. But it's Stu's own fault for not writing goals. Why didn't he sell some when the stock was going up in value? Or why didn't he hang on and wait for the stock to go back up? The reason is because Stu's only goal was to be comfortable. He didn't feel comfortable being the only guy at work who wasn't in the stock market. Then when the market crashed, he got uncomfortable again, so he sold and put his money back in the bank. If you invest solely to be comfortable, then you will *always* get burned. Think about it. How could poor Stu possibly come out ahead?

Before you invest, you need a reason to invest. Hopefully you scribbled down some reasons in Secret #1. Now here are seven basic investments you can use to reach your goals. They are:

- **You:** Investing in You means investing in products like insurance to protect you, what you have, and those you love. It also means investing your time in planning and organizing to be sure you can reach your goals. If you made it this far in the book without skipping around, you have done much of the necessary investing in You.

- **Bank/money market accounts:** Bank and money market accounts are to be used for goals that will be achieved within one year. One of your goals is probably to pay your phone bill this month. Where do you get that money? From your bank or money market account. Trying to save $50 a month for that South Padre Island spring break trip? Trying to finance a new snowboard or a day at the spa? Save it in your bank or money market account.

- **Bonds:** I'll explain these investments in detail in the upcoming secrets. Just remember that bonds are vehicles to help you reach goals in one to five years. If you want to buy a car in three years, you could save up for it using bonds. Bonds also provide income, which we'll need when we retire. I will let you know that I don't get too excited about bonds, and I feel young investors can, for the most part, get by without them. But after reading Secret #36, you'll be able to judge for yourself.

- **Stocks:** Stocks are investment vehicles for goals that lie beyond the five-year mark. Money you don't need in the next five years should be in stocks. This five-year window protects you from the ups and downs of the stock market.

- **Real estate:** Like stocks, real estate is an investment vehicle to help you achieve goals that lie beyond five years. Many real estate investments have high minimum investment requirements, but I'll show you a way around this in Secret #35. But real estate does offer a way to *diversify*—minimize risk by buying several different types of investments. Real estate, like bonds, can also provide income.

- **Education:** Education is often a goal and an investment. The more education you have, the easier it will be to achieve your goals. This may come in the form of treating an expert to a free lunch or a full-blown graduate degree. Unlike all other investments, there is never a time when you *aren't* investing in your education. Please don't overlook education as an extremely lucrative investment. A friend of mine invested $10,000 in a computer training course that increased his salary by $25,000, all within four months. You won't find returns like that on Wall Street.

- **Your own business:** Your own business can't be tied to a timeline. Some businesses are profitable in five years, others, like the proverbial lemonade stand, are profitable in five hours. But just as you're always increasing your education, you should always be looking for business opportunities. In Secret #46, you'll learn how to spot business opportunities.

Secret #30 at Work

Once again, grab that goal sheet. Look at the time limits you attached to your goals. Jot down the name of the investment that will help you reach each goal. For instance, your goal is to retire at age fifty-five and you're twenty-six. Next to that goal you may write, "stocks and real estate." Your goal might be to earn more money in the next six months. You might write down "education and start my own business." Whatever your dreams are, try to find the investments that will help you achieve them.

 ### Secret #30 in a Nutshell

Use NyQuil to sleep better. Use money market accounts for goals that lie less than a year away, bonds for goals one to five years away, stocks and real estate for goals more than five years away. Always invest in You, in education, and always be on the lookout for business opportunities.

ease up on economics

I was in search of a one-armed economist so that the guy could never make a statement and then say: "on the other hand."

—HARRY S. TRUMAN

Why It Works

Everything you need to know about economics can be learned by watching the movie *Jurassic Park*. Basically, that film is about a bunch of guys who tried to do a very complicated thing, and, though they did their best to prepare for every conceivable possibility, everything got screwed up.

Such is the case with economics. As much as the experts try to predict what's going to happen next, the reality is that the world of economics, just like the world of genetically engineered dinosaurs, is too complex to predict.

Economics is a theory game, while *Getting Loaded* is a practical game. In fact, the purpose of this secret is to show you how the close monitoring of economic factors can actually hurt your financial life as opposed to help it.

How It Works

Economics is the study of how we use our scarce resources. The goal of economics is to make the best use of these scarce resources, be it oil, timber, gold, labor, or manure. Economists study a boatload of factors and then recommend to governments, corporations, and even individuals how they can best use their scarce resources.

Imagine Janet Jackson is president of the Rhythm Nation. Rhythm Nation has a limited supply of crude oil. President Jackson and her economists sit down and try to figure out the best use of that oil. Should they stockpile it in case prices change? Should they use it to manufacture goods? Or should they sell the oil to another nation and use the profits to buy copies of Latoya's workout video?

Every system has scarce resources. In your life, money may be a scarce resource. In a ninety-six-year-old woman's life, time may be a scarce resource. On many television shows, quality acting is a scarce resource.

Every system has scarce resources. In your life, money may be a scarce resource. In a ninety-six-year-old woman's life, time may be a scarce resource. On many television shows, quality acting is a scarce resource.

So how do economics affect you and me? Minimally, is the short answer, which brings me *to the most important thing you can know about economics*. It can be expressed in this simple rhyme: "Visions, not conditions, make decisions."

The reason I talk about economics is because investors try to use economics to their advantage, but it never works. I've heard things like, "Oil prices are going up, time to sell my auto manufacturing stocks," or "Interest rates are going up, time to sell my stocks."

Crap! Crap! Crap!

Why? Because *visions, not conditions, make decisions.* Remember, this book is about living life on *your* terms. We invest our money because we are trying to achieve our goals, *not*, to use a familiar expression, because of a change in the price of tea in China. Don't sell because they cancel *Seinfeld*. Don't buy because George Bush won the election. Don't convert your assets to bonds just because we find out Elvis is alive. Whenever you buy an investment, you must always look at the investment and how it relates to your goals.

Don't agree with me? I got two words for you: **dot com.** What happened to the dot com economy? Same thing that always happens when people look solely at the economy and not at the individual investment and their individual goals. I won't pick on anyone specifically just yet (but I will later) so I'll make up a company with traits similar to those we saw in the new internet economy. Suppose I started a company called Cinderblocks.com. At Cinderblocks.com we sell bricks, cinderblocks and unmixed concrete over the internet. And the best thing about our company, we offer free overnight shipping! The brick/concrete/cement market is a multibillion-dollar industry! If our company can capture just 1% of this multibillion-dollar industry's business, we'd make over $10 million dollars a year! What's more, we're looking to merge with Sand.com, and Steelgirders.com, two internet companies that have adopted our free overnight shipping policy!

We invest our money because we are trying to achieve our goals, not, to use a familiar expression, because of a change in the price of tea in China.

My parody falls not too far from the real situation. How did companies like my satiric startup even get started? It happened because people thought we were in a new economy. An economy that wasn't bound by the old rules. An economy in which profits didn't matter. An economy in which you don't need to pay attention to your goals because the never-ending upward trend of the market will take care of everything. I admit business has changed drastically over the past decade and I'm certainly not a hold-the-fort kind of guy. But no matter what the condition of the economy, how can anyone possibly make money by offering free overnight shipping of *concrete*? Yet people looked right past such obvious warnings and threw their money at these incompetent companies.

So much money is lost on Wall Street because investors don't bother looking at their investments or their goals. They look at the entire market thinking they can actually make sense of such a large system. They jump in because everyone else seems to be in, and they jump out after everyone else has already gotten out. How do you know the best time to jump in and out of the market? *You don't.* So stop jumping.

What's worse, when you have your hand on the heartbeat of the economy, you're likely to trade more. Every time you trade (buy or sell) you will pay: 1) a commission and 2) taxes on your profits. Few people recognize the big boots of taxes and commission stomping on their profits. At your next keg party, some greedy guzzler will brag, "I bought ten shares of Yahoo! at $75 and sold them at $150. Doubled my money in less than a year."

No you didn't, you alcoholic accountant. You sold a stock for twice what it was worth, but it cost you $70 in commissions and $210 in taxes. Our Pilsner Pal did walk away with $470 in profit, which isn't bad, but certainly not the $750 he thought he made.

Secret #31 at Work

Let's get back to apple trees. Do you dig up all your seeds if you don't see a fully grown tree after a year? No! But we do that with our investments all the time. Either dig them up too soon or plant a crop we know nothing about.

Some friends asked me for advice on what to do with their investments as we crossed over to the millennium, a time when people were worried about the Y2K problem. Particularly people wondered if they should sell in October or November of 1999, then buy again right after January 1. Their thinking was that people—in fear of Doomsday—would start to sell off investments as January 1, 2000, approached. Prices would plunge. My friends planned to buy back everything right after January 1 when prices would be really low. Their hope was that the public—realizing that Doomsday never really shows up, he just has an incredible publicist—would start buying again and prices would rise. My friends would get to buy stocks at a discount, and all the other suckers would be stuck trying to catch up.

The trouble is that my friends would have paid taxes when they sold their investments and they would have paid commissions when they sold and also when they bought back again. So they would've had to make enough money to justify these lost taxes and commissions. In addition, it's impossible to pinpoint the best time to sell and the best time to buy. In attempting to pinpoint that time, you can easily lose out.

Most important, how would selling and then buying back after the New Year have related to their goals? It probably didn't, so I advised my friends against it. When it comes to timing, fahghedaboudit.

Secret #31 in a Nutshell
The only thing you can predict for certain is what you want. So invest based on your goals. And remember, "Visions, not conditions, make decisions."

---

take pete's stock market crash course

In the course of evolution and a higher civilization we might be able to get along comfortably without Congress, but without Wall Street, never.

—HENRY CLEWS

Why It Works

We finally get to the stock market—the easiest, most affordable, and most efficient way for young investors to build a fortune. But some of you may be wondering how it works . . .

How It Works

The stock market is just like any other market. Like the flea market or the supermarket, it's a place where things are bought and sold.

You won't find cans of tuna fish or old comic books for sale at the stock market, but you will find *shares* of companies.

A share is simply a piece of a company. One who holds shares in a company is said to be one of that company's *shareholders*. (This ain't rocket science.)

You buy shares in a company because you think that company's shares are going to go up in value. You're trying to make money.

 Hey Pete, why would business people want to sell parts of their company if it's profitable? Wouldn't they want to keep the shares and make money themselves? The reason a company sells shares is because it is trying to *raise* money.

The stock market is just like any other market. Like the flea market or the supermarket, it's a place where things are bought and sold.

Imagine you're a rap star who wants to get into the hairbrush manufacturing business. You're going to call your business P Diddy Combs. But you need cash to get started. You figure you need $20 million to build a factory.

You could go to a bank and get a loan. On the up side you'd own the entire company. On the down side, the bank would charge you interest, and if things go wrong at P Diddy Combs, you're on the hook for a lot of money.

Instead of going to a bank, you choose to sell shares or *stock* in your company. On the up side, you get a bunch of cash with no obligation to pay any of it back. On the down side, you give up some equity (ownership) to shareholders, who will be sharing in the company's profits. These shareholders will (in most cases) have voting rights as to how the company should be run.

There are two ways to sell these shares. You can do it privately, by selling to your friends and neighbors and other individual investors, or you can take the company *public*, which means you would sell your shares to the general public. Selling to the public is how the stock market fits in.

When you take a company public, you hold what is known as

an *initial public offering* or *IPO*. You are trying to raise $20 million for P Diddy Combs, so you may sell one million shares at $20 per share to the public at your IPO. The shares are sold, and you get your money. You use it to build your factory and kick some serious butt in the hairbrush biz.

Now the shares are out of your hands. They're in the hands of the new owners who can do with them what they want. If these owners want to sell some or all of their shares, they can do so over a *stock exchange*. The people who originally bought shares at the IPO now sell to other investors who sell to other investors and on and on. The prices now fluctuate up and down, but as president of P Diddy Combs, you don't get any more money as they're traded. But since P Diddy Combs is now a public company, you are legally responsible to your shareholders. You continually try to improve P Diddy Combs so that both you and your shareholders make money.

What determines the price of the shares? Only one thing: the number of buyers and sellers.

So shares of P Diddy Combs are out there trading on the stock market. But what determines the price of the shares? Only one thing: *the number of buyers and sellers.* Lots of people buying means the price is high. Lots of people selling means the price is low. When lots of people are buying and prices are rising, it's called a *bull market*. When prices are dropping, it's called a *bear market*.

But Pete, why do people buy and sell P Diddy Combs' stock, or any other company's stock? Because they either think that the company will make them more money (in some circles this is known as *greed*) or that it will lose them money (in some circles this is known as *fear*). Remember that behind every stock is a company trying to make money. When that company makes money, people take notice and buy the stock of the company. As people buy the stock, the price of that stock rises. Demand always makes the price of a stock go up and demand for a stock is usually created by the superb company lurking behind it.

Usually.

The truth is that demand is created because of several factors and the underlying company is only one of them. Take, for instance, the beer, tobacco, and food company Philip Morris. In 2000, the company was performing quite well, yet its stock price was at a five-year low. Part of the reason was because people were trying to avoid investing in tobacco companies. What's more, old-school companies, like Philip Morris, were being ignored as people focused their attention—and their money—on technology stocks.

 So it's quite possible to have a superb company with a low stock price and a lousy company with a high stock price. That's because *the number of buyers and sellers is the only thing that determines the price of a stock*. People buy and sell based on fear and greed, and this fear and greed comes from a number of sources ranging from a thorough financial analysis to what cousin Vinnie had to say at the family barbecue. This is a big-picture idea. This is the reason why picking stocks is difficult—because people don't always think with their heads. Emotions play an enormous part in stock selection, and the recent internet craze/crash is only one of many examples.*

So, the only reason a company is traded on a stock exchange is because at one time that company needed to raise money, and decided to sell shares instead of borrowing it from a bank or elsewhere. The only thing that affects a company's stock price is the number of buyers and sellers. The only people who sell stocks are stockholders and the only people who buy stocks are wanna-be stockholders. The only reason people buy the stock of a company is because they believe, for whatever reason, that that company's stock will make them money. The only reason people sell the stock of a company is

---

* Here's a quick rundown. In the 1980s, people wanted technology stocks and Japanese stocks. In the 1970s, people wanted big well-known companies like IBM. Bell-bottom buyers wanted these big companies because many of them got burned buying the fads of the sixties, which were technology stocks. In the 1920s, it was airline stocks. In the mid 1800s, it was railroads. In the late 1700s, it was bank stocks. Whatever the "next big thing" is, please remember the number of buyers and sellers is the only thing that determines the price of a stock.

because they believe, for whatever reason, that company's stock will no longer make them money or will even lose them money. Okay, that's not the only reason. Many times people sell a stock because they need the money for retirement, college tuition, or the down payment on a car.

That's the stock market. Sort of.

Remember that investments are either growth investments or income investments. Stocks are growth investments, but the cool thing about them is that they provide growth with the possibility of income. When you buy a stock (or any investment) and it goes up in value, that's called *appreciation*. That's one way you can make money off investments. Buy them at one price and sell them at a higher price. (Remember the difference in price is called a *capital gain*.)

Remember that investments are either growth investments or income investments.

You know the other way you can make money off an investment is through income.

Some stocks pay income in the form of *dividends*. Dividends are simply a share of the company's profits. When a company makes a profit, it can do any number of things, like pay off its debt, use the cash to buy new equipment, or pass this profit directly to its shareholders in the form of a dividend. Sometimes investors take their dividends and spend them, other times investors reinvest their dividends back into the company to buy more shares. As a rule of thumb unless you are actually living off the dividend income, it makes sense to reinvest your dividends. When people take the dividends, they typically spend them on purchases that decrease in value.

Which companies appreciate and which pay dividends? Well, some do both. But one key factor is the size of the company or the company's *market capitalization*. Market capitalization (or market cap) is basically the current price of the company—as in how much would it cost to buy the whole thing. P Diddy Combs has one million shares that are currently selling for $20 a share. So P Diddy's market cap is $20 million, or the price it would cost you to buy every share. In other words, market cap equals the number of outstanding shares times the price per share.

Small cap companies are those with a market cap of $1 billion or less. These companies tend to pay little in dividends. This is because they're trying to grow. Every dollar of profit goes right back into building the business. *Mid cap* companies have a market cap of $1 to $5 billion. Mid caps may or may not pay dividends, depending on the particular company. *Large cap* companies have a market cap of over $5 billion. Typically, large caps pay the biggest dividends. Large caps have already built up their business so they just pass the profits right on through to the shareholders.

There's really only one thing left to know about the stock market. Just as there is more than one supermarket, there is more than one place to buy and sell stocks. The most popular market is called the New York Stock Exchange (NYSE). The NYSE is an actual market in an actual building that you can visit the next time you're kickin' around in Manhattan.

The other major market is called the NASDAQ, which, if you care (and you shouldn't) stands for the National Association of Securities Dealer Automated Quotations. Unlike the NYSE, the NASDAQ doesn't have an actual marketplace; it's simply a network of computers all linked together. We also have the American Stock Exchange, which can be found in the Big Apple.

There are other markets, some of which are overseas, but you don't need to know them now. I will show you an easy way to invest in foreign stocks in Secret #44.

Okay. There's the stock market. Well . . .

Secret #32 at Work

 Hey Pete, what's all this stuff Peter Jennings talks about on the ABC nightly news, like "volume" and the "Dow?"
Individuals use volume and the Dow to analyze the market. It would be impossible for the average person to examine every stock every day to determine how the market is

doing, so people created *indexes*. These indexes are used to track the market's overall performance. Here are some of the major indexes:

> **The Dow Jones Industrial Average** (a.k.a. the DJIA, the Dow) is a list of thirty large cap stocks traded in the United States. Though horrifically unrepresentative,* this is probably the most popular index for evaluating the stock market.
> **Standard & Poor's 500 Index** (a.k.a. the S&P 500) is a list of five-hundred large companies traded in the United States. The S&P 500 is a much more accurate reflection of the market's performance.
> **The Wilshire 5000 Index** is probably the most comprehensive index in the United States. It tracks not 5,000 but roughly 6,000 small-, medium-, and large-sized U.S. companies.
> **The NASDAQ** is a market, and the NASDAQ Composite is an index of companies traded on the NASDAQ exchange. The NASDAQ composite consists primarily of smaller companies and technology companies.
> **The Morgan Stanley EAFE Index** is another important index. This index is helpful when monitoring foreign markets. EAFE tracks companies in Europe, Australasia (Australia and New Zealand), and the Far East. There are approximately 1,000 companies in this index.

Volume measures activity. It's the number of shares traded (bought and sold) in one day. While every nightly news show announces volume, it's of little use on a day-to-day basis. If volume is low, it just means that not much happened that day on Wall Street. High volume means there was a lot of activity, which means the companies you own could be significantly higher or lower in price. You'll die young of a heart attack if you watch the day-to-day changes in the market, so don't worry about volume too much.

Whew! There's the stock market.

---

* Horrifically unrepresentative because it only holds thirty stocks, and the index is weighted, which means some stocks count more than others. Basically the Dow is stereotyping at its worst, a handful of companies speaking for them all.

Secret #32 in a Nutshell

A company sells stock to the public in an initial public offering or IPO to raise money to build its business. Investors who bought shares during the IPO now sell their stock to other investors. People buy to make money and sell either to take their profits or to avoid losing money. The only two ways to make money with stocks are through dividends and capital gains. Large caps are big companies, mid caps are mid-sized companies, and small caps are small companies. The S&P 500, the DJIA, and the NASDAQ Composite Index are indexes that help people get a quick fix on the market. Volume measures activity—the number of trades made.

take a random walk

Chance favors the informed mind.

LOUIS PASTEUR

Why It Works

I've only been to Atlantic City once. Though I was underage, I waltzed right into a casino ready to play. It was one of Trump's casinos I believe. Then again, doesn't he own them all? But as I neared the tables, I chickened out. Mind you, I wasn't afraid of the casino, the police, or even the Donald himself for that matter. See, because I was underage, I knew that the moment I won something, they would bust me. Even worse, because I was underage, I knew I would win *big*, which magnified the getting-busted concern. I mean, it's one thing to get busted after losing a $5 bet. It's another thing to get busted after winning $5,000.

Needless to say, I retired to my room without betting a dime. And needless to say, when I did return to a casino (this one being on an Indian reservation) at the ripe age of twenty-one, they took my money from me in less than twenty minutes. I knew that if I played underage, I would win but get caught. And yet when I was legal, I would obviously never get caught, but I would never win either.

The stock market is much like my casino quandary. It's easy to win when you break the law, but rather difficult when you abide by it.

We've talked about the best way to save your money for retirement. The best way is using an employer-sponsored retirement account. Next best is a Roth IRA. But what specifically do you do with your savings? What do you invest it in? Coins? Collectibles? Real estate? Perhaps. But for most people, a great place to start investing for the long term is in the stock market. Before we get too far into stock market investing, you and I have to have a heart-to-heart about the *random walk theory*.

The random walk has stirred up quite a bit of controversy in the investment world. This theory answers the following question: "Is it possible to beat stock market averages by selecting your own stocks?" The entire stock market encompasses thousands of stocks, some that do really well, and some that perform poorly, but the performance of all stocks is reflected in the averages (such as Standard & Poor's 500 Index). Is it possible for individuals like you and me to consistently find the stocks that will outperform the average? Based on the information we have, from the internet, from newspapers, and the like, can we find the winners and avoid the losers consistently?

According to the random walk theory, the answer is no. In other words, on average, you will not generate better results for yourself with a few stocks than the overall market returns on average. The random walk theory is based on the idea that it is not possible to determine where stock prices will be tomorrow given the information you have today. Hand in hand with the random walk theory is the *efficient market theory*, which posits that everything that is known about a company is immediately reflected in the price of the stock. For instance, if a publicly traded energy company discovered a way to turn sand into pure energy, then the stock price would shoot up reflecting this new information so quickly that no one could profit from it. Obviously, those lucky investors who already owned this company would profit substantially, but to consistently pick the winners is impossible. Since the market is perfectly efficient, it's impossible to find an undervalued stock. Thus

> *The stock market is much like my casino quandary. It's easy to win when you break the law, but rather difficult when you abide by it.*

researching and investing in a selection of individual stocks is a waste of time.

Random walkers say that an investor is better off buying an *index mutual fund*, which in essence is a way to buy every stock on the market. You'll buy all the winners and all the losers and still come out ahead of the majority of stock pickers. Random walkers live by the edict, if you can't beat 'em, join 'em.

So why should you take a random walk? It is important that you take a few minutes and think about this theory because it will direct the way you invest for the rest of your life. If you believe the market is beatable, then you'll focus your energy and resources trying to beat it. If, however, you think the market is unbeatable, then you won't waste any time doing something you believe is impossible.

> *So why should you take a random walk? It is important that you take a few minutes and think about this theory because it will direct the way you invest for the rest of your life.*

How It Works

Before you start scouring the *Wall Street Journal* looking for stock picks, ask yourself:

1. Is it possible for *me* to separate the winners from the losers?
2. If it is possible for me to separate the winners from the losers, how much extra money can *I* reasonably expect to earn by picking my own stocks?
3. Based on this extra money, is it worth the extra time and the extra money *I* will spend on investment research to pick individual stocks?

Still unsure? Consider these arguments:

Arguments for the Random Walk Theory

- 66% of all professionally managed mutual funds failed to beat the S&P 500 Index average—in the past two decades.
- The use of privileged information for the purchase and sale of

securities is illegal. This process is called *insider trading*, and it's what got Charlie Sheen busted in the movie *Wall Street*. In the film, Sheen was asking his old lawyer buddy James Spader to tell him what lawsuits were going down on which companies. Seems harmless, but he actually broke the law. You can only buy and sell stocks based on information accessible to the general public. The question then becomes, if you can only trade stocks using information that anyone can find out, how are you supposed to ever gain an advantage?

Arguments against the Random Walk Theory

- What about Peter Lynch, the former manager of Fidelity's Magellan Mutual Fund? Lynch beat the stock market during his reign as captain of the fund. And he did it buying a lot of consumer stocks that we all know, like Chrysler and Dunkin' Donuts.

- How about billionaire investor Warren Buffett, one of the richest men in America, whose simple commonsense approach to investing has returned him a compounded annual gain of nearly 30% since the 1950s? Here's a guy who has beaten the market by overwhelming margins, year after year. And just like Peter Lynch, he did it by buying stocks of well-known companies, like Coca-Cola, Disney, and Gillette.

- The number of buyers and sellers is the only thing that determines the price of a stock. At times, the masses buy companies simply because they're popular and overlook great companies that may not be popular (the recent internet craze/crash being the perfect example). So the market may not be as efficient as the efficient market theory says.

Secret #33 at Work

 Hey Pete, what do you think? I can't make this decision for you, but here's my take. The theme of this book is that you should live life on your own terms; you should not be a slave to money. Picking your own stocks is anything but easy. I'm okay with the fact that people are willing to spend some extra time to get a little extra money, but being pissed off every time the stocks you picked go down and happy every time the stocks you picked go up is being a slave to money. Personally, I invest most of my money in index mutual funds. They still go up and down in value with the market, but I never worry I made the wrong choice, because my choice was to buy everything. They're not exciting, but they're safe. If you want excitement, try bungee jumping.

The other theme of this book is that you should use your youth as an advantage over everyone else. When you search for individual stocks, you don't really have the edge over the eighty-four-year-old guy in the nursing home. In fact, nursing home guy actually has the edge over you, because he's got more free time than you do to do research.

Here's another question: If you do believe you can beat the stock market, is the stock market the best market to beat? What about the supermarket? That's a much easier market to beat. In the stock market, you have to figure out which stocks are selling at a discount. In the supermarket, they advertise all the discounts. In the stock market, deciding between Coke or Pepsi will take a few hours. At the supermarket, deciding between Coke and Pepsi will take a few seconds. While you won't become a millionaire in the soda aisle, it is impossible to lose money.

It's time I told you about *the prostitute factor*. Recall the film *Pretty Woman* starring Richard Gere and Julia Roberts. In one scene, Julia is trying to justify the advantages of being a prostitute. She claims, "We say who, we say when, we say . . . who!"

She's right. A prostitute doesn't have many options, besides the ability to say who they sleep with and when. So it is with stocks. You get to say "who." (Who will you buy—Disney? Microsoft? Nike?) And you get to say "when." (When will you buy? When will you sell?) But that's it. Once you buy the stock, your investment is in the hands of the company's management or, more accurately, the emotions of the market.

There are many markets that don't fall victim to the prostitute factor. In the real estate market, you can say who and when, but you also get to say "what." What will you do with the property you bought? Rent it? Fix it up and sell it? You get to say "how?" How will you pay for it? With cash? Taking out a loan? Bringing in investors? The same advantages arise when you own your own business. Where will your business be located? What markets will you expand into? Remember that control is important in investing because it allows you to exercise a creative advantage. If you spend all your time searching for stocks, once you buy those stocks, you can't use your creativity to make them more profitable.

I'm not saying you shouldn't invest in stocks. Stocks are a great investment, but in my opinion, individual stock picking isn't so great because of the prostitute factor. Index mutual funds are a great way to buy stocks. You get to be fully invested in the stock market without the hassle of worrying over something you can't control. How do you invest in index mutual funds? The first thing you do is turn the page.

Secret #33 in a Nutshell

The stock market is beatable because certain people have beaten it. But can *you* beat it? Decide if you want to take the time to pick your own stocks. If not, go with an index mutual fund. One other thing to remember is that there are other markets, markets free from the prostitute factor, that are easier to beat. Two of these markets are the supermarket and the real estate market.

---

go broker

The possession of gold has ruined fewer men than the lack of it.

THOMAS BAILEY ALDRICH

Why It Works

When I say "go broker," I'm not talking about losing money. I'm talking about partnering up with a company that will help you buy and sell investments. You see stocks and other investments must be bought through a *broker*—a person who brings buyers and sellers together for a fee.

In the past, people turned to stockbrokers to help them select and trade stocks. Today, brokerage is becoming less and less a stock selection business and more and more an administration business. Today, finding the right broker is about centralizing your money so it can be managed easily and cheaply.

How It Works

Stockbrokers bring people who want to sell their stocks and people who want to buy those stocks together for a fee commonly known as a *commission*. In exchange for their advice and the service of buying and selling stocks, the brokerage company deducts their commission from every order you make through them. If they charge a 10% commission (relax, commissions typically don't go that high), that means that when you buy $100 worth of stock, you really only buy $90 worth of stock, because the brokerage company kept $10 as their commission. Let me make that clear. Brokerage companies make their money when you buy and when you sell, *not when you make money*. There are two different types of brokers; full service and discount brokers.

Full service broker. This is where it all began. When you have a full service broker, you have an actual living breathing human being advising you on your investments. He takes a percentage commission of every purchase and sale you make. You want to invest $1,000; you only get to buy $960 worth of stuff because $40 goes to your broker. Full service brokers can cost up to ten times what a deep discount broker can cost.

 Hey Pete, should I use a full service broker? Wrong question. The question is, will they use you? Here's why. First, if you recall from the movie *Wall Street*, Charlie Sheen (who played a full service broker) is trying to "bag the elephant" (a.k.a. the big client with lots of dough). You and I aren't elephants; we're more like mice. As a young investor, I'm assuming you're like me and don't have $500,000 to invest into stocks (yet). Brokers don't want a thousand $5,000 accounts; they want ten $500,000 accounts. Think about it. Would you rather take complaint calls from ten angry clients or a thousand angry clients? For most young investors, using a deep discount or online broker is the best bet. Still some people like talking to a living human. If you're one of these people, but you don't have the money to sign up with an experienced full service broker, you may be able to get in via a family member or relative. If, for instance, your grandfather uses a full service broker (as everyone did in the good ole days), the broker will often take on your account (no matter how small it is) simply as a favor to your grandfather.

But please, avoid doing business with anyone who claims, "I'm a joker, I'm a smoker, I'm a midniiight broker."

Discount broker/deep discount broker/online broker. Slowly these types are being blended into one, due to that thing we call the internet. With these brokers, you do not have an actual person to help you select investments. Online brokers simply handle all the administrative work for you, like mailing you reports from the stocks you own, or your annual tax forms, plus they provide research reports on a variety of investments. These brokers do charge you when you buy and sell, but instead of it being a commission, it is a flat fee, usually less than $35.

 In the opening pages of this book, I mentioned one of the benefits of youth was our computer savviness. Discount brokers are the way to go. For one, discount brokers welcome young investors like you and me, and an account can be opened with as little as $50. In addition, discount brokers allow us to centralize our money. We can buy stocks, bonds, and mutual funds, and write checks from our cash management accounts. Every day, discount brokers offer more services, like traditional banking and ATM cards.

Remember from Secret #23 that financial service firms are becoming like Wal-Mart superstores. They're all selling everything. If you decide to go with a full service broker, chances are they offer some sort of discounted online trading. Conversely if you plunk your money into an online broker, I'll bet that online broker offers you the option of speaking with a full service broker.

 Other things to look for in a brokerage account:
- It should have a money market account with *sweeps*. (Sweeps mean that when you sell an investment, the cash from the sale automatically goes into your money market account. This way you're always earning interest.) Remember, a money market account at a discount brokerage firm is often called a *cash management account* (CMA)
- You want a money market account with the highest interest rate you can find *averaged daily*, with check-writing abilities. Be sure to find out if there are a maximum number of checks you can write each month. (There shouldn't be.)
- A commission for an online broker runs from as low as $2 to around $35. A full service broker will charge about a 2%–4% commission.

- When dealing with an online broker, you want the option to trade over the phone at internet prices if their server goes down.
- You want the ability to buy mutual funds from America's most popular mutual fund families, like Fidelity and Vanguard. Again, since the financial world is becoming one big melting pot, I doubt you'll run into a company that *won't* let you do this. Depending on the broker, they may or may not charge you a commission for buying mutual funds. To make it more confusing, many brokers charge commissions on some funds while others are commission free. Try to find a brokerage company that will allow you to buy *index funds*. We'll talk about these more in Secret #35, where I'll explain why they are a super deal.
- You want your account insured. Stock accounts are often insured, but it's different from bank account insurance. Stock insurance does *not* cover you if the *value* of your stocks goes down. However, if

Stock account insurance is different from bank account insurance.

your broker goes out of business, he can't just sell off your stocks to pay his debts. If he did try to do this or any other funny act with your money—like trade without your authorization—your account insurance would protect you, and you would get your money back.

All the companies recommended below carry insurance.

E*Trade (1-800-387-2331; www.etrade.com)
Schwab (1-800-225-8570; www.schwab.com)
Fidelity (1-800-343-3548; www.fidelity.com)
American Express (1-800-297-7378; www.americanexpress.com)
Ameritrade (1-800-454-9272; www.ameritrade.com)

Of course the brokerage company with the best name I've ever seen is BuyandHold.com (1-800-646-8212 www.buyandhold.com). These firms are all good places to do your comparison shopping.

I take this time to explain brokerage accounts because I find an overwhelming amount of people want to try their hand at trading individual stocks. If you're not planning on trading individual stocks (and I applaud you if that is the case), you can set up your base of operations at a mutual fund company, like Fidelity (1-800-343-3548; www.fidelity.com), Vanguard (1-888-285-4563; www.vanguard.com), or T. Rowe Price (1-800-225-5132; www.troweprice.com). A mutual fund allows you to own stocks, but you give up the privilege (or pain) of selecting them. At a mutual fund company, you'll still have access to the money market in the form of a money market mutual fund. But there will be more on mutual funds in Secret #35.

A mutual fund allows you to own stocks, but you give up the privilege (or pain) of selecting them.

Secret #34 at Work

First, call up three to five online brokerage firms or three to five mutual fund companies, either that I recommend or that you've seen advertised. Tell them you want to open an account but you want to ask a few questions first. Be sure to take notes so you can compare when you're done.

But Pete, what questions should I ask?
Here's your script:

Fade In:

INT. BEDROOM—DAY

Under the gentle yet economically friendly glare of a compact fluorescent lightbulb sits a YOUNG INVESTOR amid a sea of brokerage house propaganda. He checks one brochure again for a number, picks up the phone, and dials.

INT. CUSTOMER SERVICE HEADQUARTERS MAJOR ONLINE BROKERAGE FIRM——DAY

Camera dollies through a maze of office cubicles until we meet ERIN, a suspiciously perky employee. The décor of her cube reveals little, aside from a fixation for Dilbert. But, unlike the corporate comic, Erin's excitement is unbridled. She speaks into her telephone headset.

ERIN   Thank you for calling *&^#%$ brokerage. My name is Erin. How may I help you?

YOUNG INVESTOR   I just have a few questions about opening an account.

Erin, despite countless calls like this, bleeds of enthusiasm

ERIN   Ask away.

INT. BEDROOM——DAY

The young investor smiles to himself at Erin's spunkiness. He lifts a coffee mug from his desk, revealing a copy of *Getting Loaded*, which apparently has doubled as a coaster. He sets the mug down on the other side of the desk and picks up *Getting Loaded*. He opens to page 239 and begins reading off questions to Erin.

YOUNG INVESTOR   What is the minimum amount needed to open a cash account?

ERIN   (o.s.) $500. But if you commit to a monthly investment plan, we'll waive the minimum fee. You can start with as little as $50.

YOUNG INVESTOR   Cool. Now this account has a money market account with sweeps right? A cash management account?

ERIN   (o.s.) Sure does.

YOUNG INVESTOR   What's the interest rate and how is it
                  calculated?

ERIN   (o.s.) It's 4.5% and it's averaged daily.

YOUNG INVESTOR   Can I write an unlimited number of checks
                  each month for any amount?

ERIN   (o.s.) You betcha.

YOUNG INVESTOR   Any way I can get an ATM card?

ERIN   (o.s.) You can get one if you open a bank
                  account at our online bank. You need $500
                  to open the bank account, but it pays a
                  really good interest rate and you can easily
                  move money around.

YOUNG INVESTOR   Hmmm. I see that your commissions start
                  at $14 for a market order. Can you tell me
                  ALL other fees I may incur?

INT. CUSTOMER SERVICE HEADQUARTERS MAJOR ONLINE BROKERAGE
FIRM—DAY

Erin's eyes fill with a thankfulness so infinite it is as if she
spent half her life memorizing these fees.

ERIN   I sure can. $17 for a limit order or a stop
                  order. If you don't make at least two trades
                  a year, there is an account fee of $10 per
                  year. That's it.

YOUNG INVESTOR   That's it? I want to be sure those are all of
                  the fees I can be charged.

ERIN   That's it.

YOUNG INVESTOR How much is the account insured for?

ERIN   Every account is insured for $100 million.

YOUNG INVESTOR Can I trade over the phone for the online price?

ERIN   Yep.

YOUNG INVESTOR Can I buy no load mutual funds through my account and am I charged for this?

ERIN   You can buy over a thousand funds through us. On about half of these funds, you'll pay a commission. The other half you won't.

YOUNG INVESTOR Erin, just in case I need to call back, can I have the first letter of your last name?

ERIN   No problem. It's "R."

YOUNG INVESTOR Erin R., do you have an extension?

ERIN   3246.

YOUNG INVESTOR Erin, I have one more question. Why would you use your discount brokerage firm as opposed to the others?

ERIN   Well we offer . . . blah blah blah . . . (here's where you let her sell you)

INT. BEDROOM—DAY

The young investor enjoys his final sip of coffee as Erin rattles off her company's credentials.

YOUNG INVESTOR   Thanks Erin. Erin, could you please send me the information on opening a cash account with your firm? My address is 123 Happy Street, Notting Hill, Montana 01234

ERIN   (o.s.) Got it. Thanks for calling. I'll send that out right away. Have a great day.

YOUNG INVESTOR   Thanks Erin.

The young investor hangs up the phone and folds his hands behind his head. He leans back in his swivel chair and smiles.

FADE OUT:

Done! If you do this with about five brokerage firms or mutual fund companies, you'll get an idea of what the industry is charging for their services.

There are two types of brokerage accounts, a *cash account* and a *margin account*. A cash account means you can use only the money you already have to buy stocks. A margin account allows you to borrow money from your broker to buy stocks. If you wanted to buy $1,500 worth of stock, but you only had $1,000, you could borrow the other $500 from your broker. He'd charge you interest, but ideally you would make enough of a profit when you sell the stock to pay back the $500 plus interest and still make a decent profit.

The key word here is *ideally*.

It's tough enough to make money by picking individual stocks, now you have to make enough money to pay the interest on the money you borrowed from your broker? Dumb. Never borrow money to purchase stocks. Stick with a cash account. If nothing else, they can be opened for less money.

 Hey Pete, what's a market order, limit order, or a stop order? An *order* is simply a command to buy or sell a stock. You not only get to give the order to buy or sell a stock, you also get to choose the way you want to buy or sell it. The more complex the order, the higher commission you will pay. Here are the basic types of orders:

Market order. You agree to pay the market price when your order hits the floor. (What floor? The floor of the exchange, where stocks are actually bought and sold.) You may look on your computer and see Coke trading at $50 a share, but by the time your order gets to the floor (read: your order gets processed), the price has gone up to $50.50 a share. This is the cheapest and most common order.

Limit order. This allows you to put a specific price on your order. A $50 per share limit order means you will only pay $50 per share for this stock. If, by the time your order is processed, the stock has sky-rocketed to $60, you're protected, and you won't buy. This is a more complex trade than a market order, so the trading commission is higher.

Stop order. This order is kinda like a limit order in that it controls the price. The difference is that a stop order does not set a specific price; it simply sets a boundary. A stop order commands the broker to buy or sell once the stock moves above or below a certain price. A sell stop order of $20 means that when your stock drops below $20, the broker will sell it at the next available price.

It's tough enough to make money by picking individual stocks, now you have to make enough money to pay the interest on the money you borrowed from your broker? Dumb. Never borrow money to purchase stocks.

Stop and limit orders—do you need them? That's up to you. As a rule of thumb, I'd say you're safe enough without these orders. But if you're trading extremely volatile stocks, they're probably a smart idea. Then again, trading extremely volatile stocks is not a smart idea.

Secret #34 in a Nutshell

By opening a cash account at a discount brokerage firm, you'll be able to centralize your finances. You can buy stocks, bonds, and mutual funds through your discount broker and you can also get a money market account with check-writing privileges. To find the best brokerage deal, call several companies and take notes on their fees and services. If you don't want to trade individual stocks, you can set up your base of operations at a mutual fund company. The basic way to buy a stock is a market order, while stop and limit orders cost more but can protect you from violent market swings.

master mutual funds

The stock market is the creation of man which humbles him the most.

—ANONYMOUS

Why It Works

One way to protect yourself from investment loss is to buy stock in many different companies in many different industries. That way, if one stock goes down in value, you still have a bunch of others to make up for that one stock's poor performance. This is known as *diversification*. The trouble is if you bought stock in fifty companies, at an average price of $50 per share, you'd have to come up with $2,500. That's a lot of money. But a *mutual fund* offers a way around this. It allows you to buy shares in hundreds, even thousands of companies for just a few dollars.

A mutual fund is a fund headed by a professional money manager. Investors like you and me buy shares in the fund and in doing so, we surrender the responsibility of investing over to the money manager. Some funds invest in stocks, some in bonds, and some in a combination of both. All funds are invested according to stated objectives or guidelines. Note that investors don't buy the actual stocks and bonds, the fund buys the actual stocks and bonds, and investors buy shares in the fund. Mutual funds are one of the most popular investments available today. Here's why:

1. They provide instant diversification. When you invest, it's important that not all your money is in one place—what happens if that investment turns out to be the suckiest suck that ever sucked? Funds own many companies, of many different sizes, and in many different industries. So your risk is spread out. If one stock tanks, it can be offset by others doing well, so overall, you'll be alright.

2. They allow you to invest in profitable businesses you may not understand. Imagine a person avoided investing in the cell phone industry because they thought analog roam was a suburb of Italy's largest city. This person should buy mutual funds (and an atlas).

3. You get professional money management for pennies on the dollar.

4. You save time by not having to select individual stocks.

5. Your money is fairly liquid because remember, you're buying and selling shares in the mutual fund, not the actual stocks themselves. You can get in and out with ease.

How It Works

 People serious about getting loaded with mutual funds only invest in *no load mutual funds*. No load means no sales fee. Don't buy a mutual fund that has a load. There are front end loads, where you pay a sales commission when you buy it. There are also back end loads, where you pay a sales commission when you sell it, and of course there are funds that charge you when you buy and when you sell. Don't listen to the salesperson's load of bull either: "Oh, load funds can afford to hire the better managers" or "People are more committed to long-term investing when the fund has a load." Mutual funds that carry a load just don't make sense, because there are thousands of great no load funds out there. The only people that get rich off loaded mutual funds are the people that sell them.

There are two types of mutual funds: *open ended funds* and *closed ended funds*. Open ended means that the fund issues an unlimited amount of shares. They calculate the value of the shares by adding up the total value of the fund's holdings and dividing it by the number of outstanding shares. If the fund has $10 million worth of assets and one million outstanding shares, the price per share is $10 ($10 million divided by one million shares equals $10 per share). This value is called the *net asset value* (NAV), and it is calculated on a daily basis.

Closed end funds issue a limited number of shares. These shares are traded over markets like the New York Stock Exchange. The beauty of closed end funds is that at times shares can be bought at a discount. If the fund has a hundred shares selling—because of investor demand—for $10 a share, then the price of the entire fund is $1,000. But the total value of the assets held within the fund may be $1,200. So you could buy $1,200 worth of investment for only $1,000. Mind you, every rose has its thorn, and closed end funds are no exception. The shares can also be sold at a premium, when the total NAV is less than the total price of all the shares. Money can be made in closed ended funds but they are a little more complex than open ended funds and your money may not be as liquid in a closed end fund.

> **People serious about getting loaded with mutual funds only invest in no load mutual funds.**

So you're only interested in no load mutual funds. But how do you find out if a fund is a no load fund? All this can found by reading the fund's *prospectus*. A prospectus is simply a pamphlet that outlines how the fund will invest your money. It's horrifically boring, so I've provided the highlights.

The first thing you want to know is *what type of fund is it?* And the categories are:

Money market mutual funds. You already know about these. This is where you're investing your emergency cash reserve. These funds are the lowest risk, but also provide the lowest reward. They only buy shares in the money market and they work like a bank account. Often you can write checks against the amount of money you have invested in your money market mutual fund. Since it pays more in interest, consider swapping your traditional bank account altogether for a money market mutual fund.

Bond funds. One guess what these babies invest in. Bond funds sometimes buy government bonds, corporate bonds, tax-free bonds, or any combination of the three. There's not much growth with bond funds, but they do provide income. I don't get too excited about bonds. I get even less excited about bond funds. I'll explain why in Secret #36.

Balanced funds. These funds will mess around with anything, stocks or bonds. Since balanced funds invest in bonds and stocks that pay dividends, their goal is usually income, but they do offer some potential for growth.

Real Estate Mutual Funds. These are somewhat new to the investing scene. Real estate mutual funds obviously invest in real estate, but they do so by buying several *real estate investment trusts* or REITS. REITS are companies that buy real estate properties, like office buildings and shopping malls. They're kind of like mutual funds, but instead of buying shares of stock, REITS buy a bunch of different real estate properties. A real estate mutual fund then buys a bunch of REITS. Since it's important to spread your money over a variety of different investments, a real estate mutual fund is often a great way to diversify into real estate. As I mentioned in Secret #30, real estate often scares people away because it has such a high minimum investment. Not so with a real estate mutual fund. Consider putting some of your money into a real estate mutual fund. How much money? Check out Secret #44.

Equity funds. These are funds that invest primarily in stocks. Equities vary greatly; some invest in large caps, some small caps, some in one sector of the economy, like technology stocks, while others invest in foreign companies. Equity mutual funds offer the highest reward at the highest risk. They are not for short-term goals, but they are an excellent way to build up a large fortune.

Index funds. Without a doubt, these are the coolest equity funds. These funds are also known as *unmanaged funds* or *passively managed funds* because they don't really require an intelligent manager. Index funds buy all the companies within a stock market index, such as the S&P 500. Simple. Index funds will never outperform the market averages, but they'll never under-perform them either. In fact, history has proven that they'll make you more money than the majority of actively managed funds. Why? Because picking the best stocks year after year is very difficult. While some managers may have one great year, they often follow it up with a lousy year, which evens out the performance of their great year. Index funds take all the guesswork out of buying stocks.

> **Index funds take all the guesswork out of buying stocks.**

The other advantage of index funds is that they have a low *turnover*. Turnover is simply the rate that a mutual fund buys and sells investments each year. If a $100 million fund bought and sold $50 million worth of investments in one year, its turnover is 50%. Turnover is one of the lousy characteristics of mutual funds. Don't get me wrong, every investor buys and sells so every investor has turnover. But mutual fund managers are often forced to turn over. Let's pretend the Christmas Mutual Fund has $100 million under management in January. $50 million of that is invested in Coke and the other $50 million is invested in Microsoft. (It is illegal for a mutual fund to have such little diversification, but this is a hypothetical example.) Now the fund is doing well until about October, when the market goes down. The shareholders in the Christmas fund notice the market is going down, and they want to cash in their shares. Christmas is around the corner, and it's time to stop shopping on Wall Street and start shopping on Main Street. So people tell the fund manager they want to sell their shares. The fund manager must raise the cash to pay these investors who are selling their shares. How does he do this? By selling raffle tickets? Having a bake sale? No, he has to sell some of the fund's investments and with the proceeds from these sales, he'll pay the investors who are selling their shares in the fund.

Now the manager may be screaming, "No, no! Don't sell. I've picked two winning stocks here! You'll make a fortune if you stick with me until next March!" But no matter how loud he shouts, he must sell the shares in Coke and Microsoft in order to pay the shareholders. He's forced to turn over the fund's assets.

While some turnover is inevitable, index mutual funds have a much lower turnover rate. The reason is because people who buy index funds aren't always worrying their money is in the wrong place, like the people who buy actively managed funds are.

We'll talk about which type of fund is right for you in a minute (cough! index funds), but there are two other key numbers in the prospectus:

 **Total operating expenses:** Funds charge a fee in order to pay their managers for research and their customer service people for taking calls. At the end of every day, the fund company multiplies the NAV by its fee (divided by the number of days each year) and takes this amount right out of the NAV. Let me explain. Imagine a fund charges 1% a year for its total operating expenses. 1% divided by 365 days equals a daily fee of .0027%. At the end of every day, the fund multiplies the NAV (let's pretend on this day the NAV is $100 million) by .0027% (the daily fee) to get a total of $2,700. The fund company then takes $2,700 out of the fund to pay its managers and customer support people. The mutual fund industry spent some time on this one and decided to call these fees *total operating expenses.* By law, the prospectus must tell you what the operating expense fee is. The lower this fee, the more money in your pocket. As a rule of thumb, avoid any funds with operating expenses over

1%. If you search, you can find plenty of great funds with fees less than 0.5%. Some index funds, because they don't have to pay some smart manager, have fees less than 0.3%.

12-b1 fees. They couldn't just make it simple. 12-b1 fees are fees charged for marketing expenses, and the bottom line is less money in your pocket. Avoid any fund that charges 12-b1 fees.

In terms of the best type of mutual fund for you, so far we're down to *no load mutual funds with operating expenses of less than 1%, and no 12-b1 fees.*

You don't have to read the prospectus cover to cover. No one does. But read enough to feel comfortable investing in the fund. Who are the managers and what are their credentials? What is the fund's track record? What companies does the fund invest in and do you understand these companies?

Secret #35 at Work

Hey Pete, I guess you're going to tell me I should buy index funds, huh?

Consider this one final argument for index funds. I said that the stock market is just like any other market where things get bought and sold. However, index funds offer an opportunity in the stock market I have not seen in any other market. Imagine you walked into the supermarket knowing that you were going to spend $20 on dinner. But as you stroll down the aisles, you really can't decide what to eat. Should you go healthy, or TV dinner? Chicken or fish? Beans or beef? Is Tuesday or Wednesday Prince Spaghetti day? These are all tough decisions you must make, yet you must decide on *something* because you only have enough money for one meal.

But in the stock market, with $20, it is possible to buy nearly everything in the market. It's the only market in the world that has this feature. Can you buy every outfit at Macy's for $100 just because you're not sure exactly which ones will be in style next year? Can you buy every book at Barnes & Noble just because you don't know whether it's going to be a Clancy night or a *Getting Loaded* night? However, when it comes to stocks, for the price of one, you can have them all via an index mutual fund. I'd take advantage of this rare feature.

You can buy mutual funds from just about anywhere—from your broker, from your bank, or directly from the mutual fund company. Try to avoid paying a commission when you buy shares in a mutual fund—that's just a waste of money.

In Secret #44, I'll recommend which index funds to buy. I won't recommend any managed funds, first because, by the time you read this book, who knows what the good funds will be, and second because I hope my silence will steer you toward index funds.

 ### Secret #35 in a Nutshell
Mutual funds pool your money with hundreds of other investors to buy a variety of investments. You don't own the investments, you simply own shares in the fund. No load, open ended index mutual funds are often your best bet. Don't buy a fund with operating expenses over 1%. Don't buy a fund with 12-b1 fees.

---

escape from bondage

During the first period of a man's life, the greatest danger is not to take the risk.

—SOREN KIERKEGAARD

Why It Works

Stocks and stock mutual funds are the big picture. They're the investments that are going to bring you into a comfortable retirement. Just as important, money market funds are the small picture. They're going to carry you day to day until you reach retirement. Bonds and bond funds are the middle picture, a little more risky and a little more rewarding than money market funds, but a little less risky and a little less rewarding than stocks.

Hey Pete, bonds don't sound so bad to me. Why then should I try to "escape from bondage?"
    Because historically bonds have paid out about half what stocks have paid. Bonds are not bad investments, but it's inappropriate for young investors—those of us who have plenty of time to ride out the ups and downs of the stock market—

to pad their portfolios with bonds. Remember, being too safe won't solve your problems, it will just delay them.

 As a rule of thumb, bonds may be worth considering when your retirement or a major purchase (for example, home, car, college education) is less than five years away. As long as you have more than five years before you need your money, stocks are going to be the better place for your cash. Bonds do have a small place in everyone's portfolio for diversification. You know because of my index fund infatuation that I'm a big fan of buying a little of everything, and therefore I can't leave out bonds.

it's

inappropriate

for young

investors—

those of us who

have plenty of

time to ride out

the ups and

downs of the

stock market—

to pad their

portfolios

with bonds.

How It Works

Bonds are IOUs issued by an entity, such as a corporation, or government. They're lending investments. When you buy a bond, you lend your money to the entity that issued the bond. They pay you interest for a fixed amount of time, and when that fixed amount of time is over, you get all your money—your principal—back. In general, the longer the time and the shadier the entity issuing the bond, the higher the interest rate.

In general, bonds share the same attributes:

Maturity. You buy a $1,000 one-year bond that pays 5% in interest. Unlike your little sister, at the end of one year, the bond actually *matures*, which means you get your interest of $50 plus your principal of $1,000.

Interest rate. (a.k.a. coupon) Most bonds pay interest; otherwise no one would buy them. For the most part, interest rates on bonds do not change.

Callable or not callable. How would you feel if the person you had a crush on said to you, "I'll date you as long as you know that as soon as someone better comes along, I'm outta here." That's what the issuers of callable bonds are basically saying to you. A callable bond is one where the issuer is allowed to pay you back early. You buy a $1,000 bond that matures in three years and pays a juicy 11% per year. If it's callable, then the issuer has the right to give you back your principal plus the interest owed *up to the date they call in the bonds.* If the bonds are called after a year, the issuer only owes you your principal plus one year's interest. Callable bonds blow. Here's why. Your $1,000 bond pays 11% in interest. Then interest rates drop. Now new $1,000 bonds are being issued with a 4% interest rate. All new bonds get 4%, and you've locked in an 11% interest rate. You got a good deal, right? Wrong. Because your bond is callable, the entity that is-sued your 11% bond will call it in and reissue a new bond paying only 4%. It's up to you if you want to buy the new bond or not. Just remember that entities that issue callable bonds, like that shal-low person you have a crush on, are always look-ing to trade up.

Face value. This is the value of the bond. It is from the face value that interest payments are cal-culated. If you have a $1,000 bond paying 5% in interest, you can expect to get $50 a year. Even if you bought this bond at a discount—we'll talk about how to do this in a second—you would still get $50 a year, because the interest payment is cal-culated using the face value, not the price you paid for the bond.

Rating. Just like movies, bonds are rated. But bond rat-ings aren't designed to keep people under seventeen from buying them; rather bonds are rated for their credit qual-ity. Two companies that rate bonds, as well as many other

How would you feel if the person you had a crush on said to you, "I'll date you as long as you know that as soon as someone better comes along, I'm outta here." That's what the issuers of callable bonds are basically saying to you.

investments, are Moody's and Standard & Poor's. Remembering bond ratings is simple, it's just like your report card: an "A" rating (or multiple "A's") equals awesome, a "B" (or multiple "B's") equals be careful, and a "C" equals crazy (as in you are if you buy a "C"-rated bond). Stick to "A"-rated bonds.

 **Taxable or nontaxable.** Some bonds are exempt from taxes—either local, state, federal, or even all three. As a general rule of thumb, tax-free bonds usually only benefit those people in the highest tax brackets. Investors like you and me don't usually have high enough incomes to need the tax break of a tax-free bond.
Still, I hope after reading this book, your income will shoot through the roof, and tax-free bonds may make sense down the road.

So that's bonds. Now here's why they can suck:

- Bond returns have historically been much lower than stocks. Many bonds pay just a bit over inflation—you're hardly making any money. In the history of the stock market, despite many different presidents, many different wars, *and* the movie *Waterworld*, stocks always outperformed bonds.
- Remember that bonds are only as good as the entity that issues them (a.k.a. the *guarantor*). Imagine you buy a $1,000 bond from Smokey's Tobacco Friendly Family Fitness Centers. If Smokey goes out of business, you may be out of luck. Always find out what happens if the only thing Smokey can cough up is a lung. If you do decide to put yourself in bondage, please stick with "A"-rated bonds.
- If you sell the bond before it matures, you may lose money. Contrary to popular belief, bond prices fluctuate. They move in the opposite direction of interest rates. *When interest rates go up, bond prices go down, and vice versa.* Think about it. If you have a

$1,000 bond paying 5% and rates suddenly shoot up to 9%, why would anyone pay $1,000 for your bond? They wouldn't. So if you want to sell early, you have to drop your price to maybe $600 to make your bond more attractive. Of course, you can win out. If interest rates drop to 2%, then your $1,000 bond that pays 5% in interest is going to be worth more. The point is that since bonds are fixed income investments, it seems as though what you can earn on them won't change, when in fact you can lose dough if you bail out early. And remember, if your bond is callable, the issuer may bail *you* out early to take advantage of lower interest rates.

- Bond ratings can also cause prices to fluctuate. Imagine you buy a $1,000 bond in the Exaggeration Tire Company with a 5% interest and a AAA rating. Now, even though the Exaggeration Tire Company assured you that their tires were a hundred billion times better than the competition's, they run into financial trouble. Your bond price will have to come down—why would anyone buy your CCC-rated bond paying 5% in interest for $1,000? They wouldn't—you'll have to lower the price. Should you sell out at a loss or keep it and risk that the company defaults? Risk, risk, risk.

- "Good Lord, that's a lotta money!" Bonds have a high minimum investment. Many bonds start at $1,000 and some can hit $25,000. At $1,000 per bond, how can you possibly diversify? You can't, unless you're holding the winning ticket for the Powerball. (And if you are holding the winning ticket for the Powerball, are you really going to say, "Yes! Finally I can diversify in bonds"?)

- *Hey Pete, how about bond mutual funds?* They're not that great. You shouldn't buy bonds unless you plan to hold them until they mature. Prices will go up and down, but if you hold them until maturity, you'll get all the interest plus principal back. A bond fund eliminates the opportunity to hold bonds until their maturity. If shareholders in the bond fund want cash, the fund manager might have to sell some bonds before their maturity at a loss.

With bond funds, you lose the most attractive quality of bonds, which is the predictable income they provide. *Don't buy bond mutual funds.*

Secret #36 at Work

It's not that bonds eternally suck, it's that they just suck for right now. For young investors like you and me, most of our money should be in stocks. We need most of our dough in growth investments, like stocks and real estate. But there will come a day, many moons from now, when we switch our money to bonds because we need the income—nice, steady, reliable, secure income. And, true, some of your money should be in bonds (the old let's-just-be-sure-and-buy-a-little-of-everything strategy). So here are the rules for buying bonds:

But there will come a day, many moons from now, when we switch our money to bonds because we need the income—nice, steady, reliable, secure income.

- Unless retirement is close, don't buy bonds that mature in ten years or more. You're simply better off putting your money in stocks.
- Beware of bonds that are callable. The trouble with callable bonds is that the moment they become a sweet deal, the issuer calls them back. You can't win. U.S. government bonds (a.k.a. Treasuries) that I recommend below are not callable. Corporate bonds usually are.
- Which reminds me, stay away from corporate bonds—taxable, callable, most likely bought paying a commission, and issued by entities that have a less-than-rock-solid future. If the company does have a rock-solid future, then what in the wide, wide world of sports are you doing buying that company's bonds? Buy the company's stock and make a real profit!

- I like treasury notes and treasury bills, issued with the full faith and credit of the U.S. government. But like most bonds, they're expensive with a minimum investment of $1,000. Treasury bills mature in one year or less, treasury notes mature in two to ten years. They are completely safe and are not subject to state and local income tax. What's more, you can buy them without paying a commission through a program called treasury direct. Visit www.usbonds.gov and click on treasury direct to find out how you can save on commissions by buying directly from the U.S. Treasury.

- You may already own U.S. Savings Bonds (a.k.a. Series EE). I call these birthday bonds because these are the gifts that grandma gives you on your birthday. Double E's are cool because they can be bought in small increments, as low as $25. They offer the cash-strapped investor the overrated joy of diversifying into bonds without paying a management fee. They won't make you rich, but you won't go broke either. The new I bonds are like Series EE bonds in the sense that they are inexpensive government bonds. I bonds can be bought for as little as $50 and they're guaranteed to pay a rate of return over and above the rate of inflation. Both I bonds and Series EE bonds can be bought at most banks. What's more, you don't have to pay taxes on these bonds until you cash them in. For information on both types of bonds, check out www.savingsbonds.gov.

A popular rule of thumb when it comes to bonds is to subtract your age from a hundred. The answer is the percentage of your portfolio that should be invested in stocks. The rest should be in bonds. So if you're twenty-five, subtract twenty-five from a hundred and you get seventy-five: 75% of your money should be in stocks, 25% in bonds. I wouldn't balk at all if you decided to put even less money in bonds—unless you need the predictable income for an upcoming purchase.

But Pete, what if the stock market crashes? Then it's probably a great time to buy stocks at a bargain. Which stocks you and I won't know, so we'll just buy them all with an index mutual fund.

But Pete, what if the stock market stays in the dumps for eight years? Then the brave souls with written goals will have eight years of discount shopping. If Wal-Mart had an after-Christmas sale that lasted eight years, would you complain?

But Pete, what if the stock market finally collapses and ceases to exist? Look, if this does happen (next to impossible), then most likely it will be because a catastrophic event has occurred (like tanks are rolling down Main Street and they're not *our* tanks). If such a catastrophic event happened and the stock market collapsed, chances are all your bonds and government-insured bank accounts would be worthless as well. Regardless, if catastrophe strikes, are you really going to be worried about your stocks? I doubt it. The good news? If you follow my advice, you'll have some money in foreign stocks.

> *If Wal-Mart had an after-Christmas sale that lasted eight years, would you complain?*

Secret #36 in a Nutshell

Bonds are good for generating steady fixed income and for diversifying but they should be a small part of a young investor's portfolio. If and when you buy bonds, buy treasuries and hold them until maturity. If you can't afford Treasuries, consider I Bonds or Series EE bonds, which can be bought for very little at your local bank. Don't buy bond mutual funds. When interest rates go up, bond prices go down and vice versa. A bond's credit rating can also change its price. Over the long, long run, stocks will outperform bonds.

stock up

Part One—The Research Process

I'm a great believer in luck, and I find the harder I work the more I have of it.

—THOMAS JEFFERSON

Why It Works

Unlike writing an episode of *Saved by the Bell*, picking a winning stock is a tough and time-consuming thing to do. Before you start crunching numbers, looking at charts, and cursing Mr. Coffee for not working as hard as you are, you should go through the thinking process outlined in this secret to make the seemingly unmanageable amount of stocks out there a little more manageable.

But wait, why even try to pick stocks? We already talked about the random walk theory. We already went over how easy it is to buy an index mutual fund. Why subject yourself to the extra work of reading reports and doing math—*in your free time?*

Only one answer—money. There is a slight chance you will be able to beat the market returns. And I do mean slight. According to Burton Malkiel, author of the highly recommended *A Random Walk Down Wall Street*, more than two-thirds of professional mutual fund managers don't beat the market on a consistent basis.* And these managers do nothing all day but try to beat the market. Ask yourself, is it worth it? While I can't say for sure, I bet the goal sheet you wrote for Secret #1 doesn't say anything about reading stock reports on a Sunday morning. Is it worth spending several hours looking for stocks, continually worrying about the ones you bought and the ones you didn't, all for the possibility that you may squeeze a few extra percentage points out of your annual returns? I say no, that's why I like index mutual funds.

But.

I bet the goal sheet you wrote for Secret #1 doesn't say anything about reading stock reports on a Sunday morning.

I'm here to make recommendations, not to give orders. Okay, so you didn't invest in a hundred shares of McDonald's in 1965, turning your initial investment of $2,250 into over $2 million by the year 2000. But there will be others, and I understand the temptation to search for the next McDonald's or the next Microsoft. Part of my portfolio is invested in individual stocks, so who am I to be lecturing you? In my defense, however, many of these stocks are ones I have held for many years, before I learned more about index funds. But I haven't abandoned individual stocks altogether and I doubt you will either. I hope what I can share with you briefly here will keep you out of trouble.

First, hot tips belong in the recycle bin. I am one for three on my hot tips. Many years ago, I bought a company called Boston Life Sciences. I bought it because a friend told me they had just received a patent for something I didn't understand. But the word "patent" was enough to get me. Even though this tip wasn't as hot as I thought—my friend read about it in a magazine—in a year, the stock doubled, and I took my profits.

---

* Malkiel, *A Random Walk Down Wall Street*, p. 15.

With regard to my other two hot-tip purchases, I have lost quite a bit. I can't tell you the names of these two companies. To do so would be a violation of journalistic integrity. It would appear as if I deliberately mentioned the stock in this book for the sole purpose of pumping its price up in an effort to recoup my losses. So you won't hear me mention Saf-T-Lock and Timberline Software in this book. No sir.

> *Hot tips belong in the recycle bin.*

How It Works

This secret is more about avoiding the losers than picking the winners. My hope is that out of the thousands of stocks, you will be able to select twenty or thirty that show potential and demand closer examination. That closer examination will come in the next secret. For now, let's just focus on finding those twenty or thirty. Keep in mind that to thoroughly show you step by step how to evaluate a company's financial possibilities would take a separate book (which is on the way!). But there are some basic points to keep in mind even before you begin. Let's start with the three basic rules of thumb in investment selection:

1. Never invest in something you don't understand. Suppose you didn't know anything about music and you invested heavily in a record company that boasted, "We just paid $10 million for Limp Bizkit to compose Barbra Streisand's new album!" If you didn't understand this industry, you'd have no idea this was a bad move. (At least in my humble opinion.)

2. Never invest in more investments than you can keep track of. There is no point in owning a hundred different stocks—even if they're all winners. You'll never be able to monitor them all. For individual stocks, holding between five and ten is a reasonable number. This assumes, however, that you have additional money invested in mutual funds.

3. When you buy a stock, pretend you are buying the whole company. This is billionaire Warren Buffett's creed. When you pretend you're buying the whole company, you're forced to look past the economic and market conditions that burn so many investors who buy a company simply because everyone else is buying it. Ask yourself, "If there was no stock market, would I buy this company?"

Just go through your lifestyle and make a list of companies you already do business with.

Hey Pete, now that I know the three basic rules of stock picking, how do you find a few potential companies out of the thousands that are out there?

You need to make what I call a who-is-my . . . ? list, which is a list of the companies you already do business with. Peter Lynch, who managed one of the most successful mutual funds in history—Fidelity's Magellan Fund—made this idea famous with his investment philosophy, "If you like the products, you'll love the company."

So ask yourself, "Who is my phone company?" "Who is my power company?" "Who is my favorite clothing company?" "Who is my favorite car company?" "Who is my shoe company?" "Who is my toothpaste company?" Just go through your lifestyle and make a list of companies you already do business with. Don't worry about looking at any financial reports. Just generate a list of companies you are comfortable with.

Once you've got a lengthy *who-is-my . . . ?* list, your next job is to find out what is behind the products and services you use every day. Ask yourself the following questions about each company on the list:

1. What other companies offer similar products and services, and why would someone use them?
2. Do I understand this company's products and services?
3. Do I ever patronize its competitors? Why?

4. Are its competitors bigger or smaller than the company I like?

5. What is it that makes me choose this company's product/services over another? Is it price, quality, brand name, or something else?

6. How does this company make money?

7. What are some things that would prevent this company from making money?

8. Who uses this product?

9. What do I like and dislike about this company's products?

10. How long have I liked this company's products?

11. Can the company grow or diversify into other products? (In other words, what can this company do to make more money?)

12. Are the products and services competitively priced?

13. What is their market niche? Are they the cheapest, the highest quality?

14. Can a competitor easily copy the products?

15. What do my friends think about this company and its products?

16. How do my answers compare with theirs and why?

17. What would make this company go out of business?

18. Is this company a target of government regulations?

19. Does this company piss anyone off? (Environmentalists? Unions? Civil rights activists?)

20. Is this company heavily dependent on another industry for success? (For example, a tire company—like Firestone—may be heavily dependent on auto sales for its success.)

Feel free to add to this list. You're just trying to weed out the lousy companies by asking questions. For instance, imagine you have five companies on your list when you get to question #17. Of those five companies, you come up with probable answers for three of them as to why they would go out of business. The other two, you figure could go bankrupt, but the possibility is a long shot. You have narrowed your list down from five to two.

Hey Pete, suppose I want to invest in a company that I don't do business with as a consumer? For instance, what if I want to invest in a missile company?

I hope none of you own your own missiles. (If so, please turn yourself in.) The biggest problem with nonconsumer companies (sometimes called business-to-business companies) is that you personally cannot evaluate its products. No one is going to let you shoot a missile at your ex-boyfriend's house just as a test (hmmm, imagine that). Still, there are many great business-to-business companies, and it is possible to conduct research on them. You can ask the same twenty questions. Just put yourself in the shoes of whoever buys that company's products. You'll have to think like a military general or a tractor-buying farmer or a warehouse manager looking to buy a forklift.

After screening your stocks through these questions, you've hopefully narrowed down the list a little more. You're beginning to see which companies are solid and which are shaky. Take what's left of your list and bounce them off the following ideas:

• Beware of companies that sell commodity products (products where the lowest-priced product always wins, like airlines and oil companies). The trouble with commodity companies is that they can't just raise prices if they need more money. If one airline has cheaper seats, you'll fly with them. But how much will prices have to rise before you switch from Coke to Pepsi? Sure, no one is going to pay $12 for a Coke (unless you're in a movie theater), but Coke at least has a little room to raise prices because there are so many loyal Coke drinkers.

• A *monopoly* is often the best business to own because it has no competitors. In the United States, monopolies are illegal, but they do exist. AT&T used to be a monopoly and even though it was broken up, investors could hardly complain about owning AT&T. In discussions with some hockey fan friends, I thought I uncovered another monopoly. If you've ever been to a hockey game, you may have seen a Zamboni Ice Resurfacing Machine drive by. But can you name another company that makes ice resurfacing machines? Zamboni seems to enjoy a bit of a monopoly, doesn't it? Unfortunately, Zamboni is a family-run company; you and I can't invest in it. The point is that at times monopolylike companies do exist.*

- Brand names are cool. Brand names are like a pseudo monopoly. Sure *Snow White* isn't the only cartoon in the world, but the only company you can buy a copy of *Snow White* from is Disney. People will pay more for brand-name items, which gives the companies that own these brand-name items a monopolylike advantage. And it's legal.

- What does *Consumer Reports* say? A great investment magazine is *Consumer Reports*, which is a magazine that rates products for consumers. They accept NO advertising, so they are truly unbiased in their ratings. Consumers turn to *Consumer Reports* for the straight story. Not only is the mag a great way to research a company's products, but it will help with your shopping skills as well. See what *Consumer Reports* has to say about the companies on your list.

- Remember the lawyers, guns, and money evaluation technique. Warren Zevon sang the song "Lawyers, Guns and Money." In it, he keeps talking about situations that neither lawyers, guns, or money can get him out of. If you hear about a company that is in trouble, so much so that the proverbial lawyers, guns, and money can't get that company out of trouble, take a second look. Wall Street often overreacts to bad news, like lawsuits, oil spills, or defective products. Great stocks like Philip Morris (I mean great in a financial sense) can take an unwarranted dive when bad news hits the street. When a company seems to be in so

---

* While Zamboni may seem like a monopoly, it does have competitors. For your backyard ice rink, there's the Bambini Ice Resurfacing Machine as well as the Olympia, made by the Resurface Corporation.

much trouble that not even lawyers, guns, and money can help, look closer, there may be a bargain opportunity.

Secret #37 at Work

Remember that individual stock picking is not easy. On the other hand, you only need to be right a few times. Snatch up a Coca-Cola, a Disney, a Dell, a Nike, a Wal-Mart, The Limited, an IBM, a Microsoft, a Berkshire Hathaway, a Subaru, an AT&T, or any number of Wall Street's success stories and you'd ensure yourself a healthy retirement (not to mention an attentive cocktail party audience).

Stock picking is a little like marriage.

Stock picking is a little like marriage. Sure you can get divorced (sell) at any time, but you really want to find a person (stock) you can stick with for the long haul. One that has a bright future.

 ## Secret #37 in a Nutshell

Start with companies you already do business with. Screen through them using your own judgment of their potential and your own opinions of their products. Monopolies and brand names are often good buys, as are stocks that have been beaten down by bad news. Don't invest in something you don't understand. Pretend you're buying the whole company. Buy only as many stocks as you can watch.

stock up

Part Two—The Numbers

A statistician is someone who can draw a
straight line from an unwarranted assumption to a foregone conclusion.

—ANONYMOUS

Why It Works

The second half of any successful stock pick is in the numbers. The
reasoning process is an easy way to find out which companies *should*
be making money; the numbers will show you which companies actually are.

How It Works

Hopefully the last secret helped you weed out the losers. Now we're
going to cut your list down a bit more to find the winners. I'm going
to point out the key numbers used to analyze a company and give
you an idea of whether you want these numbers to be high or low,
going up or going down.

All the numbers I talk about here can be found in a company's *annual report* or *research report*. But forget annual reports. They are written by the directors of the company, who are eager to get you to buy their stock. Plus, you'll have to do any math calculations on your own. Much easier is the research report, written by an independent monitoring company like Standard & Poor's or Value Line. Research reports pack all the info you need on one page. Plus, they do the math for you. You can get research reports fo' free from your broker, from the internet, or from your local library.

So you got your research report. Basically, when examining any company, you want to ask yourself three questions:
1. Can I buy the company (or shares in the company) at a good price?
2. Does this company make a lot of money? Is it profitable?
3. Is this company financially stable? (Does it have a little debt or a lotta debt?)

I'll start with question number one. How do you tell if a stock is a bargain? By no means is there one and only one way of answering this question, but four numbers to look for are:

Earnings Per Share (EPS). This is the company's net revenue (a.k.a. profit) divided by the number of outstanding shares. EPS is helpful when you put it on a timeline. A rising EPS often means the company is increasing its profits.
P/E ratio. This is the *price to earnings ratio*. To find it (and it is usually calculated for you), simply divide the stock's price by its earnings per share (EPS) in the last twelve months. If the price of a company is $50 per share and the EPS is $5 per share, then the P/E ratio is ten. Typically, the lower the P/E, the better.

While the P/E ratio won't tell you everything, it is a simple way to spot an overpriced stock. A high P/E means that the company is not earning much money compared to its price. Avoid companies with extremely high P/Es—the online auctioneer Ebay once had a P/E of over two thousand—as it is most likely a signal that the stock has been bid up to a price over and above what it is worth. Many investors could have avoided getting burned in the internet technology crash if they paid a bit more attention to P/E ratios.

P/S ratio. This is the *price to sales ratio*. This is the company's stock price divided by sales per share over the past year. If the P/S ratio is high, that likely means the shares are expensive and the company is not selling a lot of its product. Like the P/E ratio, the lower this number, the better.

Price to book value. This is the company's stock price divided by its book value per share. *Book value* is the number you get when you subtract a company's liabilities from its assets. It's just like your net worth. The lower the price to book value, the better. This means a company has a lot of assets compared to its price. This means that if the company were to dissolve tomorrow it could sell its assets for cash which it could pass on to investors.

You have to be careful when looking at book value. When I asked you to figure out your own net worth, I didn't let you include everything. I suggested you leave out CDs, clothes, cars, and the like and only write in assets that were likely to go up in value. But when companies calculate their net worth, or book value, they can include a lot more. For instance, imagine your company is in a building that has a one-of-a-kind self-cleaning, solar-powered toilet signed by Tom Hanks and worth over $2 million. This doesn't help the company make any money, yet it could show up in the calculations as a $2 million asset. Conversely, suppose a bio-tech company had Albert Einstein's long-lost twin brother, Manuel, working for them. This undiscovered genius would not show up on the books either, even though his mind is invaluable to the company. Remember that the price to book value ratio is just one of many numbers you will be looking at.

One big-picture concept to remember is that price is relative. The actual price of the company means nothing. A stock selling for $200 could be a great bargain, while a stock selling for 34 cents might be way overpriced. What we're looking for here is *value*. How much the company is actually worth, compared to its price. That's why we use ratios to help us determine if the price is high or low.

One big-picture concept to remember is that price is relative. The actual price of the company means nothing.

Okay, so now you've gotten a quick fix on price. Let's try to answer question two. Does this company make a lot of money? To figure that out, look for:

Return on equity (ROE). The higher this number, the better. ROE measures a company's profitability. The higher the ROE, the more profitable the company. Find it by dividing net income by *shareholder equity*. What's shareholder equity? That's just the company's net worth. Just like your net worth, it's the difference between company assets and company liabilities.

Return on sales. Da higha, Da betta. Companies make money by selling goods and services at a *profit*. In other words, they sell things for more than it cost them to create those things. The return on sales ratio gives you a glimpse of how much profit a company is earning on the stuff it sells. To calculate this ratio, divide a company's net income (its profit) by its sales revenue. If you mowed your neighbor's lawn for $100, that $100 is your sales revenue. But imagine you had to rent a mower for $65 for the day, plus you paid $5 in gas. Your profit is $30 ($100 in sales minus the $70 you spent for gas and rental of the mower).

So your return on sales would be 30% ($30 in profit divided by $100 in sales).

Return on assets. To find this number, divide net income by total assets. Normally, the higher the ROA, the better. ROA helps you determine how well a company is doing with the stuff it's got—its assets. Sticking with the lawnmower theme, let's pretend you own the lawnmower, and it's worth $200. That's the total assets (or asset since one mower is all ya got). You charge $100 per lawn and you spend $5 in gas. Your profit or net income is $95. Your return on assets is 47% ($95 or your net income divided by $200 your total assets). At 47%, you're making pretty good use of that asset. But suppose you spent $5,000 to buy the Red November, the world's first Magneto Hydro Propulsion Lawnmower. If you still charged $100 a lawn, your ROA would be a lousy 2% ($95 or your net income divided by $5,000 your total assets). You did not employ your assets very well. Like every other number, ROA varies greatly between industries.

You invest a lot in a relationship (a lot of time, a lot of love, a lot of whatever) and you expect a lot in return. Stocks are the same.

Typically, the higher these return numbers are, the better. An easy way to remember return is to think about a relationship. You invest a lot in a relationship (a lot of time, a lot of love, a lot of whatever) and you expect a lot in return. Stocks are the same. You invest your money and you expect a lot in return for the investment of your money.

The only thing left to answer now is, is the company financially stable? Can it pay its bills? Can the company survive if the economy slows down? Here are some numbers to look for.

Cash and cash equivalents. This is basically how much money a company has in cash or in investments that can easily be converted to cash. If a company has lots of cash, then it can protect itself from unexpected downturns in the economy. If you had $1 million in cash in the bank, would you be worried if you were fired from your job? But if you had $1 in cash in the bank, wouldn't you be terrified if you lost your job?

Liabilities. Liabilities are a company's debt. *Current liabilities* is money the company must pay back in less than one year. *Long-term liabilities* are liabilities due after a year or more. Debt is not such a bad thing, but the company better make a lot of money to justify the debt. Rising debt and shrinking sales are a bad sign. If a company has no debt, it cannot go bankrupt; if a company has a lot of debt, it may be in trouble if the economy slows down since, like you, even if you're laid off, you still have to make those credit card payments.

Be careful of companies with debt to equity ratios above one. Likewise, be careful when your debt to equity ratio goes above one.

Debt to equity ratio. Of course comparing actual debt dollar amounts is pointless. $1 million of debt is nothing to a billion dollar company, but it is a frightening amount for your lemonade stand. So a good way to get an apples-to-apples comparison is to use the *debt to equity ratio*. Remember, debt is what you owe, equity is what you own. To find the debt to equity ratio, divide the total liabilities by shareholder's equity. When the answer is high, that means the company has a lot of debt, compared to its equity. Why is this bad? Well think of your own financial situation. Wouldn't you be a little nervous if all you owned was a fading wardrobe of Abercrombie and Fitch currently valued at $800, yet you borrowed $2,000 on your credit card to buy that wardrobe? In this case, your debt to equity ratio would be a whopping 2.5! $2,000 (your debt) divided by $800 (your equity in clothing) is 2.5. Be careful of companies with debt to equity ratios above one. Likewise, be careful when *your* debt to equity ratio goes above one.

Current ratio. Quickly find this number by taking current assets and dividing by current liabilities. In general, the higher this number, the better. A high current ratio means a company can meet the obligations of its short-term debt. It means it can pay its bills. Once again, think of your personal life. If your current ratio was one, that would mean you would have $1 in cash (in a bank or money market account) for every $1 of debt due within a year. You're cutting it close. It would be better if you saved a little more and spent a little less to move your current ratio to two, which would mean you have $2 in cash for every $1 of debt due within a year.

Inventories. Ever go to buy a pair of shoes and just when you find the pair you like, you can't find your size? Sensing your frustration, the clerk shuffles up to you and offers to look "in the back" for your size. This room "in the back" is filled with *inventories*—the stuff the company is trying to sell. In the realm of shoes, inventories consist of Nike sneakers and all the materials used to make those sneakers, like leather and rubber. You need to be careful the company's products are not just sitting on shelves in warehouses. Remember that there's money tied up in those inventories, money that's not earning anything. Rising inventories are a problem if sales aren't rising with them. This means the company is making products that it cannot sell.

Acid test. This is a stricter version of the current ratio. The equation is current assets *minus* inventories divided by current liabilities. Here's where this is useful. Imagine if I owned a lemonade stand business valued at $100. But suppose that in that $100 value I included $40 worth of plastic promotional mugs printed with the logo "Year 2000 Celebration Mug." These mugs were a hot item during the millennium celebration, but now, they're just about worthless. The acid test won't let me count them in my calculations. To "pass the acid test," companies must

Rising inventories are a problem if sales aren't rising with them. This means the company is making products that it cannot sell.

Stock selection gets complicated because different companies have different needs.

have a one-to-one ratio. In other words, for every $1 in cur-
rent liabilities, the company has $1 of current assets minus
inventories.

Secret #38 at Work

If you've read this far, I bet mutual funds are starting to look better
by the word. But if you're still fixin' on stock pickin', let's sort all
these numbers out. Stock selection gets complicated because different companies have different needs. Some companies will need to
carry a lot of debt, just to operate, while others will have none. But
in general, here's what you're looking for:

- Always look at the same numbers from several companies that
  compete with the company you're thinking of buying. By doing
  this, you'll get an idea of what, on average, is typical for that industry and how your pick measures up. If the average P/E ratio
  for airline stocks is twenty and the company you picked has a
  P/E of fifty-one, you've got some explaining to do.
- The management is always a tough thing to evaluate—it's not
  like the CEO is going to meet with young investors like you and
  me. Even if she did, would she honestly tell us she just made a
  big mistake last week and we should take our money and run?*
  For a while, I searched for an easy way to evaluate management.
  Then I attended a seminar where money master Peter Lynch offered a wonderful way around this dilemma—just buy a simple
  company. As an example, Lynch mentioned he made a lot of
  money off Dunkin' Donuts, commenting that he never had to
  worry about the Japanese inventing a better donut. In other
  words, find a company that can be run by idiots, then you don't
  have to worry about management. Maybe that will be my next
  book, *The Complete Idiot's Guide to Buying Companies That Can
  Be Managed by Complete Idiots.*

* No, she wouldn't because that's insider trading and that's illegal.

- Rising earnings means that the company is either expanding, raising prices, selling more, cutting costs, or doing any combination of the four. All good things.
- When in doubt, draw a table. Here's a good one:

1. High Return on Equity High Debt to Equity	3. High Return on Equity Low Debt to Equity
2. Low Return on Equity High Debt to Equity	4. Low Return on Equity Low Debt to Equity

- Put the companies you're considering into one of the four squares. Each square represents possibilities. Some companies will have high returns on equity, and lots of debt (square 1). This might be a company like Ford Motor Company. Others will have low debt and low returns on equity (square 4). This might be a company like Disney.

  Find a company that can be run by idiots, then you don't have to worry about management.

- By looking at this chart you can see that square 3 is the place to be, because it represents companies that have a high return on equity, and low debt (companies that can make a lot of money and don't have to borrow a lot of money to do it). Microsoft is an example of a company that may be found in square 3.
- You can also see that square 2 ain't for you. You need to be careful when buying in square 2. Square 2 contains companies that don't make much money on their equity, and to make what little money they do, they need to borrow. General Motors might be an example of a company that falls into square 2.
- Be on the lookout for companies that reside in square 3 and beware of those the fall into square 2.*

---

* Keep in mind that things change. Who knows what debt Microsoft will take on tomorrow, or how high General Motors' return on equity will go. These companies are only examples of the current situation as I write this. These are by no means long-term benchmarks.

Finding the perfect stock is the same as finding the perfect companion—often you have to give something up. Yes, we're all searching for the good-looking, honest, rich, caring, funny, supportive person who owns a beach house. But that person can be rather difficult to find, so we have to take less of one thing for more of another. Admittedly, your boyfriend Fred ain't the sharpest knife in the drawer, but after years of being lied to, you're looking for an honest guy, and that's Fred. And true, Ashley isn't the most faithful of girlfriends, but you value your freedom as much as she values hers, so it becomes a good match.

Like the world of dating, stock selection is a matter of give and take and only time will tell who is right.

Stocks are no different. We're all looking for a cheap, simple, cash-rich company that makes a lot of money by selling a monopolylike brand-name product without borrowing any money to do it. But rarely does a company offer everything you want. You'll probably have to give something up. You might trade a high P/E ratio (basically an expensive stock) for a high return on equity (a sign that the company is likely to make a lot of money). Or you might buy a low P/E ratio knowing that company is about to undergo a major lawsuit. Will they win? You happen to think so, and that's why you've bought the stock. Others, those who sold all their shares once the lawsuit was announced, believe the company is likely to lose, and that's why they got out.

Like the world of dating, stock selection is a matter of give and take and only time will tell who is right. But, unlike the world of dating, there is a way around stock selection—the index mutual fund. That brings me to *the most important sentence in this book:*

The best advice I, or any other financial advisor, can give you is to invest in a tax-favored retirement account via no load index mutual funds.

Did I convince you? No? Okay. Meet me halfway. Invest the bulk of your bread in index mutual funds. Then sink a small amount of cash into an online brokerage account and trade stocks. This is what I do. This is your computerized casino. Good luck.

Secret #38 in a Nutshell

You want a company with little debt (low liabilities) that makes a lot of money, high return on equity, high return on assets, and high return on sales. Lots of cash is good, so are rising earnings. Compare several companies within the same industry to get an idea of going rates. When you buy, you may have to give up one thing to get more of another.

be careful if you go clubbin'

There is no easy way from the earth to the stars.

—SENECA

Why It Works

"It's official," writes Chuck Carlson in his book *60-Second Investor*. "There are more investment clubs than there are people in China." The popularity of investment clubs is on the rise. But investment clubs can create problems. For one, money, friendship, and business are all buzzing about in the same room, which can lead to problems. But the even greater picture is that you should not even bother with investment clubs until your credit card debt is dead, your insurance is up to par, and you have funded your retirement accounts. Still, as the popularity of these clubs climbs, it is important to learn a little about their good and bad qualities.

How It Works

There are basically two types of investment clubs: those with money and those without money. An investment club with money means the club members have pooled their money into one account. Once a month (or once a whatever), everyone gets together to discuss the stocks they researched. At the end of the meeting, the members vote on what to do with the cash and stocks in the club's account. Should they sell their Home Depot stock? Should they buy more Hewlett-Packard?

Clubs without money meet on a regular basis, but it is up to individual investors how they will invest their own money. They can take all or none of the recommendations from the club.

> *Investment clubs are good for spreading the research over several people.*

Secret #39 at Work

Human beings are social creatures, so it's no wonder why these clubs are so popular. And how good would you feel if your club voted to buy the stock *you* recommended? Even better, wouldn't it be great if that stock went through the roof and you made everyone in the club a ton of money?

Of course you can guess what I'm going to say next. Imagine a dim-witted but verbally persuasive club member named Al. Al has been pushing to buy stock in a butter company. What if your club voted against your stock and instead bought Al's? Even worse, what if Al's butter company stock (poor Al confused profit margin for profit *margarine*) totally crashes? You trusted your money to a group that voted against you in a decision that lost you money.

My advice on investment clubs is this: use them for what they're good for and don't use them for what they're not good for. Investment clubs are good for spreading the research over several people. They're a good sounding board for ideas. They're even a bit of a social event.

What they're not good for is protecting your money from taxes, increasing your chances of financial aid, or paying off your credit card.

By all means, join an investment club. You can research stocks, listen to the picks of others, even socialize without forking over any money. If the club won't let you join without contributing money, then start your own, nonmoney club. Check out the National Association of Investors Corporation (NAIC) at www.betterinvesting.org. They have information about starting your own investment club.

Secret #39 in a Nutshell

People can contribute money or information or both to an investment club. A club is a great place to share information, but it doesn't make much sense to share money. Consider contacting the NAIC if you want to start your own club.

buy all the time

Why It Works

 You could make a fortune in the stock market if only you could be certain which stocks would shoot up in value. But we've already discussed that this is very diffi- cult. A way around this dilemma is to buy an index mutual fund, which is a way to buy every stock. Simple enough. But *when* do you buy shares in the index mu- tual fund? I mean, you could make a fortune if only you knew ex- actly when to buy. But, as you can probably guess, deciding when to buy is even more difficult than deciding what to buy. The good news is there is a way around this.

Our strategy for deciding what to buy is simply to buy every- thing. Why not use the same strategy in deciding when to buy? Why not buy all the time? If you use *dollar cost averaging*, you make a lot of money by buying all the time.

How It Works

Dollar cost averaging (DCA) is the only way to ensure you buy less when the market is high and more when the market is down. DCA simply means that you invest the same amount of money on some predetermined regular schedule—for example, on the first of every month—regardless of whether the market is up or down. You do this month after month, year after year. The idea is that over the long term, you'll buy more shares at lower prices, because whenever the market is down, you'll automatically buy more with the same amount of money.

To begin dollar cost averaging, simply sink a chunk of each paycheck (hopefully 10%) into the market. This is easy for scheduling, since your paychecks fall on the same days of every month.

Paycheck not big enough? No problem, just invest 10% of three paychecks, or invest four times a year on the same days every year. That's it.

To begin dollar cost averaging, simply sink a chunk of each paycheck (hopefully 10%) into the market.

If you follow my advice and stick with index mutual funds, dollar cost averaging is easy. But if you are picking your own stocks, the process is a bit more difficult. For individual stock selectors, I recommend dollar cost averaging quarterly rather than monthly. Unless you are investing several hundred dollars every month, you just won't have enough money to spread out your investment evenly over all your stocks. So let your cash build up and invest four times each year using the same times every year.

*Yeah, yeah, yeah Pete, but this time I **know** the stock is a bargain. I'm gonna sink all my money in at once when the price is cheap.* Ahhh, the temptation to time the market is unrelenting. Even if you do find a good buy, with so much money on the line, you may wait to see if it goes lower. During this time, the stock may go up again. (Then you're really pissed.) Or suppose the day after you buy the stock, the price goes down even further? Now you have no cash to take advantage of the even greater savings. You're stuck.

Secret #40 at Work

Imagine you wanted to invest in a defense company called Pachelbel's Canon Corporation, which is selling for $10 a share on January 1.

That year, you have set aside $1,200 to invest. If you purchased $1,200 worth of Pachelbel's Canon Corporation on January 1, for that year you would have 120 shares. Now compare to what might have happened if you had used dollar cost averaging and purchased $100 worth of Pachelbel's Canon Corporation shares every month of the year:

The Benefits of Buying All the Time

Month	Price Per Share	Shares Bought*	Amount Spent
January	$10.00	10	$100.00
February	$12.00	8.3	$100.00
March	$12.00	8.3	$100.00
April	$15.00	6.6	$100.00
May	$15.00	6.6	$100.00
June	$20.00	5	$100.00
July	$15.00	6.6	$100.00
August	$10.00	10	$100.00
September	$8.00	12.5	$100.00
October	$5.00	20	$100.00
November	$5.00	20	$100.00
December	$8.00	12.5	$100.00
Total	$135.00	126.4	$1,200.00

Average Number of Shares Purchased Per Month: 10.53
Average Price Per Share: $11.25
(Now here's where it gets cool.)
Average Price <u>Paid</u> Per Share: $9.50

With lump sum investing, you paid $10 per share and bought 120 shares for $1,200. With dollar cost averaging, for the same amount of money, you bought 126.4 shares. You bought more shares when the price was low (during months like September, October, November, and December) and you bought fewer shares when the price was high (during the months February through July).

* For the sake of comparison, I'm assuming here that you can buy partial shares. Even if this was not allowed, dollar cost averaging still forces you to buy more shares when the price is low and fewer shares when the price is high. Who can argue with that?

Because you bought fewer in the high months and more in the low months, you snagged 126.4 shares for $1,200. You paid about $9.50 per share, or 50 cents less than the $10 per share you would have paid with lump sum investing. And *notice*, you did this when the average share price over the course of the year was $11.25 and the price per share was higher than $10 for half the year! It only dipped below $10 for four months. Because of dollar cost averaging, you were forced to discount shop. Even though prices were higher, it didn't matter because you simply bought fewer shares. And this time I let the lump sum investor get off easy. How bad would the lump sum investor feel if they had bought everything in June when the price per share was $20?

The trouble is no one knows for sure when these highs and lows are going to happen. The only way to be sure you never pay too much for a stock is to use dollar cost averaging.

It's quite common for stocks to lose 30% or more of their value over the course of a year. Look through the financial section of your newspaper. Look at the fifty-two-week highs and lows of stocks. You'll see the numbers vary drastically. The trouble is no one knows for sure when these highs and lows are going to happen. The only way to be sure you never pay too much for a stock is to use dollar cost averaging.

Secret #40 in a Nutshell

Dollar cost averaging is the easiest way to be sure you buy more shares when prices are low and fewer shares when prices are high. Simply invest the same amount of money on the same day every month or every quarter. When prices are low, your money will buy more shares. When prices are high, your money will buy fewer shares.

avoid the pitfalls

Those who are of the opinion that money will do everything may very well be suspected to do everything for money.

—SIR GEORGE SAVILE

Why It Works

Ladies and Gentlemen, I present to you three of the most popular ways to lose money in the investment world—options, commodities and short selling. Investing in these is like smoking at the gas station. They are all short-term investments that bet on short-term price fluctuations. They're sexy, just like that girl in the movie *Species*, but they're dangerous, just like that girl in the movie *Species*. Please avoid the investments discussed in this secret. I take this chapter to describe them because the investment community peddles them quite viciously and I don't want you to lose your shirt.

How It Works

For young investors like you and me, our greatest advantage lies in our youth. Compound interest is doubling our money year after year. We're consistently buying more shares when the market is low and less when the market is high. Therefore, any investment bound by a short time limit is an investment that robs us of our most precious advantage. If you're buying and selling every six months, you're on the same playing field with a ninety-nine-year-old woman looking at stock charts and waiting for Willard Scott to announce her birthday on the *Today Show*. Here are the reasons why you should steer clear of the above mentioned short term investments.

Options. Options are rights to buy or sell stocks at predetermined prices within a given period of time. When you own an option, you do not own the stock itself, you simply own the right to purchase or sell the stock. Remember, in an option deal, the broker makes money regardless of outcome, while either the buyer or seller must lose. When you buy options (or rather, when you *don't* buy options), you can buy *puts*, which are rights to sell a stock at a specific price. With puts, you're betting—hoping and praying—that the price of the stock will go down. When you buy *calls*—the rights to buy stock at a specified price—you're betting, hoping, and praying that the price of the stock will go up. An easy way to remember this is *put* your foot *down* and *call* your friend *up*.

Please avoid the investments discussed in this secret. I take this chapter to describe them because the investment community peddles them quite viciously and I don't want you to lose your shirt.

Imagine you have a call option on a Mongolian cement company called Genghis Khan-crete at $100 that expires six months from today. This means that you have the right to buy a hundred shares of Genghis Khan-crete at $100 per share anytime within the next six months. The price of the option will depend on Genghis Khan-crete's current price, but let's assume this option is selling for $2 per share, a total of $200. Because you have a call option, you're hoping the price of Genghis Khan-crete will go up. If Genghis Khan-crete shoots up to $150 per share, your option is *in the money* because everyone else has to buy the shares at $150 and you have the right to buy the shares at $100. If, however, the price drops to $80 a share, your option is *out of the money* because what good is the right to buy an $80 stock for $100?

People buy options because they can control a lot of money using very little of their *own* money. To buy a hundred shares of Genghis Khan-crete for $100 a share would cost $10,000. To buy the right to control those hundred shares could cost maybe $200 (plus commissions). If you buy the stock for $100 and it shoots to $150, you've made $5,000 or a 50% return (excluding taxes and commissions). If, on the other hand, you owned the option and the stock goes to $150, your option is worth $5,000. That's a 2,500% return on your original investment of $200 (excluding taxes and commissions).

All the phone calls in the world to the Psychic Friends Network won't help you predict short-term fluctuations in the market.

Sounds like a cool idea, but all the phone calls in the world to the Psychic Friends Network won't help you predict short-term fluctuations in the market. Remember, your option is only good for six months. If Genghis Khan-crete goes down in value or doesn't move, you lose all your money.

Commodities. A commodity is anything that comes out of the ground—cattle, corn, oil, gold. You get the picture. Randolph and Mortimer lost their fortunes trading commodities in the movie *Trading Places*. Bryan Brown's character suffered the same fate in the movie *Cocktail*. Commodity investing isn't investing at all—it's gambling. (Although in the financial world, this gambling is called *speculating*. Same difference.) You're betting on the temperament of Mother Nature. Big mistake— remember *Jurassic Park*? Those scientists bet they could manipulate nature and turn it into a theme park. What a mess that turned out to be. The only thing worse than investing in commodities is investing in a ticket to *The Lost World*.

Commodities are traded via *futures contracts*. Futures contracts are agreements to buy or sell commodities at a specific price at a specific time. But unlike options, which are the *right* to buy or sell, futures contracts are an *agreement* to buy or sell. They're a legal contract, which you must adhere to. The idea is that you'll buy a contract and then sell your contract to a real buyer, like a health food company, at a profit, before it expires. Otherwise—and I mean this literally—you will have to buy and take delivery of the commodity. Imagine one thousand of bushels of soybeans in your apartment!

Commodity investing isn't investing at all—it's gambling.

You cannot predict what Mother Nature is going to do and since commodity prices are dependent almost entirely on Mother Nature's mood, you're going to lose. Unless you know a good rain dance to conjure up, stay away from commodities. **Short selling.** Short selling (or shorting) sounds cool, but it isn't. You've heard the investment advice "buy low and sell high." Well, shorting is just selling high and then buying low. People short a stock when they think a stock is going to go down. Imagine a coffee company that prints legal advice on all its packaging. The company, called Grounds for Dismissal, just lost a major lawsuit, because one piece of legal advice printed on their packaging was inaccurate. So you think the share price of Grounds for Dismissal is going to go down. To conduct a short sale, you inform your broker you want to sell *short* a hundred shares of Grounds for Dismissal Corporation at $10 per share, a total of $1,000. You are now required to repay your broker with a hundred shares of Grounds for Dismissal Corporation, *not* $1,000 in cash. Remember, you believed the stock was going to go down in value. If the price drops suddenly to $5 per share, you can now repay your broker by spending $500 to buy the hundred shares at $5 per share. You get to keep the profit of $500. You have sold high and then bought low.

The trouble with shorting is that it is one of the few investments with *unlimited* risk. If the stock goes up in value, then who knows how much it will cost you to replace the shares you sold? During the dot com boom, I drove myself nuts resisting the temptation to short a few of the dismal dot coms. Luckily I saved myself from shorting any of these stocks. How did I do it? I recognized one simple fact. I knew that certain dot com companies had to come crashing down—with P/E ratios in the hundreds, even thousands, something had to give. The trouble is, even though I knew certain companies would come crashing down, *I had no idea **when** they would come crashing down.* Imagine the heart trouble I would have if I had shorted Amazon.com near the end of 1998 only to see it soar to in 1999. What amount of Pepto-Bismol could carry me through till 2001 to see it drop back down again?

Stay away from short selling. Even if you're right, you don't know when you'll be right.

Stay away from short selling. Even if you're right, you don't know *when* you'll be right.

Secret #41 at Work

 If a broker or investment advisor suggests that you buy options or commodities, or recommends short selling, tell him he's fired. They make no sense for young investors (or anyone for that matter). Even if they give you the sweet sell, "Oh, you know that because of the holiday season toy stocks are going to go up in value," don't buy it. No one knows for sure.

Don't be conned by the term "limited risk."

And don't be conned by the term "limited risk." Often times with these investments, you fork over $1,000 in cash but you may be on the hook for $3,000 if things don't go well. Limited risk simply means that you can lose only the money you invested.

Sounds nice, but make no mistake, you can still lose everything you invested.

If you like to gamble, go to Vegas. You'll lose all your money but you'll at least get loaded on Sin City's free drinks. You may even run into Wayne Newton—but that's a different gamble altogether.

 Secret #41 in a Nutshell
Options, commodities, and short selling are all short-term investments. Investing in these robs us of every advantage our youth offers. The only advantage your youth provides with regard to these investments is your ability to survive a mild heart attack.

forget everything else

Art is making something out of nothing and selling it.

—FRANK ZAPPA

Why It Works

There are nearly an unlimited amount of things you can invest in, but by and large, I want you to forget about them. Sure, there may be some investment out there that I haven't covered that will make you a fortune. But since you don't know what that investment is, and neither do I, let's not worry about the unknown. This book has laid the groundwork for you to begin a healthy financial life. It's by no means a stairway to heaven, but it is a rope ladder. Keep climbing, you'll get there.

How It Works

But the act of searching for that stairway to heaven is as popular as the song itself. I respect that. If it's of any help, however, below is a list of stairways that *do not* lead to heaven:

> *This book has laid the groundwork for you to begin a healthy financial life. It's by no means a stairway to heaven, but it is a rope ladder. Keep climbing, you'll get there.*

- Art. If you buy it at an auction, it's been marked up with heavy commissions. Even if you get a good deal, you'll have to pay to insure it. If it skyrockets in value, you'll have to find someone nutty enough to buy it off you while paying the auctioneer another hefty commission.
- Annuities. An annuity is like a tax-free mutual fund. The trouble with them is that they usually carry some pretty heavy commissions. Compared to an index mutual fund bought inside a Roth IRA, annuities don't look so hot. I bet someone, someday will approach you to buy an annuity. Don't bother. The stuff we already talked about is the better deal.
- Collectibles/memorabilia (For example, comics, baseball cards, autographs, Ben Affleck's socks). You have to store them, insure them, and even if you get lucky and buy a $25,000 comic book for a buck, name me five people you know that can pay $25,000 for a comic book. I'm not saying don't collect comic books and baseball cards. I'm just trying to clear up the misconception that comics, cards, and other collectibles are a way to make money. Collecting is an enjoyable hobby, not an investing scheme.

Hey, Pete, what about converting my money to foreign currency? The only time you should cash in your U.S. dollars for foreign currency is when the cab driver in Paris will take nothing else.

- Business opportunities sent through the mail are an excellent way to lose money. So are those opportunities pitched through a cold call.

- Oil-drilling operations are an expensive, risky, large minimum investment. Actually, forget mining operations of any kind, whether it's gold, diamonds, copper, or uranium. Typically, younger people don't get pitched these investments because we don't make enough money to overcome the minimum investment. But someday, when that brochure so glossy it could double as a mirror lands on your desk, you'll know to chuck it right into the recycle bin.

- Gold is for records that sell well. So is platinum. Precious metals need to be insured so they're a drain on your wallet. If you have some gold coins, don't sell them, but there's no need to buy anymore. Your money is better off in stocks.

- If you loan money to friends, you're apt to lose both. Think about it, you can't win either way—you either lose all your money, which sucks, or you make a lot of money off your poor friend.

- Lottery tickets are a tax on the mathematically challenged. (But I admit, when the Powerball or the Big Game breaks $100 million, I buy a ticket. Who knows?) Can't kick the gambling habit? Check out www.luckysurf.com. It's a free internet lottery.

- We already went over Vegas and Wayne Newton.

- Forget penny stocks. No, these aren't stocks that sell for a penny. These are stocks issued at cheap prices and often trading at less than $5 per share. While not every stock under $5 is bad (heck the mighty Chrysler once dipped below $5), often penny stocks consist of extremely volatile companies with flimsy financials. Be careful.

- You won't get loaded investing in wine. You can easily get loaded by drinking it. If you do drink a lot of wine, a wine cellar may be a good investment. It will allow you to buy wine by the case, which will result in significant savings over your drinking career.

Secret #43 at Work

If you do run into something I haven't thought of, and you probably will, you do have the information to properly screen any investment.

Okay, so, Bert and Pattie want you to invest in their pizza parlor. But what do you know about pizza? (Besides no anchovies.) Even if you do know more about pizza than the rest of us, ask yourself, what is the minimum investment/liquidity/risk/reward/control and how does it stack up to the other investments recommended in this book? From pizza parlors to pearls to plutonium, common sense in addition to the measuring sticks discussed in this book can prevent you from losing thousands over a lifetime.

 Secret #42 in a Nutshell
Stocks, bonds, real estate, education, and money market accounts are here to help you reach your goals. Comics, art, wine, and Beanie Babies *are* your goals.

---

know when to sell

Let's just be friends.

—SOMETHING WE'VE ALL HEARD

Why It Works

By now, you know the best time to buy is *all the time*. Using dollar cost averaging, you're buying a little every month. That's easy. But when do you get rid of it? That's the tricky part. Often people either hold on too long only to watch the fortune they made dissolve into nothing, or they sell too early, only to watch the fortune they could have had soar to the heavens. Either way, they're pissed off.

When you know when to sell an investment, you'll enjoy not only more money, but more happiness. You won't curse yourself for selling too late nor will you have to endure the pain of watching your neighbors amass a mountain of riches because you pulled out early.

How It Works

Knowing when to sell is easy—just think about dating. If you don't date, consult a friend who dates a lot. If you don't have any friends who date, rent one of those cheesy romantic comedies on dating. If you can't get to a video store, then you've either been living on the moon, or you've got a parole hearing coming up. Either case, I can't help you.

Anyway, imagine you date someone for three months. And it's the greatest three months of your life. So, do you break up just in case the next three months aren't as good? No! Think about why you break up with someone. You break up because *the reasons why you originally got into the relationship are no longer there.* Suppose you enter a relationship because your partner is good looking, wealthy, and honest. Two years later, your partner is overweight, bankrupt, and telling lies. Now it's time to get out because the reasons you originally got into the relationship are now gone. Same thing with investments. When the investment you bought is no longer fulfilling the reasons why you bought it (be that steady income, a low price to earnings ratio, and so on), sell.

> **When the investment you bought is no longer fulfilling the reasons why you bought it (be that steady income, a low price to earnings ratio, and so on), sell.**

Don't sell simply because the stock has doubled. How can you be certain it won't triple without looking at the numbers? Or if you sell because the stock is in the dumps, how do you know it's not the perfect time to buy?

We've looked at investing in stocks, bonds, and mutual funds. Soon we'll get to investing in your own home and your own business. Regardless, before you sell any investment, keep the following ideas in mind:

1. **You should sell an investment when it has outlived your reasons for buying it.** If you bought McDonald's thinking it would expand into ten new foreign countries, sell it when it has done so. If you bought an undervalued stock for $20 a share and you thought it was worth $80 a share, sell it when it hits $80. Obviously, you can't cast aside common sense here. Sure Mickey D's is now operating in those ten countries, but where else can the Golden Arches be planted? Can it grow anymore? And about that $20 stock that went to $80. Before you

cash out, review the numbers to determine if it is going to go to $100.*

2. **You should sell an investment when it complements your goals or a shift in your portfolio.** As retirement approaches, so does the need to start moving money out of the stock market. You've had growth, now you want to live off the income of your fortune. Or suppose you invested in a stock as a way to save for a large expense, such as the down payment on a house. It's time to buy your dream home and time to make a portfolio shift, from stocks to real estate.

Mind you, if an investment complements your goals, the usual timelines can be scrapped. Imagine you bought $1,000 worth of the O Town Real Estate Holding Company as a way to save for a new car that you wanted to buy five years down the road. But in two months your O Town stock is worth $12,000. It's time to sell out O Town, take the $12,000 and put it somewhere super safe, like in a money market account or Treasury Bills. Remember you should buy stocks with the *plan* that you'll hold onto them for the long term. By no means must you hold onto stocks for five years. If your plan comes together sooner, sell the stocks and put the money where it's readily available.

3. **You should sell to rebalance your portfolio.** *Rebalancing* is the act of selling one investment of your portfolio that has increased considerably in value, moving the profits from this sale into the other investments in your portfolio. Imagine you own three stocks (very dangerous, but this is just an example). Let's pretend you own $1,000 worth of Coke, $1,000 worth of Disney, and $1,000 of General Motors. After a year, the Coke stock is worth about $980, the General Motors stock is worth $1,100, but after the surprising success of their new movie, *The Lion King versus the Little Mermaid*, Disney's stock soared to $4,300. It's time now to take some of those profits from Disney and put them into the other investments. You could sell $2,000 worth

---

* Much easier said than done of course. But a quick glance at the stock report and its numbers—P/E, ROE, and so on—can help.

of Disney, and put $1,000 into Coke and $1,000 into General Motors. Rebalancing would have saved many people from the dot com crash. If they had taken some of the huge profits they had made in Amazon.com, Ebay, and Cysco, and transferred it into some of the overlooked stocks (perhaps a Philip Morris or, for those who did *really* well, a Berkshire Hathaway*), the crash might not have been so painful. Or you might take some money out of a roaring NASDAQ index fund and put it into a foreign stock index fund, or money out of stocks to put into bonds or real estate.

The problem with rebalancing is just when you really should do it, you probably won't.

 Hey Pete, how often should I rebalance? Remember that every time you sell, you will pay a commission and maybe taxes, so keep it to a minimum. And your profits should be big enough to justify these commissions and taxes.

Rebalancing is a tough one to a put on a timeline. Who knows when the market will hit new highs and lows? In Secret #45, I suggest reviewing your investments every three months. If you've picked up a real winner you'll probably notice it in this three month review and you'll have to decide if rebalancing is in order.

The problem with rebalancing is just when you really should do it, you probably won't. When someone has what they think is a winner, it's tough to convince them to let go of some of it. If you bought a stock at $15 and now it's worth $85 (and climbing), you're not going to listen to me. You'll be out yacht shopping. Still, when you are making big bucks in the market, I hope this little reminder about rebalancing will pop into your head, maybe when you're trying on Rolex watches. ("The silver one balances on my arm much better. Wait a minute. Balance. That reminds me. I gotta call my broker.")

---

* One share of Berkshire Hathaway currently sells for about $70,000. Not a typo. One share. $70,000.

If it's of any help, here is a short list of recycle bin reasons why you *shouldn't* sell:

1. Because the price is high (it may go higher). Feel free to sell some of the investment to rebalance. In fact, feel free to sell all of it but *only after you have done your research.* Just because the price is high doesn't mean you should get rid of it. Remember, price means nothing; it's value we're after.

2. Because the price is low. It may go higher and it may be a great time to buy more at a discount.

3. Because you need the money. Use the three months of emergency cash you were *supposed* to put in your money market account. You did do that . . . didn't you?

4. Because you *think* the economy is going to do something.

5. Because your inner voice says so. I've never met my inner voice, but when it comes to money, I think my inner voice has horns and a pitchfork. I'd much rather focus on my research and my goals.

> *I've never met my inner voice, but when it comes to money, I think my inner voice has horns and a pitchfork.*

6. Because of the election, or the end of a decade, or because Bill Gates is taking Viagra. True, all of these could have an effect on the market, but no one knows what that effect will be or when it will happen.

Hey Pete, what about the tax angle? Is there a better time to sell for tax purposes? In most cases, you can subtract investment losses from investment profits to ease your tax bill. But don't sell just for the tax write-off. Stick with the three rules. Also, if you sell a stock that you've held less than a year, the taxes on that sale will be higher than one you held more than a year. If the stock lies inside a tax-deferred account, such as an IRA or 401k, taxes make no difference.

Secret #43 at Work

For young investors like you and me, there should not be a lot of selling going on. We're trying to build a fortune, not take quick commission-beaten, tax-eaten profits. Even if we're talking inside a tax-deferred account, selling should be kept to a minimum.

Secret #43 in a Nutshell

Every time you sell, you stand to pay a commission and taxes. There are exceptions of course, but in general, less selling is better. Sell when selling complements your goals, your reasons for buying an investment no longer exist, or when there is a clear need to rebalance. Otherwise, don't sell.

---

put it all together

Do not squander time, for that is the stuff
life is made of.

BENJAMIN FRANKLIN

Why It Works

It works because this is it. The big-picture chapter.
Listen up.

How It Works

First pay off your high-interest consumer debt. This is car loans,
credit cards, and any loans you may be paying on consumer products,
like refrigerators and stereo systems. Forget about everything—
home buying, retirement accounts, and stocks—until your high-
interest debt is dead. However, if your employer matches your
contributions to the company's retirement plan max out the matching part of the plan before doing anything else—even credit cards. If
you took out loans to pay for investments, such as a house or a college education, there's no need to pay these off. Just continue to pay
on time.

Be sure you have the proper insurance. Secret #17 can help. (No skipping disability!) You are your own best asset.

Cash is next. You need three months worth of living expenses in cash before you proceed. Ideally this money should be kept in your money market fund, but it doesn't really matter where you put it as long as it is not in your mattress and it is outside of retirement accounts.

Speaking of retirement accounts, they come next. Shave 10% right off the top of every paycheck and sink it into your employer-sponsored retirement plan, be it a 401k, 403b, Keogh, SEP, or SIMPLE. If you don't have one of these plans, that 10% (up to $3,000 a year) should go into a Roth IRA. This is long-term money, so that means you invest in stocks or stock mutual funds. At the end of this secret, I suggest some specific investments you should buy.

You need three months worth of living expenses in cash before you proceed.

By now you are more financially secure than 95% of all Americans. Congratulations!

Other than that, you should be:

- Systematically switching your traditional light-bulbs for compact fluorescents (and doing all the other money-saving tips you've learned).
- Investing outside your retirement account if there's money left over. Remember, one-year goals are funded by the money market account. One- to five-year goals are funded by bonds—preferably Treasuries. Over-five-year goals are funded by stocks or stock mutual funds.

If you're under twenty-one, treat yourself to some legal activity that gives you pleasure. If you're over twenty-one, treat yourself to a cold one. Whatever your age, you deserve it. You're not at the mercy of your creditors, or your boss, or anyone else for that matter. You can live life on your own terms. You're getting loaded.

Secret #44 at Work

Here are three rule-of-thumb portfolios for getting loaded:

The World's Easiest Investment Portfolio

- Three months' cash in a money market account. This account should not be in a retirement plan. This is money you need to be able to get at if an emergency arises. Wherever you set up your brokerage account is where your money market account should be.
- 10% of your paycheck into a retirement account. Divided like this:

  - Half the money invested in any index mutual fund that mirrors the performance of the Wilshire 5000 Index. Remember this index consists of small-, medium-, and large-sized companies.
  - The other half of the money invested in any index mutual fund that mirrors the performance of the Morgan Stanley EAFE Index. This is an index that tracks foreign stocks in Europe, Australasia, and the Far East. Several foreign markets have grown faster than the U.S. market, and an EAFE Index Fund is the cheapest way to take advantage of these foreign profits. Which fund? Pick the one with the lowest operating expenses.

- Try to put some money in a real estate mutual fund that diversifies over a large number of real estate investment trusts. As always, pick the fund with the lowest operating expenses. Lost? Try the Vanguard REIT Index Fund.
- Any leftover money you manage to save can be placed in treasury notes or treasury bills bought directly from the Federal Reserve or in your money market account. This will generate income for upcoming purchases, like tickets to the upcoming Dallas

Cowboys/Cleveland Browns Game, *The Phantom of the Opera*, or those given to you by the Los Angeles Police Department.

The World's Second Easiest Investment Portfolio

- Three months' cash in a money market account.
- 10% of your paycheck into a retirement account. Divided like this:

  - A third of your retirement money into an index mutual fund that mirrors Standard & Poor's 500 Index, an index of 500 large American companies.
  - A third of your retirement money in any mutual fund that mirrors the Morgan Stanley EAFE Index.
  - The final third of your retirement money in any fund that tracks the Russell 2000 Index. This is an index of small cap companies.

- Try to put some money in a real estate mutual fund that diversifies over a large number of real estate investment trusts.
- Any leftover money you manage to save can be placed in treasury notes or treasury bills bought directly from your local Federal Reserve or in your money market account. This will generate income for upcoming purchases.

Mr./Ms. Vegas Portfolio

- Three months' cash in a money market account.
- 10% of your paycheck into a retirement account.

  - Of that 10%, put 45% into any index mutual fund that mirrors the performance of the Wilshire 5000 Index.

- Put another 45% into any index mutual fund that mirrors the performance of the Morgan Stanley EAFE Index.
- So 90% of your money is in index mutual funds. The remaining 10%? Well that's yours, Ace. If you think you can beat the market averages, here's your chance to prove it. Please do your research and even though taxes don't matter (because this is a retirement account), please keep your trading to a minimum.

- Try to put some money in a real estate mutual fund that diversifies over a large number of real estate investment trusts. (This is starting to sound familiar.)
- Any leftover money you save can be split between T bills or T notes or put in your money market account.

 Hey Pete, my employer-sponsored retirement plan doesn't offer any mutual funds like the ones you recommend. What do I do?

First, don't panic. Regardless of what your company offers in its plan, you're trying to diversify by investing some money in small-sized companies, some money in medium-sized companies, some money in large-sized companies, and some money in foreign companies. Tell your plan administrator that your goal is to diversify over small, medium, large, and foreign.

This isn't all that tough. In fact it reminds me of a famous quote from *The Karate Kid*, "wax on, wax off." Remember that one?

For those of you who missed the film (where ya been?), Mr. Miyagi, the karate master, teaches Daniel, the hero, the martial arts using everyday movements. The arm motions you use to wax a car are the same arm motions you use to block a punch. (Hence, "wax on, wax off.") It's a great flick, and we all knew that Daniel would win in the end, but did you buy it? I mean the guy learned karate in like six weeks. Can wax on, wax off really get you that far? I didn't think so, so I decided to find out for myself.

Shortly after the film hit theaters, I enrolled in karate class, along with the rest of America. Turns out, the film is more accurate than I thought. My karate instructor (he was no Mr. Miyagi, but what can you do?) told me that martial arts is not about knowing a textbook of tricks. It's about being able to do a few simple moves perfectly. So the answer is yes, if you can get wax on, wax off down to a science, you can defend yourself quite well.

So it is with personal finance. You really need to do a few simple things over and over again. Selecting an index mutual fund portfolio couldn't be simpler. But how many people will actually discipline themselves to invest in that portfolio year after year? Wax on—get your paycheck. Wax off—invest 10% of it in index mutual funds. Wax on, wax off.

So it is with personal finance. You really need to do a few simple things over and over again.

If you can do that consistently, you will be able to live life on your own terms. Life will get easier. Think about how good it would feel to be thirty-nine and have $75,000 in a stock portfolio. The even better feeling is that in seven years, that money (assuming an easy 12% interest rate) doubles to over $160,000. Sure that's retirement money, not to be touched for many years, but life will be much easier knowing that it is there. If you want to tell your boss to go to hell, you have a three-month emergency reserve to back it up. If you want to venture into your own business, you have some financial support. Or if you want to take a year off to paint, write, sculpt, or surf, the decision will be a lot easier knowing you have no debt and that retirement is pretty much taken care of. Money, at a base, increases your options. If you take care of the big stuff, the little stuff will fall into place. This is *your* financial life. Find a portfolio that works for you and stick with it.

Okay, Pete—reality check. You do realize I just got laid off from an Internet Company and I've been doing temp work and waitressing on weekends. I have student loans weighing in at $148 dollars a month, credit card minimum payments of $70 a month, plus rent, food and all the usual expenses. I think it's gonna take me five years just to get out of credit card debt and save up this emergency cushion you're so adamant about. What the hell am I supposed to do?

How about get started? If you've read this far, you have forty-four secrets to help you get on the path to investing for retirement. I know you're temping now, and it's tough these days to get a job with just an undergraduate degree, but now that you know about the tax savings of the Lifetime Learning Credit maybe you can afford those part time computer courses that you need to get the job you really want. And that credit card debt, what's the interest rate? How about switching to one with a lower APR? You're out of school and your folks have an empty nest? Can you organize a yard sale? And remember chain reaction shopping. In the glory days of the dot coms, you might have made a salary that could withstand the rental payments of an apartment right in the city. But after you got laid off, you don't have the job, but you still have the high rental payments, which cause everything else in your life—groceries, movie tickets, and so on—to be more expensive. Hang in there though, because one buying decision can affect many others. Once your lease is up, grab a much cheaper place and watch nearly every expense on your budget decrease. And so what if it takes you eight years to pay off those student loans? Once those are paid off putting that $148 into an investment account should be no sweat. You've been writing a $148 check for the past eight years anyway. It's in your blood.

Money, at a base, increases your options.

This does not happen overnight. It probably doesn't even happen over a month. It may take several years to get your financial life in order. But get started because doing it now only makes it easier in the long run because of compound interest.

Secret #44 in a Nutshell

Pay off credit card debt. Properly insure yourself. Put three months of living expenses in a money market account. Invest in the S&P 500 Index, The Wilshire 5000 Index, the Morgan Stanley EAFE Index, and the Russell 2000 Index via no load index mutual funds. These investments should be inside a retirement account. Money for shorter-term goals should be in the money market or Treasuries. Adjust your portfolio to fit your personal goals. Wax on, wax off.

review

Nothing endures but change.

—HERACLITUS

Why It Works

Why do you go to see your doctor each year? Why do you call your boyfriend several times a week? Why do you take the "Chick Magnet" in for an oil change every 3,000 miles? All for the same reason. To be sure everything is cool.

If you just buy investments and never bother to review them, you'll soon find you ain't got no money.

Same deal with your investments. You want to be sure everything is cool. If you never go to the doctor, then you're gonna get sick. If you never call your boyfriend, then you guys are gonna break up. If you neglect the "Chick Magnet," you'll soon find it perched on cinder blocks. If you just buy investments and never bother to review them, you'll soon find you ain't got no money.

How It Works

Every three months, I want you to set aside a half hour for a financial checkup. I want you to do two simple things:

1. Grab some paper and a pen and write answers to these six basic financial checkup questions:

   - "Am I on track for my goals?"
   - "Am I overspending in any areas of my life?"
   - "What new opportunities are out there, and how can I take advantage of them?" I'm not talking hot stocks here. I mean stuff like savings opportunities and educational opportunities.
   - "Do these investments continue to support the reasons I had for buying them?"
   - "How am I doing?" How much did you save this month by wrapping your water heater in a pre-fab blanket? Any stores your consumer buying pool forgot to hit up?
   - "What can I do to better prepare for my financial future?"

   To answer these questions, you may have to do a little research. Perhaps you've gotten some junk mail offering you a new credit card with a lower interest rate. Is it worth it? Your research will tell.

2. Once you have your written answers, write a quick game plan to readjust your finances. For instance if you do find a better credit card, your plan might be to switch cards.

Secret #45 at Work

When it comes to review, my worry is not that people won't take the time to review. No, I worry that people will review *too* much. Now that we have the internet, we are all able to check our stocks two, three, even five times a *day*. I have seen many people do just that.

One big-picture thing to remember about the world of finance is that it is a world just like any other. As much as we wish to ignore this fact, logic, common sense, and sanity are just as important in finance as they are in any other part of your life. The main difference with the world of finance is that illogicalness, blatant stupidity, and insanity often go unpunished.

Here's what I'm getting at. If I check my stocks five times a day, I'm known as "guy who is into the market." However, if I check up on my *girlfriend* five times a day, I'm known as "guy who needs psychiatric counseling." But what's the difference? In both situations, I'm obsessing about something I cannot control. Unfortunately, there isn't any treatment program for me if I check up on my stocks five times a day. Fortunately, there is a treatment program for me if I check up on my girlfriend five times a day. It's called jail.

Remember that personal finance *is about financing your personal life*. It is *not* about personalizing your finances. You're trying to manage your money to create a lifestyle. You're not trying to create a lifestyle to manage money. As simple as it may seem, many people get this backward. Looking at your stocks five times a day is creating a lifestyle so you can manage your money.

You're trying to manage your money to create a lifestyle. You're not trying to create a lifestyle to manage money.

Secret #45 in a Nutshell

Review your finances and your goals every three months. Look for new opportunities in education, or savings. Write answers to the checkup questions to be sure you're on track for your goals. If you're a bit off track, make the necessary adjustments. Don't worry about your investments on a day-to-day basis.

last call

These last four secrets may seem unfair to you, since they're really more for my older readers. But it would be just as unfair to leave them out. Remember that one financial advantage of youth is that we haven't lost our money yet. Simply by skimming these secrets, you *can easily save yourself several thousand dollars.* Most people buy life insurance, then pick up a personal finance book to find out that they not only bought the wrong kind of life insurance, they also bought too little or too much. Even more people forego the drafting of a will. When the "Big Day" comes, their loved ones are left sitting in the courtroom trying to figure out what the word "intestate" means and why such a large chunk of the family fortune is being paid to some hotshot lawyer the family doesn't even know.

Why not do it the other way around? Find out what you need to know *before* you need to know it. You may not need life insurance right now, but someday you will. You might as well be prepared for it when the salesperson rings your doorbell.

mind your own business

Imagination is more important than knowledge.

—ALBERT EINSTEIN

Why It Works

It works because you're young. It works because you're creative. It works because you can afford to take more risks than people your parent's age. It works because you have control. It works because of the tremendous tax advantages. It works because if you love something, it isn't work at all. It works because if you truly believe in it, you won't let it fail.

I'm talking about starting your own business.

 Many people follow the dogma, "I'll get some experience in the real world before I start my own business." What these people overlook is that the older you get, the more creativity you lose because society has dumped more of its rules on you and the less risk you can take because you have taken on more responsibilities (for example, husbands, wives, mortgages, children, and full-time jobs). So while you may not have as much business experience, which you can learn along the way, you have fewer responsibilities, more creativity, and more energy than those seasoned business people twenty years older than you.

So while you may not have as much business experience, which you can learn along the way, you have fewer responsibilities, more creativity, and more energy than those seasoned business people twenty years older than you.

You may or may not make more money working for yourself than you will for someone else. But even if you make less money, you may still come out ahead because of the tax advantages. Working for someone else, you may make $50,000 a year and take home $35,000 of that. But as a business owner, you can enjoy so many tax write-offs that you may only take home $30,000 a year, but your car is paid for, your computer is paid for, your lunches are paid for, and even some of your vacations are paid for. If your business allows you the luxury of working when you want, you'll enjoy even more savings. You can go to amusement parks on the weekdays, when rates are cheaper. You can come into work late and leave late, cutting a half hour off your commute. I'll bet you'll work harder when you work for yourself because you'll see the fruits of your labor (as opposed to slaving away in an underwear factory and seeing only the Fruits of Your Loom).

Even if you don't make as much money working for yourself, I think you'll enjoy work (and life) much more. I know several self-employed people who make less money being their own boss. But they get their enjoyment not from a fat paycheck but from their freedom from the prostitute factor. No longer do they just get to say who? Or when? They now can say how? (How should I run my business?) Where? (Where do I want to work?) What? (What do I want to do today?) Even why? (Why am I doing this?)

By the way, the government *wants* you to start your own business. That's why they have made two types of taxes, those for business owners and those for business workers. Business workers are taxed much more heavily than business owners. Why? Because business owners create (as in create jobs, create new products), and the government (rightly so) has deemed that creation and innovation are important to the general welfare of the country. By writing favorable tax laws for business owners, the government is saying they *want* you to invent this year's equivalent of the lightbulb and they *want* you to start your own business and create jobs for people. And this isn't all dollars and cents; there are tax savings available to social innovators, like artists, writers, musicians, and anyone who creates.

Another reason: *there has never been a better time in the history of the human race to start your own business.* How's that for an argument? Because of the internet, you are able to reach customers all over the world for almost nothing. And as young people, we are on average more familiar with the internet than any other generation. We grew up with it. Yes, yes, I know we are just coming out of the dot com disaster. But many of the dot coms failed because they forgot the one key factor to starting any business. (What's that one key factor? Stick around, I'll get to it in a minute.)

The government wants you to start your own business.

Finally, look at the top dogs. How did billionaire Warren Buffett make his money? By starting *his own* investment partnership. How did Bill Gates make his money? By starting *his own* company called Microsoft.*

Not enough? How's this one: when do you think Britney Spears made all her money? When she was taking orders in the Mickey Mouse Club or when she went out on *her own* to become a musician?

---

* I'm not going to go through everyone here, but whenever you get a chance, grab the latest issue of *Forbes* magazine that covers The Forbes 400—a list of the 400 richest people in America. Some make the list because of divorce or inheritance, but an overwhelming number are on the list because they started their own business.

How It Works

 There are a few rules of thumb you should know about getting loaded with your own business:
*   Do something you love. You'll work longer and harder, and it won't even seem like work.
*   Start small. You've probably heard that more than 50% of all new businesses fail. This is a garbage statistic. I could just as easily say more than 50% of all employees don't become the CEO of the company they work for. But don't be stupid. When I say start your own business, I don't mean bet the farm and buy a sports bar for $250,000 just because you like sports and you like to drink. A business can be started for nothing. Yes, absolutely nothing. "Hey, can I shovel your driveway for ten bucks?" Congratulations! You now own a snow shoveling business.

*   It's better to lose $100 ten times than $1,000 once. Feel free to make as many small mistakes as you want, just don't make any big ones. I'm all about taking risks, just take small ones. If you lose $100 ten times, you'll know ten ways not to do business. Lose $1,000 once; you may be out of business.

*   Don't go it alone. Be sure to tell your family and friends that you're trying to start your own business and ask them to help you in any way they can. Depending on your business, it may make sense to take on a partner, share the wealth, and share the risk.

*   Don't quit your day job, if you have one. If you don't have one, you're either already rich (in which case you should be on a beach reading a Harry Potter book, not this one) or you're still being supported by your parents, which puts you in a prime position to start your own business. The fact is when you start your own business, you will make mistakes and you may need more cash than you thought. Keeping the day job or staying on good terms with the folks will solve this problem.

*   When you own your own business, you are allowed to subtract expenses from the business's total income. Imagine your business made $100,000 last year. Imagine last year you took a busi-

ness client out for a $20 lunch three hundred times, a total meal expense of $6,000. You ate lunch every day, and now your business's taxable income is only $94,000. If you were an employee whose salary was $100,000, that entire $100,000 is subject to tax (and you'd still have to buy lunch!). Tax advantages are one of the many beauties of running your own business. Instead of you paying for everything with your after-tax income, the business pays for everything with its *pretax* income. Beware however, that while deducting business expenses is legal, the IRS does not take the process lightly. If you own your own business, or you start one and want to start deducting business expenses, you must see a tax advisor.

- Interview at least one winner and one learner. A winner is someone who started and is now running a successful business. A learner is someone who tried to start a business and learned from it. Buy each of them lunch (*Yo quiero* Taco Bell?) and ask what they did wrong, what they did right, and what they would do over. The more of these winners and learners you can find and interview, the better. Since you're young, you'll see people are happy to help you.

- Start acting like an entrepreneur today. Maybe you are still in school. Maybe you are already working for someone else. Even if you already work for yourself, start pretending there is opportunity all around you. Even if you don't agree with me, force yourself to believe it. Try doing things a different way. Drive to work a different way. Shop at a different store. Hang out with a different person. Anything that mixes up your routine. Even if it seems stupid or if it seems to be more work than the norm, just try it. See, when you screw up your daily routine, you'll begin to see what's wrong with your daily routine and you'll want to fix it and when you start trying to fix what's wrong, you're an entrepreneur.

Interview at least one winner and one learner. A winner is someone who started and is now running a successful business. A learner is someone who tried to start a business and learned from it.

Secret #46 at Work

I believe that everyone should at least try to start their own business. I mean what the hell. Being a business owner may not be for you, but at least you'll know. Remember you can either win or learn. You can't lose.

So here's what I want you to do. First, be sure all your other finances are in order, credit card debt, retirement plan contributions, and all that jazz.

> *Now I want you to make a P.O. list. This is simply a list of everything that pisses you off. The creation of a P.O. list will lead to more opportunity than any other single action you can do.*

Next, make a here's-what-I-am-good-at list. This is a brief list of your natural and learned talents. Make it as long as you like, but it should be honest. Lying will only hurt you later.

Now I want you to make a P.O. list. This is simply a list of everything that pisses you off. The creation of a P.O. list will lead to more opportunity than any other single action you can do. More ideas are generated by people who are pissed off than from any other state of emotion. Think about everything that bothers you and write it down. "It pisses me off that I always have to drive my little sister everywhere." "I hate washing the dishes." "My apartment has no room." The more you write down, the easier it will be.

Once you've got your own P.O. list, start talking to friends and family and ask them what they're pissed off about.

When you've completed this, you should have a gigantic list of business opportunities. True, you won't be able to solve them all tonight, but look closely at your list and the lists of your friends, and ask if there is some sort of problem you could solve by starting your own business. For this exercise, this does not have to be your dream business. I just want you to free yourself from any excuses and just go out there and do it. Who cares what it is? Just try it.

If you don't find a business somewhere on your lists, just keep writing and asking more people. You'll find something.

Once you've found your business, start it. That's right. No more talking, no more wishing, no more hoping, just go for it. This (finally) brings me to the key factor that many of the dot com bombs ignored:

when you start a business, you have to take it slow. Secret #32 talked about companies going public to raise money for their operations. Normally, companies are in business for a few years before they go public. They have a proven track record and have shown a profit. Such companies go public thinking, "Hey, we're making money, and if we can go public and raise some cash, we'll be able to make even more money." In the dot com economy, many companies went public thinking, "Hey, we're not making money yet, that's why we need to go public to raise money. Once we do that, *then* we will make money." When Netscape went public, it was not making a profit. When Amazon.com went public, it was not making a profit. When Pets.com went public, get this, it actually began selling products for *less* than what they cost. Basically, they were selling $10, at the bargain price of $8.

> **When you start your own business, it's important that it starts making a profit immediately.**

When you start your own business, it's important that it starts making a profit *immediately*. Sounds obvious, but we just had a whole slew of companies ignore this simple fact. They focused on expanding the business as opposed to making money.

So for this exercise there is only one rule: *under no circumstances can you spend more than $500.* If you can't start your business for less than $500, find another business. Yes, I love your idea for a full contact savings bank called Cross Checks. But that's going to cost a fortune to get going. First, prove to me that you can run a profitable business for $500, then we'll talk about combining the inseparable worlds of violence and finance.

Please, no cheating. If your business makes a profit, you can use that profit to grow the business but you may not put any more than $500 of your own money into the business. Don't worry about tax write-offs or incorporating or any of that crap until your business starts making a profit. For now, just start.*

---

* *Yeah sure Pete, what business can possibly be started for $500?* Hmmm . . . well Gary Dahl started the Pet Rock for . . . actually I'm not sure. What's the going price for a North American rock these days? Peter Hodgson, the man who gave the world Silly Putty, started with $147. That was in 1949, so that's just over $1,000 in today's dollars. If you find the next Silly Putty, just take on a partner.

But Pete, should I spend the $500 on advertising? On supplies? Should I save some of it as an emergency fund?

Who knows? Who cares? There are no right or wrong answers here. The most you can lose is $500, so go ahead. Take risks and make mistakes. Now that brings me to *the most arrogant sentence in this book:*

I think this little $500 business start up exercise is just as important, if not more important, than a business degree from an accredited university.

You know I'm a big fan of formal education, but informal education is just as important. This exercise will take away your fear of starting your own business. That is half the battle. It will teach you things no classroom can teach you, like how to deal with rejection, fear, failure, success, and, most important, people. Think of it as an investment in education. I bet an entrepreneurial class at your local college would run you at least $500 (including course fees, books, and the dreaded, yet mysterious student activity fee). Why not cut out the middle man and go for it? If you continually examine what you're good at and if you continually generate P.O. lists, you're sure to find a business that works for you.

Many personal finance books offer a questionnaire to use in determining if starting your own business is right for you. There's no harm in a little soul-searching, but it doesn't compare to the real thing. I say just try it and see what happens.

One word of caution with this "jump right in with both feet" exercise. Please start a safe business, one that will put you as far away from potential lawsuits as possible. I'd say you're pretty safe with your term paper typing service, but I'd be careful with your idea about a trampoline rental business. Mind you, I have nothing against a trampoline rental business or any high adventure business for that matter. But with only $500 to blow, you just won't be able to buy the proper insurance a high risk business demands. So keep it simple and safe on this one.

Secret #46 in a Nutshell

Think about what pisses you off. Think about what pisses your friends off. Find a way to solve whatever it is you or they hate. Find a way to solve it for less than $500. Then solve it until you make a profit or run out of the $500. You are (or at least were temporarily) a business owner. Alter your lifestyle to find new business opportunities.

get a crib

Propria domus omnium optima (*One's own home is best of all*).

—LATIN PHRASE

Why It Works

While it is possible to lose money in real estate (as it is with any other investment), you are guaranteed to lose money if you rent.

Just as every investor serious about getting loaded should consider investing in stocks via equity mutual funds, every investor serious about getting loaded should make the effort to purchase their own home.

Look. You gotta live somewhere so you might as well make a profit (or at least not lose any money) on your living arrangements. While it is *possible* to lose money in real estate (as it is with any other investment), you are *guaranteed* to lose money if you rent. Rent is a purchase, like food or clothing, but buying a home is an investment. The nice thing about buying a home is that if you live there long enough, it's very difficult to lose money.

Here is why buying your own home is the greatest idea since Cliff's Notes:

- A *mortgage* is the loan you get to pay for a house.* Mortgage interest and property taxes are tax deductible. (Remember though, if you are taking the standard deduction, you won't be able to deduct interest and property taxes.)

- You build up equity as you pay off your mortgage. You can borrow (carefully) against this equity to buy things, like cars or college educations. Interest rates on a home equity loan will usually be more attractive than other loans, like car loans. Plus, the interest on these home equity loans is tax deductible.

- The Good Lawd ain't making any more land. The land that we have now is all the land we will ever have. Real estate has gone up in value an average of 5% per year for the last twenty years. And you can bet your Pedro Martinez rookie card that demand for real estate, over the long haul, is only going to continue to go up.

- If you sell your home at a profit of less than $250,000 ($500,000 for couples), you pay no capital gains tax. When you think about it, that's a pretty big tax break. If this break didn't exist, you'd be looking at over $75,000 in taxes on a profit of $250,000. (Remember that capital gains tax is the money you pay on the difference between the purchase price and the selling price, assuming of course that the latter is higher.) If, however, you sell your home at a loss, you do not get a tax break.

- Since there are so many voting homeowners, your interests as a homeowner will continue to be protected.

- Spending money on your home (for repairs, additions, decks, and so on) will often give you an immediate benefit as well as long-term appreciation. It is one place you don't have to feel guilty spending. This is all within reason of course. Sure, in your eyes, what could be more valuable than a swimming pool shaped like a donut? But beware if you sell to a croissant lover.

---

* Okay, this is actually a lie. When you buy a home, you take out a loan. The mortgage is the legal document that allows the bank to take your home away if you don't pay that loan. Now you know. But since everyone is used to saying, "I'm paying my mortgage," I won't try to change the world here.

- The alternative to home buying is renting. When you rent, you're still buying a home; you're just buying it for someone else, namely, your landlord. Sure, real estate has its risks, but renting is a guarantee that 100% of your rent money will be lost. (It has been argued that people who live in low-rent or rent-controlled areas should avoid buying and instead invest the money they save in mutual funds. This is not a bad argument, except that very few people have the discipline to do this. Owning a home forces you to save.)

How It Works

 The first thing to know is when you *shouldn't* buy a home. Assuming you are making an income, and that you can afford the down payment, the only time you should not buy a home is *when you will not be in the same area for five years or more.*

Buying a home costs money. I'm not talking about the actual price of the house you're looking at; I'm talking about the costs incurred during the process of home buying, like lawyer's fees, real estate commissions, inspections, and insurance. I'll get to these fees in a minute, but realize that when you own for at least five years, you lessen the blow of these costs.

Five years also protects you from downturns in the real estate market. If you buy just before prices plummet, the last thing you'll want to do is sell at the bottom. When you're able to hang on for at least five years, the market is likely to recover. This is by no means guaranteed, but you have a much better chance of getting your money back, maybe even more, if you hang on for half a decade. Keep in mind another rule of thumb: the longer you own a home, the more likely you are to make money. While I believe a home is an asset, one could easily turn it into a liability by continually upgrading to a better home every couple of years. Just as stock trading should be kept to an absolute minimum, home buying and selling should not become commonplace.

Don't worry about whether the real estate market is up or down, because *no one* can predict the market. It doesn't matter if you're married or single. As long as you're going to be in the same place for five years or more and your finances are in order, buy.

Ahem, there is of course the 20% down payment that you'll need to come up with. The bank will loan you the rest. 20% of a $100,000 home isn't chump change. You could put down less and borrow more, but that will cost you more money in the long run. How do you get this camel hump of cash? Besides working hard and saving diligently, I recommend you call two banks. One is called Mom, the other is called Dad. No luck? "Well Mom, I guess I'll need my old room back . . ." (For some readers, a loan from Mom and Dad is totally out of the question. But about a quarter of first-time homebuyers get their down payment as a gift. If this quarter isn't you, the next secret will be of some help. I'll show you some other ways to get it.)

In a minute, I'll take you step by step through the home-buying process. But for now, let's keep some general home-buying concepts in mind.

> *You have a much better chance of getting your money back, maybe even more, if you hang on for half a decade.*

- Be sure to use the negotiation skills you sharpened from Secret #15.
- If you can find it, seller financing is great. This is when you buy a home and the owner allows you to pay him off slowly over time, instead of going to a bank for the money. It eliminates many hassles, namely that 20% down payment. I don't want to kid you, though. Despite what anyone will tell you, seller financing is tough to find unless you're in a lousy market. Most often it will be offered by owners with dead-end properties (properties they believe they can do nothing with or are desperate to get rid of). Still, if you can find a flexible seller, or you're willing to take a chance on that property no one else wants (remember more risk, more reward), by all means go for it.

- Single-family homes appreciate faster than condominiums. But condos are easier to maintain because most of the upkeep is done through the condo association. They're also easier to evaluate because all the condos are the same. Just knock on everyone's door in the condo association and ask them what they like and dislike about their place. If you're looking to buy unit twenty-one and the woman in unit twenty tells you her roof leaks and her heating bills are off the charts, chances are unit twenty-one will have the same problems.
- The more you know about the seller and their reasons for selling, the better. The less the seller knows about you and your reasons for buying, the better.

> *The more you know about the seller and their reasons for selling, the better.*

  - Get a home inspection. It costs a few hundred dollars and can save you countless headaches. An inspector visits the house, before you buy it, and checks the roof, the heating system, and the foundation. He points out any potential problems in the house and gives you a written report on what he finds. While it's possible he can overlook something, an inspector adds an inexpensive level of assurance to your home-buying process.
  - Think ahead. Right now you're single so you're thinking you only need one bedroom. But what are your plans five years from now? You may get married. Remember, your goal is to stay in this place five years, so look down the road a bit.
- Three letters you want to learn are DOM. Sounds like a rap group, but it really stands for days on market. Find out how long homes have been on the market in your area. This will give you an idea of how hot the market is. If homes sell within five days, you're in a hot market and you should expect to pay full price. If, however, the average DOM in your area is a hundred days, there's much more room for negotiation. DOM varies throughout the country, so get an idea of what the average is for your area. Ask your real estate broker for this info.
- Speaking of real estate brokers, use one. Remember:

- Brokers are licensed by the state and they can get in big trouble if they act in a sleazy manner.

- They've done the home-buying process dozens of times, so they have all the answers to all your questions.

- Some brokers work for the seller (a.k.a. seller's broker or listing broker) and some for the buyer (a.k.a. buyer's broker), but all are required to be ethical. If you are using a selling broker, just be careful what you say aloud to them. They are loyal first to the seller, so keep the mouth shut. (How do you find a good broker? Ask your friends who just bought homes, or ask your financial advisor for suggestions.) Feel free to meet with several agents before selecting one you feel comfortable with.

- Don't sign an agreement to work exclusively with one broker unless you feel comfortable with that broker, and make sure the agreement allows you to find and purchase a property on your own without paying the broker a commission.

- Remember chain-reaction shopping? Buy an expensive home in an expensive neighborhood and everything, from the stores to the taxes, will be expensive. I'm not saying head for the projects, just buy reasonably. A good rule of thumb is to buy the cheapest house in a nice neighborhood. The other nicer homes, because of a process known as *progression* will add to the value of your home.*

- Never fall in love with a property. But when you do fall in love with a property (as everyone does), *never* let anyone know you've fallen in love. The moment the seller or the real estate agent know you want it, the price is going to go up.

---

* The opposite of progression is called *regression*, which is the lowering of your property's value owing to its neighbors. Regression happens when you own the nicest house on the street and the other not-so-nice houses drag down the value of your house.

Secret #47 at Work

So you're sticking around for five years and Banco de Parents has agreed to help you out with some of the down payment. You're looking to buy your own crib. Here's how you do it:

Never fall in love with a property. But when you do fall in love with a property (as everyone does) never let anyone know you've fallen in love.

1. Hop on the internet for an hour. Go to www.homes.com or www.realtor. com. Look at the price of single-family homes and condos in your area. What has stuff been selling for? Also check out www.iown. com, or www.lendingtree.com to get an idea of what you can expect to get for a mortgage. You can also grab the Sunday edition of your local newspaper to see what homes are selling for.

2. Review your finances. How big of a down payment can you make? (The bigger your down payment, the lower your mortgage. For first-time homebuyers, plan on at least 20%, and more if your credit is lousy.) Be sure to factor in taxes, insurance, maintenance, as well as mortgage payments. How do you find all this stuff? You can visit the town tax assessor's office to get an idea of property taxes you're likely to pay. Your real estate agent or the yellow pages should provide you with the names of a few insurance companies to give you estimates. (Secret #17 also lists a few insurance companies.) The seller might give you copies of heating and electrical bills. If he does, that's because he's proud of how fuel efficient his house is. If he doesn't, that may mean he's hiding something. Maintenance is tricky because you don't know when your roof is going to leak any more than you know when your Nike stock is going to double. Carlton Sheets, author of the highly recommended real estate course "No Down Payment" suggests a maintenance budget of $25 to $35 a month for condominiums and $35 to $50 per month for single-family homes. One last thing, if you're buying a condo, there is probably going to be a condo association fee. Your agent or the seller should be able to tell you what this is.

3. Ask your friends and family for recommendations on real estate brokers in your area. If any of your friends have recently purchased a home, ask them who they used.

4. Get some names together and meet with agents. Pick the one you feel most comfortable with. One warning about agents, though. They may avoid showing you properties sold by people who refuse to pay a real estate commission. Like every other area of finance, why would someone sell you something if they can't make money off the deal? When your real estate agent says, "I've shown you every house on the market," he most likely means "I've shown you every house on the market *that will pay me a commission.*"

 So Pete, how do I ensure I see every house on the market? There are two ways to do this. One way is to work with a real estate agent, and then scour the internet and the classifieds to see all the noncommission-paying properties (most often these are "For Sale by Owner" properties) on your own. Or you can agree to pay your agent a commission if, for whatever reason, the seller will not. This way, he'll show you everything. Whether or not this is worth it is completely up to you.

5. Once you select a broker, meet with them briefly to tell them your needs. Remember that if they work for the seller (something they MUST disclose to you before you begin working with them), you need to be careful what you say. Just be vague, "I'm looking in the $100,000 range" as opposed to "I can afford $125,000." The broker will probably invite you onto his computer to view homes on the Multiple Listing Service (a computer database of homes for sale). You and your broker will select some houses to look at and make arrangements to see them.

> **When your real estate agent says, "I've shown you every house on the market," he most likely means "I've shown you every house on the market that will pay me a commission."**

6.   Ask your broker to:

- Recommend a real estate attorney.
- Recommend a mortgage broker.
- Give you an idea of how much you'll expect to pay in closing costs (legal fees, commissions, title fees, inspector's fees).
- Email or fax you when new homes in your price range come on the market.

7.   Once you've found the best mortgage deal, (and yes, you should compare your broker's suggestion with at least two other companies you find on your own) ask to be *preapproved* for a loan. This is when a mortgage company locks in a loan amount and an interest rate that will not change for a predetermined period of time (such as sixty days). Having a preapproval makes you a more attractive buyer than if you were just *prequalified*. A prequalification is just a phone interview that really means nothing. Go for the preapproval right away.

8.   Call a few attorneys and introduce yourself. Find out what they charge and how much you can expect to pay for the entire home-buying process. Work with the one you feel most comfortable with.

9.   Find a home inspector. Look in the phone book or ask friends. Don't ask your broker, because he may recommend the most alcoholic, lackluster "oh everything's fine" home inspector he knows.

10.   By now, you have more solid info about what homes cost and what it will cost you to buy one. Ask yourself, can you afford it? If not, you may have to rent a little longer to save up. If so, jump to step 11.

11.   Ahhhh, now you can start looking at houses. The more you see, the better. You can go with or without your broker, but if you go without your broker, be sure to call him and talk about the homes you saw and what you liked and disliked.

 12. See at least five homes. Be sure to look at the neighborhood. Schools, libraries, public transportation—all that stuff is worth checking out. The local police department should be able to provide you with crime statistics. Feel free to talk to people who may be your potential neighbors to see how they like where they live and to see if you like who you'll be living next to. And if you're buying a condo, knock on some doors and ask people how they like their condo.

13. When you find the home you like, it is time to make an offer. Your broker can help you fill out the offer, which is a standard form (but read the whole thing anyway!). If you can, it would be good to know the following bits of info before submitting your offer:

- How long has the house been on the market? Just look for DOM.
- Why is the seller selling?
- Has the seller received any other offers and for how much?
- What homes similar to yours have recently sold for. Your broker should be able to answer this, just ask him to provide you with "comps" (recent comparable home sales).

14. Your offer should be subject to the following:

- A home inspection.
- Acquiring financing (but since you're preapproved for a mortgage, you're all set).
- A pest inspection (if it's common in your area).
- Property delivered vacant and broom clean (this way they can't leave any of their crap in the house).
- A walkthrough. This means before everything is finalized, you get to walk through the house and make sure it's okay. (If you saw the Richard Pryor film *Moving*, you'll realize the importance of this advice.)
- If it's a condo, your lawyer's satisfactory review of the condominium documents and budget.

15. *Hey Pete, how much should I offer?* I can't effectively answer that because it depends on the market and the property. Your research will be the best indicator—are other homes going for full price or are all offers coming in under the asking price? Just remember that if you want the property, your offer should be strong. When you submit the offer, you'll most likely have to put down a $1,000 deposit.

16. The seller will either accept, reject, or counter your offer. If you get flat-out rejected, that usually means your offer was way too low. A counteroffer is a rejection of your first offer, but it means your offer was close enough that the seller wants to keep the deal going by suggesting a slightly higher price than what you offered. Truly, it's up to you to decide whether it's worth offering a higher price. My advice here is if you want the property, don't nickel and dime too much. Sure, $1,000 is a lot of money but not for a $150,000 home you're going to live in for five years.

17. Remember that price isn't everything. Okay, you won't go up $10,000. What about letting the seller live in the house an extra sixty days? What if you help the seller move? I don't know! Be sure to ask.

18. Congrats! You and the seller reached an agreement. *Que pasa* now? Well, now the attorneys get to beat each other up for a few weeks while they draw up the *purchase and sale agreement* (P&S). While an offer is binding, it is a general one- or two-page contract. The P&S is many pages and covers everything about the house. Your lawyer will read and make changes to the P&S. Before signing it, please read the P&S. It's as boring as the Nature Channel, but it's important. Lawyers make mistakes too. While the P&S is being signed, you'll be conducting a home inspection.

Congrats! You and the seller reached an agreement. Que pasa now? Well, now the attorneys get to beat each other up for a few weeks while they draw up the purchase and sale agreement (P&S).

19. Once the P&S is signed, you'll have to fork over more money, between 5% to 20% of the purchase price, which is held in an escrow account. When money is held "in escrow," that means it is held by a third party until the contract is fulfilled. No one can take the money while the deal is going on. In most cases this 5% to 20% comes out of the down payment. If the deal falls apart for reasons out of your control, you get this money back. However, if you back out of the deal, you may be out some cash.

20. Now what? The selling broker is conducting a fire inspection, and your mortgage company is doing a *title search*—a process to ensure that the seller is actually the owner of the home. Your mortgage company is also doing an *appraisal* of your home, which means they calculate the value of your home to be sure it's worth the amount they loaned you. You, of course, are negotiating the purchase of a pallet of hot dogs for your housewarming cookout ("Listen buddy," you tell the hotdog salesman, "you got about thirty seconds to throw in free mustard or I'm hanging up and calling Kentucky Fried Chicken! You think I'm joking? Ask your friend who sells pasta salad about me. Then you'll know who you're dealing with!").

You do not have to close until the house is empty and broom clean.

21. All this work is inching you toward the *closing*. The closing is the transaction to buy/sell the house. The morning of the closing, do a walkthrough. This is a no-brainer here. Go to the house and poke around. You want to be sure the house is in fact vacant and that they haven't left anything in there, like old furniture, garbage, or dead bodies. It's the seller's job to move this stuff, not yours. You do not have to close until the house is empty and broom clean.

22. At closing, you, your broker, and your attorney show up to meet the seller, the listing broker, and the seller's attorney. (Although not everyone needs to show up at the closing—it all depends.) The seller will give you the keys to the place, and you give the seller the rest of the money. This may include some of

your own money—the rest of your down payment—and will include the bank's money—your mortgage.

23. You are now a homeowner.

This is a home-buying crash course, but the process really isn't all that complex. Take it slowly, see a lot of properties, and learn the market. A good broker who can guide you through the process will prove to be as valuable as the home you buy.

Secret #47 in a Nutshell

If you're in the same place for more than five years, buying probably makes sense. Plan on a 20% down payment. See Mom and Dad or the next secret for help. Use a real estate broker. The DOM is an important number to tell you how strong your offer will have to be. See at least five houses. Get a home inspection. Buy the cheapest house in the neighborhood. Take the whole process slowly.

---

mingle with a mortgage

A bank is a place where they lend you an umbrella in fair weather and ask for it back again when it begins to rain.

ROBERT FROST

Why It Works

Buying a home is a big step. It can be intimidating. People keep looking and looking, or waiting and waiting for the market to go down, without realizing they are losing money on their rent in the meantime. Remember that if you see yourself in the same area for five years or more, you should make the effort to buy a place. But there's still that damn down payment in the way. Here are a few tricks to help.

How It Works

If you read the footnote in the last secret, you'd know that contrary to popular belief, you don't pay off a mortgage when you buy a home. You pay off a loan. The mortgage just secures the home to the loan. If you don't pay your loan, the bank takes your house, and they can do this because that house has a mortgage on it. As I said before, I'm not here to change the world. I'll use the word mortgage, even though I should say loan. To protect itself, the bank usually asks you to cough up a *down payment*, which is a lump sum of cash you put down to buy the property.

Imagine you wanted to buy a $100,000 house. The bank would ask you to put down $20,000 and then they would give you a mortgage for $80,000. If you fail to pay the loan, the bank figures it can sell the house for at least $80,000. The $20,000 that gets lost is your money, not theirs.

The biggest obstacle for most people buying a home is the down payment. Where do you get such a sum? The first thing to remember is that mortgages, like everything else, are negotiable. I knew of a seventy-six-year-old gentleman in Florida who got a thirty-year mortgage to buy a home.* Anything is possible.

I said that one out of every four first-time homebuyers get some help from their parents or relatives to buy a home. You may think you don't even have a shot at a sum this large, but think again. Your family doesn't necessarily have to write you a check for the down payment. There are a number of ways they can help you.

- They can offer to guarantee the loan. This costs them nothing, unless you fail to pay up. With a guaranteed loan, the bank may lower the down payment to a more affordable level. Or, they may lower the interest rate.
- Family members can also pledge their assets as collateral. Perhaps your family owns stocks, which they can put up so the bank will lower the down payment. Again, it costs them nothing—unless you stop paying. Some brokerage companies—Merrill Lynch being one of them—will allow you to use your stocks as collateral for a 90% or even 100% mortgage. You can still buy and sell your stocks (some restrictions apply), even though the stocks are collateral.

---

* Why would the bank do this? Perhaps he had to make a huge down payment. Perhaps the interest rate on his loan is very high. Anything is possible.

While this is an option, it's not necessarily a good one. Borrowing 100% of the value of your home will make your monthly payments expensive.

 If your family is unable to help you, worry not. The common 20% down payment is getting less and less common. Your youth comes to the rescue. If you're young, your income is at a lifetime low. Typically people don't get excited about a low income, but buying a house is an exception. You may be able to qualify for government-sponsored programs that assist low-income and first-time homebuyers. Here are some of the more popular programs:

 • Contact the Federal Housing Association (FHA) at www.hud.gov. The FHA offers to insure the loans made by banks. You can get a loan even with a lower down payment, a low income, and some debt on your record.

• Talk with Freddie and Fannie. (Who?) Freddie Mac and Fannie Mae are nicknames for two companies designed by the government to help people buy homes. When you shop for a mortgage, ask lenders if they participate in Freddie Mac or Fannie Mae programs. Check out *www.fanniemae.com* and *www.freddiemac.com*.

 • Your state or local housing authority may have a program to help you, especially if you earn a low income. Your state and local housing authority should be listed in the phone book, or if the web is your thing, check out www.ncsha.org, known in some circles as the National Council of State Housing Agencies.

Typically people don't get excited about a low income, but buying a house is an exception. You may be able to qualify for government-sponsored programs that assist low-income and first-time homebuyers.

Remember, taking a low down payment means you'll need to borrow more. Duh. Your monthly payments could be considerably higher. If you borrowed $80,000 to buy a $100,000 home, your monthly mortgage payments (that's just mortgage payments) would be $532 per month, assuming a 7% interest rate. If you borrowed $95,000 with the same interest rate to buy a $100,000 home, you would pay $632 per month plus an additional $53 per month for private mortgage insurance (I'll explain in a minute). So the lower down payment means an extra $153 dollars per month.

Remember, taking a low down payment means you'll need to borrow more. Duh. Your monthly payments could be considerably higher.

If you put down less than 20%, the lender will probably sock you with *private mortgage insurance* (PMI). PMI is simply insurance to protect the bank in case you fail to pay the loan. PMI adds to your monthly mortgage payments. You usually can stop paying PMI premiums when your equity in the home rises above 20%. Remember, equity is what you own. When you've paid off 20% of the house, call the bank and ask them about canceling your PMI. It is your responsibility to notify your lender of this. Putting less down and paying PMI is an option, but it will cost you more in the long run.

Mortgages aren't all that difficult. Your mortgage will either be *fixed* or *adjustable*; you'll either get a lower rate but pay more in *points*, or get a higher rate with no points; and your mortgage will either be for fifteen or thirty years. (You can get various lengths on your mortgage, but fifteen and thirty years are the most common.) Let's break this down.

- Fixed rate or adjustable rate mortgage. If you have a fixed rate mortgage, your interest rate remains the same throughout the life of the loan. Your payments for the first year will be the same as the final year. With an adjustable rate mortgage, the interest rate is tied to the economy. If interest rates are high, your payments will be high and vice versa. Unless interest rates are offensively high, a fixed rate mortgage is going to be the better bet. There is a lot to be said for predictability. Even if you don't save every last penny going with a fixed rate, you'll at least know exactly how much you can be expected to pay for the life of the loan. If you do get an adjustable rate mortgage, try to lock in the rate for at least five years. You could for instance get a thirty-year adjustable rate mortgage with rates locked at 7% for the first seven years. After those seven years the rate will fluctuate based on the conditions of the economy. But at least you've locked in some predictability. Should rates hit rock bottom, you can always *refinance*. Refinancing is the art of paying off your old mortgage with a new one that carries a better interest rate. Refinancing costs money up front, but as a rule of thumb, if rates are at least 1% lower than yours and you intend to stay in the home for a while, it is usually a good bet.

Unless interest rates are offensively high, a fixed rate mortgage is going to be the better bet. There is a lot to be said for predictability.

- Rates or points? *Points* are an up-front fee charged by the lender. One point equals 1% of the loan. If you have an $80,000 loan with one point, your fee will be $800. This is a one-time fee you pay when you close on the home. Normally when you pay points, your interest rate on the loan is lower. If you pay nothing in points, your rate will most likely be higher.

- *Hey Pete, what's it going to be, rates or points?* The answer lies in how long you're going to be in the house. Taking more points with a lower rate gets better and better the longer you're going to stay in the house because your points get spread out, while you're enjoying a lower rate. Here's what I mean. If you pay $1,200 in points and you're only in the house one year (I hope not), then those points cost you an extra $100 a month. If you're in the house for two years, that $1,200 is spread over twenty-four months ($50 per month) and so on. (www.lendingtree.com has a handy calculator to help you decide between rates and points.)

- Fifteen or thirty years? Overall, you'll save more money with the fifteen-year mortgage, but it will be more expensive each month (even though it is for fewer months) and it is tougher to qualify for. A nice thing about a fifteen-year mortgage is that it is an aggressive forced saving program. You're forced to build up equity quickly. In just fifteen years, you've saved a huge sum of money. Only, you didn't save this money in a bank account, you saved it in a house. Some financial advisors argue that one may be better off with a thirty-year mortgage and investing the difference in stocks. Great idea, unlikely reality. There is a middle ground on this timeline topic. Get a thirty-year fixed rate mortgage with no prepayment penalty. That means you're allowed to pay the loan off whenever you want. You could pay off your thirty-year loan in fifteen, twenty, twenty-five, or thirty years, whichever works for you. If you want to put more into your home, you can; if you want to put more into your investments, you can. And if you know the Yankees are going to win (again), you can put your money in that too.

A nice thing about a fifteen-year mortgage is that it is an aggressive forced saving program. You're forced to build up equity quickly.

Secret #48 at Work

There are big rewards for doing your homework when it comes to mortgages. Surf the web for an hour or so. A great site is www.lendingtree.com. Not only will lenders fight for your business, but the site also has all the handy calculators you need to decide between rates or points, fixed or adjusted, and fifteen or thirty years. Also check out some of the government sites to see if you qualify for any government-sponsored programs.

You can get a loan from several different places, but two of the most popular are mortgage brokers—people who work with several lending companies to find the best deal—or your online or local bank. One is not better than the other, because it all depends on which one offers the better deal. That's why an hour on Lending Tree can prep you to separate the good deals from the bad ones.

 ### Secret #48 in a Nutshell

The lower your down payment, the higher your monthly payments. It is difficult, but often wise to slap down the standard 20% down payment. Go to your parents, your local and state housing agencies, and the federal government for help reducing the down payment. Points are up-front fees paid to the lender. One point is 1% of the loan. More points make sense if you will be in the home for a while. Get a fixed rate thirty-year mortgage with no prepayment penalty.

---

don't lose your life

Life insurance isn't bought, it's sold.

—OLD SAYING

Why It Works

This secret offers two pieces of advice. Its most literal meaning is don't die. Wisdom does not get more solid than this. But the hidden meaning of the title is that I don't want you to lose your life, as in your social life, trying to pay for life insurance you really don't need. While I hope you remain on this earth a very long time, I can offer no advice that you haven't already heard on how to do that. Perhaps the book you're looking for is *Immortality for Dummies*. But this thing about not overpaying for life insurance I can help you with. I need just four pages of your time.

How It Works

 I've never sold life insurance, but I imagine it's a pretty easy thing to sell. I mean, talk about getting emotional. All the salesperson has to say is, "Isn't it important for your loved ones to be taken care of when you're gone?" and your check-writing hand gets twitchy. But the big-picture line to remember when you buy life insurance is the same line you used when you first broke up with someone: it's not you, it's me.

When you buy life insurance, it's not a question of how valuable your kids and your spouse are to you, it's a question of how valuable *you* are to your spouse and your kids. That's the big mistake people make when buying life insurance. It's not about your loved ones, it's about you. Life insurance is a way *to provide income to your dependents because you passed away.* That's its purpose. So to buy life insurance, you must have 1) an income and 2) people who depend on your income (a.k.a. dependents). If you don't have both, you don't need life insurance and you can skip to the final secret to start learning about wills. Note that when I say "income," I don't mean just a paycheck. I mean that you should consider the cost to replace what it is you do. If you take care of children, cut the lawn, and do the housework, but receive no paycheck for this, you still need to account for that when buying life insurance. These services may have to be paid for in the future. Ask yourself, how much would it cost to replace what I do? How much to hire someone to take care of the kids, cut the lawn, and do the housework?

Suppose you buy a policy that pays out $1 million in the event of your death. This amount is called the *death benefit*. A safe 4% annual interest rate would pay your dependents $40,000 a year in interest—forever! But if you were still alive, how long would you really be supporting your loved ones? If the answer is forever, then

When you buy life insurance, it's not a question of how valuable your kids and your spouse are to you, it's a question of how valuable you are to your spouse and your kids.

you should stop here. Your dependents can live off the interest from your invested death benefit without ever dipping into the principal.

But $1 million may actually be *too* much money, because that amount implies your dependents will be dependent on you for the rest of their lives. Your spouse might remarry and your children will grow up someday and hopefully earn their own living. That's why before you buy life insurance (before you meet with an agent), you need to answer these questions: How many years will my dependents be dependent on my income? Will there be any big costs, like college, coming up?

To determine the amount of your policy, use the chart below. Column one indicates the number of years of annual income you need to replace. Column two indicates the number to multiply by the annual income. So if you need to replace $50,000 worth of income for fifteen years, the chart tells us that you would need a policy for $600,000 ($50,000 × 12).

Here's the chart:

Column One	Column Two
Years of Income to Replace	**Multiply Replacement Amount by:**
5	5
10	9
15	12
20	15
25	18
30	20
40	23

Remember to factor in existing policies from work (easily found by contacting your human resources department) as well as Social Security benefits (easily found by calling the Social Security Administration at 1-800-772-1213). Also factor in any other investments you currently have, such as stocks. Let's say you earn $50,000 a year. If you die, that's $50,000 less your dependents can depend on. But then you figure that your existing policies and investments will generate $10,000 a year. So you're looking to replace roughly $40,000.

And don't forget to add in large lump sum payments, like college for your kids.

Aside from all the calculations, purchasing life insurance is an emotional activity that depends on you, your dependents, and what you can afford. Based on my suggestions, purchase the amount that makes you comfortable. And remember, if you don't have an income and people who depend on that income, you don't need life insurance!

Secret #49 at Work

The first thing to do when it comes to life insurance is to find out how much you need. The second thing is what to buy. Basically there are two types of life insurance: *term life insurance* and *cash value life insurance*.

Term life insurance is nothing more than life insurance. You pick a death benefit, pay a premium every month for a specified term, and when you die, you get that amount. Simple. Cash value life insurance (be it whole life, variable, or universal) provides you with life insurance just as term does, but it also builds up a cash value. In other words, you can get some money from it even if you don't die, because part of your premiums go toward building up a cash reserve that you can dip into.

Remember, if you don't have an income and people who depend on that income, you don't need life insurance!

 Term insurance is cheaper, and you will get more bang for your buck. The premiums for a million dollars of cash value life insurance may cost ten times more than term. The rule of thumb when it comes to life insurance is that you should buy term insurance and invest the money you save from not buying a cash value policy on your own. You'll earn more investing the difference in mutual funds than in cash policy.

Insurance salespeople want to sell you a cash policy because the commission they'll earn on it is much bigger. They argue that a cash policy is forced savings and that if you bought term you'd never invest the difference on your own. This is not such a bad argument because few people have the discipline to save and invest. If you buy a cash policy, you'll in all likelihood pay the premiums because you'll treat the premiums as you would any other bill. And most people (wrongly) pay their bills first and invest last. The problem is that cash policies are so expensive. What often happens when people buy a cash policy is that they only make the payments for a few years. Then, after suffering through these painful premiums, they decide to get their cash out of the policy and switch to term. But when they go to grab the cash out of their current policy, they find they don't get out anywhere near what they put in. Why? Because a lot of their dough was swallowed by commissions. The commission bite is especially hard in the first few years of the policy.

Insurance salespeople want to sell you a cash policy because the commission they'll earn on it is much bigger.

So buy term and invest the rest—but please invest the rest!

 ## Secret #49 in a Nutshell

Life insurance provides income to those who were dependent on you. If you have no income and no dependents, you don't need life insurance. How much to buy depends on your comfort level, your dependents' comfort levels, and your checkbook's comfort level. When you do calculate the amount, remember that your dependents may one day become independent. Term insurance is cheaper and easier to understand; cash value doubles as a so-so form of forced saving and investment.

---

protect your ass-ets

The fortune which nobody sees makes a person happy and unenvied.

—FRANCIS BACON

Why It Works

It has been said that the only things that are certain are death and taxes. I guess death is certain, but taxes at the time of death don't have to be. By filling out a few documents, you can slide right out from under the heavy burden of estate taxes and fees. You may not have a large net worth just yet, but someday you will. When you die, your dependents will pay taxes on your net worth. And even if your net worth slides under the estate tax limit, there are countless other matters that need to be addressed. Even if all you own is a guitar, you still have to decide who gets that guitar, otherwise the state will choose for you. It's also very important to find out if your folks have taken the proper measures to protect their estate. Here we go again with that no-person-is-a-financial-island big-picture idea. *Fortune* magazine estimates that our grandparents will accumulate over $6 trillion in the next ten years. At least some of this $6-trillion fortune will be passed to our parents. Then it will be passed onto us. So let's not lose any unnecessary trillions to the government. Here's how we do it.

How It Works

First, do this at your leisure. The older you get, the more important this is, so just keep the info in this secret in the back of your head. When you feel ready, take some action.

If you have no written documentation stating how you want your assets (or estate) divided up, then the government distributes those assets on your behalf. This legal process of dividing up your assets is known as *probate*. The government does its best to distribute your wealth in a sensible manner, such as dividing it among living relatives. But their idea of a fair distribution may not be yours. "No!" you scream from heaven. "How could you possibly leave it all to cousin Earl? He's going to blow it all on that statue commemorating the Denver Broncos!" Worse than the cousin Earl debacle: if you have no living relatives, the state may end up getting everything you own. "No!" you scream from heaven. "How could you possibly leave it all to the State of Colorado? They're going to blow it all on that statue commemorating the Denver Broncos!"

By filling out a few documents, you can slide right out from under the heavy burden of estate taxes and fees.

What's more, the state hires some guy (typically a lawyer) to handle the distribution of your assets. As a fee for this lawyer's services (what, did you think you get a *free* lawyer), this guy may get a percentage of the entire value of your estate. So if your estate is worth $100,000, your loved ones may lose $5,000 right off to the administrative lawyer. Plus court fees can add a few extra thousand dollars onto that. To top it off, anything that goes through court becomes public record. If you die and try to secretly leave $50,000 to the International Flat Earth Research Society,* everyone's going to know.

So what's a way around this? The most common way is to draft a *will*. A will is simply a document describing how you want your

---

* As far as I can tell, this is an actual organization. The phone number didn't work when I tried, but then again, if I were the chairman of this society, I wouldn't answer the phone either. Check out www.talkorigins.org/faqs/flatearth.html and see for yourself.

estate to be divided up. He gets this, she gets that. With a will, the court must recognize and obey your instructions.

But the problem with a will is that everything still has to go through probate, which means fees, courts, and everyone knowing about your philanthropy to the International Flat Earth Research Society. Often people need to sell investments, such as homes, simply to pay all the damn fees. But there is a way around probate altogether.

Like a will, a *revocable living trust* (RLT) is a document that describes who gets what when you're gone. But unlike a will, a RLT also names someone to control your assets while you're still alive. In most cases, this is you, the *trustee*. So you can put everything you own into the trust, like your house, car, and stocks, without changing your lifestyle. You, as trustee, are still in control, only now your assets are bundled up nicely in this trust. When you die, your *remainder beneficiaries* (perhaps your children, spouse, or cousin Earl) get this nice bundle known as the trust. But the coolest thing about a RLT is that it bypasses probate. It allows your assets to easily be transferred from one person to another without the court's intervention— so go ahead and give the International Flat Earth Research Society that $50,000. Why not make it an even $100,000? No one will know! Look, proving the earth is flat is not easy, so they could use the money.

 Hey Pete, do I really need to do all this trust crap? Eventually it'll be worth looking into. You may not have many assets right now, but your parents might. Do they have a trust? What about your grandparents? I don't know how well you get along with your family, but I'm willing to bet there ain't one family in America who wants to see the government rake through their personal finances and divide those finances up as they see fit. And if you are on good terms with your family, they probably want you to

You, as trustee, are still in control, only now your assets are bundled up nicely in this trust. When you die, your remainder beneficiaries (perhaps your children, spouse, or cousin Earl) get this nice bundle known as the trust.

have some of the wealth they worked so hard for. The simple difference between a trust and a will (or worse—no will at all) can mean tens of thousands of dollars. If I asked you to sign a piece of paper that would save you thousands of dollars, risk-free, would you do it? Sure you would! That's all trusts are. Documents that could save you thousands.* It's worth the few hours it takes to look into creating a RLT. In a moment, I'll explain some of the easier ways to do it.

I'm willing to bet there ain't one family in America who wants to see the government rake through their personal finances and divide those finances up as they see fit.

If your estate is large enough, you may have to pay estate taxes. Wills and trusts aside, one of the easiest ways for someone (like your parents, for instance) to bypass estate taxes is to give their money to you before they die. Yep, that's right. You're allowed to give up to $11,000 per year to each beneficiary tax-free. See what I mean that no one is a financial island?

I realize that this may not be the case for every family, but it does remain an option to put on the back burner. And mind you, money in your name can screw up your shot for financial aid, so don't even worry about this strategy until your campus days are behind you.

Secret #50 at Work

The first thing you have to do is get the family together. This involves everyone. Find out if your parents and grandparents have properly organized the transfer of their estate. I know this whole thing is a morbid subject that no one really wants to talk about. But it is important. It's a lot of money that a lot

---

* If you are a real dork, you'll actually do this exercise. Get together your ten richest friends and your ten poorest friends. Then ask everyone to whip out their checkbooks. You'll notice that your rich friends' checks have headings that look like this:

Joe A. Blow, Trustee
Joe A. Blow, Revocable Living Trust

Your poor friends will simply have their name and address on the checks. This exercise is of course a waste of time, but try it if you don't believe me.

of people have worked hard for, and no one wants to lose it simply because you failed to do a few simple things.

If you find that you or your family need a will or a RLT or, there are two ways to go about creating them: the expensive way and the cheap way. The expensive way is to have an attorney draw up the documents. The cheap way is to do it yourself, either by using computer software or following along in a book.

 Here's what I would do. Try it out first on your own. You can get started right away for under $50. A good computer program is Nolo's Living Trust Maker, or, if you're the book type, check out *Plan Your Estate* also published by Nolo. You can also head to www.legal docs.com to look over some trusts. Legaldocs.com charges a fee for some of their documents, but everything is reasonably priced.

If you can, try putting together a trust on your own. Later, when you have the opportunity (and the money), have an attorney who specializes in estate planning look over your work.

I know this seems like a pain in the ass. And I'm not asking you to do it right away. But it is something to think about because you know this book is about long-term thinking. I'd be cheating you if I left this stuff out. I'd also be cheating you if I didn't alert you to the fact that your parents should spend some time on estate planning. For what you and your parents can save in taxes and fees, I think it's worth it.

So I *trust* you *will* take the opportunity to plan for your estate.

It's a lot of money that a lot of people have worked hard for, and no one wants to lose it simply because you failed to do a few simple things.

You know this book is about long-term thinking. I'd be cheating you if I left this stuff out.

Secret #50 in a Nutshell
If you die without a will, the courts will rake through your finances and distribute your money as they see fit and they'll charge you for it. If you die with a will, the courts will rake through your finances and distribute your money as you see fit, and they'll charge you for it. If you set up a revocable living trust, the court cannot rake through your finances, nor can they charge you. Anyone can give anyone up to $11,000 per year without paying taxes. This is often the most convenient way to reduce the size of an estate and thereby reduce estate taxes.

bottoms up

Since I started this book with a true story, I might as well end it with
one. And though this story is about me, it's something I think we
all do.

Let's call her Sara. I had just gotten her number and I was stuck
in that all-too-familiar limbo regarding the timing of the first phone
call. You know the dilemma—I want to call her now, but if I call her
now I'll look desperate, so I'll wait a few days, but if I wait too long,
she'll either get pissed off or meet someone else.

Fortunately or unfortunately, I had some help. A small but dis-
tinguished panel of three close friends had gathered in my apartment,
and two were advising me on what to do. The original purpose of
this panel was to watch a Red Sox game, but I was offered relationship advice during the commercials.

One friend was pushing for an immediate call. He argued that
the whole "wait five days to call trick" was now useless, because so
many films and TV shows had talked about it that any attempt to
replicate this scam would be detected and scorned.

The other friend was of course lobbying for patience. He tossed
aside the argument that pop culture had exposed the waiting trick.
It's human nature, he argued, to always want what you can't have.
Let her know she can't have you and then, just when she thinks all is
lost, present yourself.

Back and forth the argument went, until the third friend (probably the smartest of the bunch, and certainly the one most interested
in the game) told me, "Pete, maybe it is better to call now. And maybe

it is better to wait. But how can you really know for sure? You can't. So just call whenever you want. If that's two hours after you meet her, fine. If that's two weeks after you meet her, fine. But don't waste your time trying to control something you can't." With that, he turned the volume back up, and I went into the other room and made the call.

I made the call because he was right. I had no idea if Sara was a "play the game kinda girl" or a "let's just be honest kinda girl." Even if I did know what kind of girl she was, that wouldn't have mattered because Sara, like every other human, is an emotional being, and emotions aren't predictable.

So it is with money. We spend so much time trying to control what we can't and ignoring that which we can. My advice to you is the same advice my friend gave me—stop worrying about the things you can't control. You have no control over interest rates, or economic conditions, or what stocks will go up and down and when. So stop worrying. Diversify over a few low-fee index mutual funds and be done with it. You can, however, control how much you save, how much you spend, how much education you get, and (to some degree) how much you pay in taxes. While nothing is certain, your time is much better spent on the latter than trying to guess the next hot stock.

> **You have no control over interest rates, or economic conditions, or what stocks will go up and down and when. So stop worrying.**

By now I hope you've realized that personal finance is much simpler than society wants it to be. Paying off credit card debt is a wise financial move. But we often don't want to hear such advice because it's too simple. Just like it's too simple to just call that newfound romantic interest when you want. No, no, we want to debate, evaluate, and reevaluate.

Thankfully, by learning the concepts outlined in this book, I understand what I can and cannot control financially and manage my money accordingly. As for Sara . . . well, I didn't write this book to talk about my romantic triumphs and tragedies. I wrote this book to help you reach your goals.

And I hope I did just that. I hope I've showed you how to use your youth to make getting those goals just a little bit easier. Once your finances are in order, you'll find it easier to be generous. Once you start achieving your goals, you'll have time to help others achieve theirs. Who knows? They may even buy *you* a free lunch.

So thanks for reading this book. I would like to hear how each of the secrets worked out for you, or even if some of them didn't. You can reach me at the address or website below. Or if you ever see me in person, please tell me about your experiences. Perhaps we'll even have a drink at a bar together and talk about—whatever. But the whole time we're sitting there, our money will be at work for us and we'll be quietly getting loaded.

Cheers,
Peter G. Bielagus

I can be reached online at www.peterbielagus.com or by mail at:

Getting Loaded
c/o Peter Bielagus
170 South River Road
Bedford, NH 03110

website directory

Banks

www.etradebank.com
www.netbank.com
www.bankrate.com
www.fdic.gov The website of the Federal Deposit Insurance Corporation, the federal agency that insures bank accounts.

To find a local bank, just look in the yellow pages or ask family and friends who they use.

Bonds

www.usbonds.gov United States bonds online

Brokerage Companies

www.ml.com Merrill Lynch
www.salomonsmithbarney.com
www.morganstanley.com
www.etrade.com
www.schwab.com
www.americanexpress.com
www.ameritrade.com

Car Buying

www.kbb.com
www.carfax.com
www.edmunds.com
www.autonation.com
www.carmax.com

Credit Rating Agencies

All three of these places will give you a copy of your credit report. In most cases you will have to pay a small fee. Do it anyway.

www.equifax.com
www.experian.com
www.transunion.com

Credit Cards

www.bankrate.com To compare rates and learn about credit cards
www.cardratings.org To compare rates and learn about credit cards
www.cardweb.com To compare rates and learn about—you know

College Costs

www.fafsa.ed.gov (Free application for Federal Student Aid)
www.debtfreegrad.com
www.cashforcollege.com
www.college-scholarships.com
www.upromise.com
www.savingforcollege.com

Cruise Ship Jobs (as promised)

www.cruisechooser.com
www.cruiseshipjob.com
www.smallshipcruises.com

Home Buying

www.fanniemae.com
www.freddiemac.com
www.homes.com
www.isoldmyhouse.com
www.realtor.com
www.hud.gov
www.iown.com
www.ncsha.org

Insurance

www.insurweb.com
www.quotesmith.com

Individual Retirement Accounts

www.rothira-advisor.com
www.moneychimp.com

Legal Advice

www.lawstreet.com
www.findlaw.com
www.laweasy.com
www.legaldocs.com

Mortgages

www.lendingtree.com

Mutual Funds

www.morningstar.com To find ratings on a variety of mutual funds
www.vanguard.com To buy funds from Vanguard
www.fidelity.com To buy funds from Fidelity
www.troweprice.com To buy funds from Fidelity . . . just kidding, obviously T. Rowe Price.

Renting Apartments

www.homestore.com
www.apartments.com

Saving

www.coolsavings.com
www.valupage.com
www.priceline.com
www.mysimon.com
www.bestdeal.com
www.lowermybills.com

Social Security

www.ssa.gov

Stock Selection

www.fool.com
www.hoovers.com

Taxes

www.irs.gov
www.taxsites.com

glossary

401k An employer sponsored retirement plan for employees of for profit corporations. 401ks offer a way to reduce total income, save money on a tax deferred basis, and perhaps the chance to receive matching funds from the employer.

403b An employer sponsored retirement plan for employees of nonprofit corporations. Much the same as 401ks, 403bs offer a way to reduce total income, save money on a tax deferred basis, and perhaps the chance to receive matching funds from the employer.

529 State operated, tax favored investment plans designed to help people save for higher education. Each state outlines the specific terms of its own plan, yet an investor can use his/her money in the plan at any college in the country.

Appreciation An increase in the price of an asset.

Asset Anything that is yours.

Balance In terms of credit cards, this is the amount of money you need to pay to even up with the credit card company. If you have a $100 balance on your credit card, you owe them $100.

Beneficiary The person who receives money as the result of being named in a will, trust, or life insurance policy.

Bond An IOU. When you invest in a bond, you loan your money to a corporation or government that agrees to pay back your investment, plus interest within a predetermined period of time.

Broker A person or company that brings buyers and sellers together for a fee.

Capital Gains Profit from the sale of an investment. There are also **capital losses** which are losses from the sale of an investment.

Cash Management Account A money market account housed at a brokerage firm and often connected to a stock account.

Certificate of Deposit A debt instrument issued by a bank that pays a specific amount of interest on a specific amount of money for a specific period of time.

Credit As in tax credit. An amount you can legally subtract directly from the taxes you owe.

Commodity Anything that comes out of the ground—corn, oil, soybeans and so on. A *commodity* business is one that competes in an environment where the lowest price always wins.

Compound Interest Interest earned on your principal *and* on accumulated interest.

Coverage What an insurance policy protects.

Debt What you owe.

Deduction As in tax deduction. An amount you can legally subtract from your total income. Deductions are good.

Direct Underwriter An insurance company that sells its own policies.

Diversification The art of diversifying. Just kidding. Diversification is the art of spreading your money over several types of investments, like cash, stocks, bonds and real estate, to spread out the risk and reward.

Dividend A portion of company profits paid to shareholders at management's discretion.

Dow Jones Industrial Average A list of 30 large cap stocks being traded in the U.S.

Efficient Market Theory A belief that the stock market is perfectly efficient, which means that everything that is known about a stock is already reflected in its price, which means that an investor cannot beat the market averages.

Equity Ownership. Equity is what you got.

Exemption As in personal tax exemption. An amount you can legally subtract from your total income for each individual you financially support.

Fear A force that makes people sell investments.

Gambling A risky undertaking for the possibility of profit.

Grace Period With relation to credit cards, the period after a purchase is made that no interest is charged. If payments are made within the grace period, a consumer is not charged interest. It is usually 20–25 days.

Greed A force that makes people buy investments.

Individual Retirement Account IRA A personal retirement account allowing individuals to put money away tax deferred. Contributors with low incomes may also be eligible for a tax deduction. See also *Roth IRA*.

Inflation A rise in the cost of goods. Inflation erodes your purchasing power.

Interest The rental fee for money, usually expressed as a percentage.

Internal Revenue Service The United States government agency in charge of collecting federal taxes.

Investment An outlay of money for income or profit.

Intestate The condition of someone who dies without a valid will. When a person dies *intestate* state law then determines how his/her assets will be divided up.

Keogh A retirement account for self employed individuals allowing individuals to save large amounts of money in a tax deferred account.

Large Cap Companies having a market cap of over $5 billion.

Lead Pricing A marketing gimmick where one product's price is lowered in order to "lead" consumers into the store.

Liability Anything you owe money on. For example cars, credit cards etc.

Liquidity A measure of how quickly an investor can get his/her money out of an investment without substantially affecting the investment's price. A bank account is a liquid investment, real estate is not.

Market Capitalization The current price of a company if you were to buy the whole thing. Find it by multiplying the total number of shares by the current price per share.

Mid Cap Companies that have a market cap of $1 to $5 billion.

Mortgage A contract that secures a property to a loan. If the borrower does not pay the loan, then the lender has the right to take the property.

Mutual Fund A fund headed by a professional money manager that invests in a combination of stocks and bonds on behalf of the fund shareholders.

Net Worth The number you get after you subtract what you owe (your liabilities) from what you own (your assets).

Option The right to buy or sell a stock at a specific price within a specific period of time. When you own an option you do not own the stock, you simply own the *right* to buy or sell that stock.

Order A command to buy or sell a security.

Premium The fee paid for insurance protection.

Probate The process by which a will is authenticated and its instructions carried out.

Purchase To obtain by paying money or its equivalent.

Random Walk Theory A belief that future stock prices cannot be predicted by examining past prices.

Return The money you receive from an investment, often calculated on an annual basis and expressed as a percentage.

Revocable Living Trust Agreement outlining how your assets will be controlled while you are alive and how they will be distributed upon your death. Most commonly used to avoid probate.

Roth IRA A variation of the *IRA*, the Roth IRA allows contributions to grow tax *free* as opposed to tax deferred. After the contributor reaches age 59 and six months, they may withdraw the money from their Roth IRA without paying any tax on the earnings.

Russell 2000 An index that measures the performance of 2,000 small U.S. companies.

Security Any type of investment product, be it stock, bond or otherwise.

SEP IRA A retirement account for self employed individuals.

Short Selling An investment strategy where an investor sells a stock he/she does not own but borrows from someone else. The investor hopes the price of the stock will soon fall, allowing the investor to buy it back at a lower price and replace the stock he/she borrowed.

SIMPLE Stands for Savings Incentive Match Plan for Employees. This is an employer sponsored plan offered by small for profit companies.

Small Cap Companies with a market cap of $1 billion or less.

Social Security Retirement plan administered by the Social Security Administration.

Speculating See *Gambling*.

Standard and Poor's 500 Index An index of 500 large companies traded in the U.S.

Taxable Income The amount of a person's income that is subject to income tax.

Total Income The worldwide total of all the money earned by a taxpayer in one year from wages, investments, alimony, rents, royalties, pensions and other sources.

Upselling A marketing gimmick wherein a salesperson tries to convince you to buy additional products after you decide to make an initial purchase.

Volume A measure of stock market activity. Volume is the number of shares bought and sold over a specific period, usually measured daily.

Will A legal document outlining the wishes of person with respect to the transfer of their assets upon their death.

Wilshire 5000 An index that tracks not 5,000 but 6,000 small, medium and large-sized U.S. companies.

index